BOATER

A Life on England's Waterways

Jo Bell

Harper
North

HarperNorth
Windmill Green
24 Mount Street
Manchester M2 3NX

A division of
HarperCollins*Publishers*
1 London Bridge Street
London SE1 9GF

www.harpercollins.co.uk

HarperCollins*Publishers*
Macken House, 39/40 Mayor Street Upper
Dublin 1, D01 C9W8, Ireland

First published by HarperCollins*Publishers* 2025

1 3 5 7 9 10 8 6 4 2

Poems on pages 2 and 44 reprinted by permission of Nine Arches
Press. Originally published in *Kith* 2015.
'Late Fragment' by Raymond Carver reprinted by permission of Penguin Random House.
Originally Published in *A New Path to the Waterfall* 1989.
Extracts from *Narrow Boat* by L. T. C. Rolt reprinted by permission of
The History Press. Originally Published in 1998.
Poems and extracts from 'The Book of Nots' (page 21), 'The Slow Machine'
(page 58), 'A diet rich in birdsong' (page 232), 'Boat in Dry Dock' (page
243), and 'Untitled' (page 264) are the author's own work.
The author acknowledges that the first line of 'No Seafarer' (page 2) is taken
from the eponymous Anglo-Saxon poem, 'The Seafarer'.
Prints: Hillmorton Locks; Farmers Bridge; Bridge 78, Audlem © Eric Gaskell.
Copyright © Jo Bell 2025

Jo Bell asserts the moral right to be identified as the author of this work

A catalogue record of this book is available from the British Library

ISBN 978-0-00-871629-5

Printed and bound in the UK using 100% renewable electricity at CPI Group
(UK) Ltd

The Other Way

Contents

For my mum, Wendy,
a true companion on
the journey: and for the navvies.

'*Thousands have lived without love, not one without water.*'
– *W. H. Auden*

'*Very little is needed for the happy life.*'
– *Marcus Aurelius*

Foreword

This is an adventure story. The adventure is a small one, and the country in which it happens is not on the usual map, because the place where I live is not on your map. It sits inside a parallel geography, on a map-within-a-map of England and Wales. It requires you to look differently at the land you live in. Its history, too, is a history-within-a-history; a rival to the chronicles of great men whose monuments are columns, and whose homes were themselves monuments. This watery nation is an idiosyncratic country, which inspires a love of place without nationalism. Its people include ordinary workers, clowns, freaks, and charlatans. All share a sense of self, time, and purpose, which makes their world different to the one that lies ten feet away, beyond the water's edge.

I have not crossed the Atlantic in a dinghy with nothing but a jar of peanut butter and a waterproof hat. I have not scaled Everest, or rescued a friend from a crevasse by cutting off my own leg. But then, adventure is not a question of scale. What I have done is travel the waterways of England (and sometimes Wales) for twenty years, meeting with extraordinary people in an extraordinary environment. I have learned a lot about human nature, including my own; about rope, and Brasso, and bravery; above all, about the necessity for a constant supply of biscuits.

The history of the canals is a history of work, and of a changing planet. It involves armies of navvies who dug out the channels; thousands of mill workers and miners, whose labour filled the waterways with cargo; and generations of boating families whose knowledge was deep and subtle, but unrecorded because writing was not their habit.

In the twenty-first century, the canal is a renewed and regenerated place populated by boaters with new needs and offerings. However, the deep and distinctive culture is still there, still rich, still funny and still tragic.

The canals of Britain are one of the great achievements of human endeavour. As an archaeologist, I maintain that they are more precious than Stonehenge. As a boater, I maintain that they are more precious than almost anything. In my partial account of their history, I touch on three other lives: those of James Brindley and Thomas Telford, canal builders at the beginning and end of the canal age, and that of the writer L. T. C. Rolt.

What I have discovered in writing my boating life is a deep stream of gratitude: for the working boaters who introduced me to this way of life, for the present-day boaters who circulate slowly with me around this wet map, and for the deep understanding of my own country that has built up, lock by lock, mile by slow mile. Come with me on this journey.

I call this metahistory. It is solid history, told by me – a historian and poet – and seen through the prism of my own experience. Plenty of boaters will disagree with my take on something or other. The boating community is full of naysayers, and has as many opinions as any other community*. This is a memoir, a metahistory, a provocation.

There is also a broken heart in this book. Like most, it healed.

---

*Not true. The boating community has far more opinions than most other communities, and we are more vocal than most in expressing them.

Working with the Dead

No Seafarer

I sing my own true story, tell my travels
small as they are, of episodes on shallow channels;
working up to Wolverhampton through the Twenty One
or drifting into Diglis, gagging for a cup of tea.

It's all about me: my boat, my slow-mo marvels,
my lockside affairs – a spaniel saved from death,
a bon mot for the fat gongoozler. That day
on the Llangollen, storm-glazed, glad together.

The overgrowing straits that carry me
from one pub to the next, the shallow river mouths
and long-dead ferry points where knackered boats
would carry sheep across at dusk;

I sing their praises daily, bank to bank.
A narrow span, a slight adventure
of slight travels, yes. But still my own, and true
and still, for all that, sung.

Kith, Jo Bell

Hold your nerve

Y**ou** don't sail on a canal, you *boat*.

The canals where I have lived my boating life have a different vocabulary to that of the oceans and rivers; yet I began that watery career on a wide, wild river. I took the helm of a narrow boat for the first time on the widest and wildest of all – the Severn.

My skipper was a dark-haired, rakish man called Richard, with a personality disorder and a glint in his eye. He invited me to join him near Worcester, for a short journey aboard a grubby seventy-two-foot-long narrow boat. It was August. Sunset pinked the water. Champagne and mangoes were taken in the coal-stained hold. The cabin was intimate, slope-sided, and smelled of varnish, paint and fresh sweat. The river swirled thrillingly under the hull of a shallow, flat-bottomed steel boat intended only for non-tidal channels.

As we approached the lock at Diglis, where the broad river meets the straits of the Worcester and Birmingham Canal, Richard handed me the tiller and told me to turn this long, rigid vessel into a channel that was transparently too short to accommodate it. 'Steer for that wall,' he commanded, 'and don't turn the boat until I tell you to.'

I was quite sure that I couldn't turn the boat, even when he told me to. I pointed its impossibly distant nose towards the brick wall at the edge of the basin. I had twenty tonnes of steel under my hand – a long, thin shape that would not be quick to turn against the current of the Severn. The tiller pushed hard against my arm, juddering as the current struck the hull. I held it steady, feeling that three miles an hour was a reckless speed at which to drive an irresistible force into an immoveable object. As we came closer to the wall, I touched the tiller but there was a growl: 'Hold your nerve. Leave it.' I waited just a few seconds more; the wall was surely upon us now, and I grabbed for the tiller. 'No. Leave it,' growled the skipper. At the point where I was gritting my teeth and preparing my defence for the damages case, Richard grinned; 'Turn. NOW!' I pushed my whole weight against the brass bar that sets the course of the boat. I held it there in the classic boater's pose; right shoulder back, arm straight to lever against the tiller bar, but torso leaning forward, and eyes looking ahead to see if the boat would clear the wall. It did. We slipped into the first lock at Worcester, with a luxurious three inches clear on each side.

Cepheus was one of a class of inland cargo boats named after constellations. The man was a colleague and sometime boyfriend. Both would appear in my story again, in contexts both joyous and tragic; and that short trip on the river shifted the balance of my life. As the swans of the Severn gave way to the proletarian ducks of the canal basin, I began to feel the strange, intoxicating loss of control that comes with falling in love. I did not yet understand how special the Severn was, nor how far my involvement in the waterways would outlive my involvement with the man. If I had known how often I would get that same manoeuvre wrong in the years to come, I might not have fallen quite so hard. But of course, it wasn't the man I was falling in love with. It was the boat.

We will come back to the boat, and perhaps to the man, but for now, let me explain how I got here.

I came to the canals because I was an archaeologist, and I became an archaeologist because of Harrison Ford. As it turned out, *Indiana Jones*

and the Raiders of the Lost Ark was not a perfect representation of life as an archaeologist in the United Kingdom (more mud, fewer Nazis). But then, Stephen Spielberg would not have made a feature film about six people breaking up frozen tarmac in a car park in Durham, which is what I did for much of the next twenty years. Most archaeology in Britain is done in advance of development. You spend a lot of time on building sites and road-widening projects, jiggling about to stay warm and waiting for a JCB to bring up a Bronze Age chariot or a medieval skull. Eventually, via a route as wiggly as the North Oxford Canal, archaeology would bring me to another life as a boat-dweller but, first, I had to serve my time.

If you run away from home to join the circus and you prove a little too peculiar, even for the lion tamers and trapeze artists, then they give you a mattock* and send you to the nearest archaeology unit. The people there will be scholarly, curious (in both senses) and dirty (in both senses). They will be funny and clever, with vastly dysfunctional personal lives and perhaps a substance abuse problem. They smell of mud and rolling tobacco. Their pockets are full of clay pipe stems and Rizla papers and unidentifiable blobs of medieval iron. Many of them know an immense amount about one minute aspect of Roman, Celtic or Jacobean material culture. They have specialist knowledge of latrines, penannular brooches, copper wire manufacture or – well, canals. These diggers, sharing accommodation in remote villages and hunching over camping stoves in a site hut at break time, have the camaraderie of intelligent, hungover people working together on a shared, often pointless, manual task. 'We are the highest qualified labourers in the UK,' grunted a colleague as she pushed a barrow of

---

*A mattock is a pick-axe with a flat blade on one side. If you have never used one, then your lower back pain must be coming from somewhere else.

soil up a slippery plank to the spoil heap. 'And the lowest paid,' said a voice from the bottom of a muddy trench.

With this team and a constantly shifting cast of others, I was part of an extended family who worked across the north of England for the next ten years. I began at the Roman fort of Arbeia in South Shields, where a scrape of my trowel showed a constellation of rusted hobnails marking the outline of a disappeared Roman boot. Our time team travelled to remote uplands to measure Iron Age ring ditches, map Neolithic stone scatters and excavate medieval grave yards. We dug trenches in urban back lanes to check for Roman roads, and found Saxon skeletons bisected by Victorian sewers.

The fieldwork team were one kind of clan, but our finds connected us to a deeper kinship with long-gone ancestors. On every site, in every trench, we found traces of the men and women who walked the same landforms long before us. Most archaeology isn't about precious objects or beautiful artefacts, but about literal trash. We study with reverence the broken pots and lost shoes that our predecessors never wanted to see again. In each case, as you lift a sherd or a clay pipe stem from the soil, there is a powerful sense of contact with the dead: *From your hand to mine*, you think. Perhaps in years to come, archaeologists will feel the same sense of mystical connection as they are wading through layers of discarded iPhone cables and left-footed Crocs.

Never was this feeling of contact stronger than on one site in a threadbare field, high above the river Coquet. As I scraped back the soil with my trowel, a toothy chip of flint flew up from the ground. Flint is not native to Northumberland, so this microlith (tiny stone) had been brought in from elsewhere, by someone travelling in the Stone Age – a time when flint was literally cutting-edge technology. I found another, and another. Now I worked slowly, gradually charting a scatter of the ancient chippings; and when I stood back to look, the pattern was clear. I was looking at a sort of flinty doughnut: a ring of translucent fragments circling an empty space. Here on this spot 10,000 years ago, someone sat down on the ground and set to work. They carried with them the means to make a useful blade; perhaps a knife to cut meat, an arrowhead, or a scraper to clean an animal hide. With a skilled hand, they struck an antler or stone against a flint core, knapping away at it to shape the tool they needed. They used their best technology to meet the needs of that day. Then, the unknown blade-maker stood up and walked off, leaving behind them this small, circular absence on a hillside. Millennia later, we diggers sat in our own circle, eating our sandwiches together, looking over the same valley as the tool maker. Their absence felt to us like a strong presence; we were fellow travellers in the same place, thousands of years apart.

Not all of the sites were so ancient. Archaeology studies the material culture of the past, and the past ends yesterday. Sometimes we were recording nineteenth-century textile mills or pottery kilns. Assessing a Leicestershire colliery that had been operational just a few years prior, I enjoyed drawing a boundary to make its control room a scheduled ancient monument – the highest level of protection that we can give to a historic place. There would, I said to myself, be one outpost left to stand for the coal industry that shuddered to a halt in my generation.

Some of our best field archaeologists had few official qualifications, and the best-qualified were idiots. The variety of experience, age, and background was an asset to our fieldwork and a joy to behold. Each of our work days drew a connecting line between dots on the history map – same place, different time. At the Roman fort excavation, one colleague would always take an abrupt turn at the same point on the site. He seemed to be avoiding an obstacle, though the ground looked to me like a spread of random rubble. 'Why do you always turn left there?' I asked him. He looked surprised, like a man who has just been told that he's wearing his trousers inside out. 'Well,' he said, 'that's where the door is.' The entrance he was walking through had not been there for sixteen centuries. The building it gave entry to was only a smudge of gravelled colour in the soil. He could *see* it. The rest of us routinely walked through Roman walls like ghosts from the future, but his deep involvement with the site sent him through the invisible door every time.

One building, one field wall, one village, one rural life is laid down on top of another. Sometimes the evidence of one survives into the next generation – a medieval church is absorbed into a growing town, the line of an ancient road preserved in the bend of a motorway – but often they are obscured by later buildings or boundaries. After a few years in this environment, time began to feel like a series of translucent layers.

In my teen years, when I still knew everything, my mother used to drive me crazy by speaking of the department store in Sheffield as 'Rackhams'. She meant House of Fraser. It had been House of Fraser for years. Why couldn't she get that into her head? Nowadays if I happen to mention House of Fraser, my younger brother shoots me a pitying glance and corrects me. 'You mean Aldi,' he says. 'It has been Aldi for years. Why can't you get that into your head?'

If the world around us changes so much in one lifetime, it can be hard to visualise the changes that happen over a longer span of years. Archaeologists have a simple tool to explore that changing world. They call it map regression, which makes it sound like a new-age therapy that requires you to sit in a field chanting with women called Rainbow or Windchime, but actually is a pleasing mixture of time travel and colouring in.

The time map

Find the spot where you live on a range of old maps at the same scale. What do you see on a map of 1832, 1850, 1910, 1964? When does your house appear for the first time? Now, get a sheaf of tracing paper and trace out the lines of anything that appears 'new' in each map. Record the black squares and dotted lines that show footpaths, pubs and hospitals. Notice what changes, and what stays from one edition to the next. Perhaps your earliest tracing shows a field with a barn in one corner and a church nearby. Thirty years later you see that the barn is gone, and there is a coal mine in the same spot: a little knot of pithead buildings, a new road. The church is bigger. Fifty years later, the next map says 'coal mine (disused)'. The big church remains. The latest map shows a black-beaded line of new houses and a school, on a road now called Coalpit Lane. The church, of course, is still there.

You and I are dots somewhere on this topmost sheet. Pretty soon another layer of lives will be laid down, and we will join all the other dots who have peopled the exact same spot. Sometimes our predecessors peek through to our layer. More often they remain unsuspected beneath our feet, like Richard III sleeping in his municipal car park for 500 years. Our successors, of course, are always invisible – but they will be able to see some of us.

In a map regression of South Shields, the earliest layer would include the parade ground at the frontier fort of Arbeia. Here is a Roman soldier, tramping the cobbled square in the middle of the fortress. On a much later layer at the very same spot, a newer dot marks the Jo Bell of 1992, a trainee archaeologist kneeling on the mud and swearing under her breath as she cleans the cobbles of a Roman ruin.

She knows about America and Australia, which the Roman did not. She knows that men have stood on the moon: but she doesn't yet know a damn thing about the English canals.

The process of finding out about the canals began long after I left Arbeia, when I found myself working for British Waterways (BW). This is the organisation that maintains the canals – and not, as we often explained, the organisation that deals with water rates or a broken mains pipe. 'That's not us madam, that's Severn Trent,' said the receptionist five times a day. Part of my job here was to give a short talk to my colleagues, sketching the history of the British canal system. I began by asking what seemed to me a patronising question for canal-side workers. 'When do you think the canals were built?' I thought there might be a bit of discussion, but that people would broadly settle on a date somewhere between 1770–1800.

'Built?' said one woman blankly. 'How do you mean, *built?*'

It was news to her that the canals were man-made at all. Two other women, sitting together at the front of the room, were long-time receptionists at one of BW's flagship offices. They did know that the canals had been built, but when? They conferred urgently, as if for a pub quiz. One of them said tentatively, 'We think the 1980s, as an amenity for leisure.'

These women had worked together for a decade in an office right next to the canal. They walked to work every day under one of the elegant bridges cast by famous ironmaster William Hazeldine, and conspicuously branded with the date 1824. Did they really imagine that a modern government – a Thatcher government at that – would spend billions of pounds building a nationwide water network that cuts through, among other places, Regent's Park, Birmingham and central Manchester, so that holiday boaters could tie up near London Zoo and grandparents walk along it with toddlers at the weekend? Did they really think that this had happened less than twenty years before, in order to place it coincidentally next to the Georgian warehouses and time-softened bridges that stood so conveniently outside the office door? They did. It turns out that for a great many people, the time map is invisible and that history doesn't matter at all. Who knew?

I was here because I had found my own obsession. Like those colleagues who specialised in Roman latrines or medieval horse husbandry, I had come to a fixation with industrial archaeology and the networks of road, rail and water that connect its components. The study of factory, mill and mine connected me to my Derbyshire and Yorkshire homeland, a place of gritstone and peak. My friends began to dread going on walks with me. 'Let us visit the millstone quarries of Padley Gorge,' I would brightly say. 'Oh, *do* let me explain what sort of water wheel operated here, what these gravelly slag heaps signify, and why the flues of North Pennine lead mines are zig-zagged.' Their eyes glazed over. 'Every day's a school day,' said one boyfriend through gritted teeth as I explained how float glass was manufactured. Ingrate.

My life on water began with a map regression in a Manchester library. I was studying a moorland clough called the Cheesden Valley where a scrummage of little water mills had stood in the late eighteenth century. Patient librarians brought me sheet after thick sheet of tithe maps, Ordnance Survey maps, estate maps. On sheet after thin sheet of Permatrace I painstakingly traced the copperplate lettering, the coal-black squares and thin threads of ink that marked buildings and streams.

It was a map of skylarks and coal dust – a layer on the time map where the sounds, the smells, the very air were different to ours. The air of this earlier age was alive with slow, organic sounds; the clop of packhorse hooves, the spill and clunk of water wheels. As time went on I saw the watermill dots of the Cheesden Valley disappear, and the neighbouring maps fill up with ink in their place. Steam-driven cotton mills and new-fangled factories fired up, closer to the grand and growing arteries of transport. Water power and horseflesh gave way to the stronger, faster, hungrier economy of coal, steam and iron. In a single lifetime, the workers who had peopled the stone mill buildings of a misty valley and worked its slow machinery, migrated to the brick mills and factory floors of a crowded, smoky and hectic Manchester. It was an incremental change, as dizzying for those living through it as the change from industrial to post-industrial in our own lifetime. I squiggled and squinted my way into the exact moment when this spot became properly industrial.

What became visible on those tracings was the change that bled across the whole of Great Britain like a drop of dye on kitchen roll. It flooded across the north, across Britain, across the world. In one long lifetime, metamorphosis. All of it changed: our relationships to time, work, each other, politics, the written word, to private relationships and individual rights. As Yeats wrote of a later translation, everything was:

> changed, changed utterly:
> A terrible beauty is born.
> – *from* 'Easter, 1916', W. B. Yeats

What effected that translation was infrastructure: roads, railways and, of course, canals. Few words in the English language are more boring than infrastructure. Who cares about turnpike road construction, the railway network, the little tramways and ferries that filled the cognitive maps of our great-grandmothers? I do. As I traced the snaking lines on these historic maps, I saw new connections between people and ideas.

Some of them were roadways or railways; but the ones that counted for me, the ones that began this national metamorphosis, were the waterways. To understand the present layer, we have to unimagine some of it and return ourselves to an earlier world; a world before canals existed.

Moving a piano in 1766

Imagine, if you will, that you wish to move a piano from Liverpool to Leeds. Why would you do that? I hear you ask. I have no idea. Perhaps your great-aunt Margaret has bequeathed it to you, in which case congratulations, and sorry for your loss. But how will you do it? You will first trace the route in your mind, consulting Google maps or trusting to the satnav to get you there without a hitch. You'll probably take the M62 and M60, ending with the A58 towards Leeds. You get someone with old-school tattoos to help you lift your piano into a reasonably sized van, remembering to lift *from the knees*. Then you drive it east across the Pennines, leaving behind the great sweep of the Mersey and travelling over a hill country of small rivers, bleak moors, and steep gradients.

The Pennines will not be a serious impediment. Warm and dry in your van, you tootle along the broad red motorways and wide blue A-roads of your mental map. If it rains, you put the windscreen wipers on. If it snows, you put the heater on. You cross the Ribble, the Douglas, the Aire, the Calder, and other rivers without really noticing, on a road-bed which barely jiggles your bottom. You do it within two hours if you're lucky. The cost is the price of van hire, and your own time. Well done. Put your feet up and have a cup of tea.

Now: imagine that it is 1766. You still wish to move a piano from Liverpool to Leeds. Let's still not worry about the why. This earlier piano will admittedly be much smaller (it will in fact be a *fortepiano* and will cause a small sensation in your Yorkshire social circle) but the task is much more difficult.

As an eighteenth-century Yorkshire person, the map you now have in your mind's eye is wholly different from the one you called up in the twenty-first. Your pre-industrial mind turns first to the wide, wet, natural resources that are, and always have been, the best way to shift an awkward load. The Trent, the Severn, the Thames, and the Tyne, the Derwent, the Fal, and, of course, the Mersey: the big rivers of 1766 are broad and clear and busy. To the modern eye, a river is a landscape feature, an amenity, a habitat, an environmental treasure, an obstacle to be crossed. To the eighteenth-century eye it's a big wet road. It is a water *way*.

However, your route between Liverpool and Leeds runs across northern hill country. Famously, large rivers are found at the bottom of hills and not at the top. They are out of the running for this journey.

The fortepiano buyer of 1766 engages with the road in a much more embodied way than the twenty-first century traveller. You will not be dashing over the watershed in a machine built by machines, protected from potholes and rainfall. You will not have watertight windows, a Jelly Belly air freshener and shock absorbers to cushion your sedentary bottom. Nor are you listening to *Drive Time* on Radio 2 and looking forward to a stop at Tebay services for a hand-crafted artisan quinoa-and-sputum energy ball. The Pennines are going to travel *through* you with every unabsorbed shock of the road. The air is very fresh, but it does not smell of jelly beans. It probably smells of horse shit.

The nation that you travel through will feel wetter, windier, sweeter and smellier than ours. There are fewer people in this earlier England[†]. There is much more poverty and starvation in it. Its infrastructure is quieter than ours – no combustion engines, no trains, no planes – but the land itself is louder. It is wildly, visibly, and audibly alive with animals and insects, with unimaginable densities of songbirds and field mice, with raptors above and fish splashing out of the rivers. Above all, it echoes with horse hooves. It is not yet intensively farmed. We haven't yet set in motion the great cycle of consumption and demand, advance and decline that will eventually put the UK's biodiversity in the bottom 10 per cent of the world's nations.

Your Georgian nation has many ways to move a piano, or indeed anything else. There are sailboats, horse boats, packhorse trains, chain ferries, heavy ox-drawn carts and sprung carriages, waggon ways sloping from the growing collieries down to the riverfront wharves. Individual travellers go by foot, by mule or donkey, or on horseback. All involve more physical effort and less comfort than the modern traveller expects. Your costly (and frankly showy) purchase will have to travel over the South Pennines through the Aire Gap, and across the exposed moorland of Saddleworth. It's remote and hilly, with what locals call 'a lazy wind' because it does not travel around you but through you. This is countryside that frowns on a piano. Perhaps you should have taken up the flute instead. At any rate, it will need to travel by road.

The old parish roads that suffice for a local journey are unpredictable. One local council might maintain its routes well, but the next

---

[†] Around 8.5 million people in 1766.

leaves them full of pot holes so deep that fast horses carrying the post can break their legs. In some places the best routes available are 1,400-year-old Roman survivals. The sturdy carts delivering food and supplies to the swelling towns often throw a wheel but you will not be putting your fortepiano on a cart because the narrow hill trails won't accommodate it.

The highways (seldom 'roads') of 1766 often follow the same routes once used by stone axe traders in the Neolithic period. Usually, such a road follows the shortest line possible across high ground. It gives travellers a good view over the country; it saves human and equine legs from the effort of dipping and climbing again. Rainwater drains away from the track bed, and good weather helps it to dry out but it will still likely be a precarious and poorly maintained transport route. Even in 1809, one traveller will describe a Peak District highway as 'extremely dangerous' with 'not above a foot and a half left for a horse to travel ... One false step would bring destruction to the rider and his horse.' He hasn't been born in 1766, and we have a piano to move. I would take the legs off if I were you.

Travel is not only more exposed and uncomfortable in this period; it is slow, labour intensive, and therefore expensive. Your delivery will take about five days, for reasons which you're beginning to understand. Five days in the rain and wind, even five days in the sun (good luck with *that* in Cheshire) is a large commitment of time. On reflection, you are not going to make this trip – simultaneously boring and dangerous – yourself. You're going to pay someone to carry it for you; and they are going to take it by packhorse.

You might catch up with them at an inn or shop on their route. A typical 1769 advert tells us that 'PENNY and WHITE's Pack-horses set out every Friday from Bath to Shepton-Mallet, Sherborne,

Dorchester and Weymouth' travelling a long circuit which would cover about twenty-five miles a day. They started from Mr Penny's fish shop, and the advert mysteriously adds, 'The proprietors will occasionally send their Fish-machines'.

Packhorses are *everywhere,* at least inland. After humans with a backpack, these little beasts are the oldest way to move goods across hill country. On a trip across moorland in 1766 one might see hundreds of them. Hitched together in short or long trains, they snake up and down the slopes, picking their way along stone-paved 'trods' or deep holloways worn into sunken lanes by their hooves. You hear them a mile off, because the lead animal wears a belled collar to warn travellers that now would be a good time to stand aside. People on foot or horseback press themselves against a drystone wall or step into a wet ditch and let six, ten, or (if they're unlucky) forty ponies pass by in a jangling single file. Some will later claim that the market town of Clitheroe might see 1,000 animals passing through on a single day.

Each animal is weighed down with panniers carrying up to 240 pounds in weight. Two hundred and forty pounds of what? What are these stolid animals carrying, as they circulate like blood cells around the body of England? *Everything.* The horse gangs carry salt and cheese from Cheshire to Derbyshire; lead and millstones from Derbyshire to Sheffield; bundles of steel from Sheffield to the scythe-makers of Ridgeway, where I grew up; bundles of scythes from Ridgeway out towards the rivers, the ports, and then onward by sea to everywhere that a ravenous empire can reach. They carry raw wool to the spinner, spun yarn to the weaver, woven cloth to the fulling mill and finished cloth from the mill to the merchant. The beasts bring luxury too. Their bundles include spices and sugar, brandy and rum, broadsheets full of political news, libellous cartoons, ballads, and gossip from the other side of the ridge.

Oh, and your piano of course. The 1760s fortepiano is a large, luxury object but it isn't the size of a modern piano. Somewhat disassembled, it will *just* fit onto the back of a sturdy horse. Pray for good weather, since bad weather will further endanger your precious cargo. Blizzards have frozen travellers to death, even on the ten-mile trip between Sheffield and Hathersage. Foot travellers are said to have drowned in the deep mud of a poor country road. Arthur Young wrote at this exact time that he had 'measured ruts of four feet deep, floating with mud only from a wet summer' near Preston. It's not just mud, either. Imagine the state and the stench of Clitheroe's roads when a thousand packhorses a day are slowly passing through, and fodder is slowly passing through them.

Water, such a precious mobilising force in the mills and new weaving sheds, is a hazard on the highways. Standing, tidal or marsh water, heavy rainfall, and river crossings are all dangerous. A seasonal flood can break bridges and erode embankments, sweep away horses, loads and the very fabric of the roadbed. All of this will extend the journey and make your costs higher. Where possible, then, the carrier might transfer your troublesome piano from the grateful packhorse occasionally and stick it on a cart, to travel the new turnpike roads. Where they exist, these are a great improvement. They are built and funded by private investors, and laid down by a new class of professionals. They recoup their cost through tolls, on a rolling licence. A typical stretch near Newark was advertised on a three-year contract in 1790; it had made £1,186 for its toll collectors in the previous year.

But even these improved thoroughfares were no good for heavy cargoes, which ruin the surfaces. In 1772 a typical 'melancholy accident happened near Little Chester Turnpike; two carts meeting on the road, one of which was loaded with coals, and the other having four

Women in it, which latter, in turning out of the road to make room for the former, (the ruts being very deep), was overturned, and one of the women killed on the spot.'

Above all other loads, in 1766 the turnpike roads and the pack-horse trains are carrying one heavy, combustible burden from its deep inland sources to the hundreds of places where it is needed. That commodity is coal. Coal to heat crucibles, to smelt lead or copper or iron, to boil water for dyeing cloth, to fire brick kilns or potters' kilns; the packhorses are carrying coal into all the places that river traffic cannot reach. These squat and stoical beasts, no matter how many of them there are, cannot possibly carry enough of it to meet even the existing demand in 1766. These roads, no matter how diligently the authorities maintain them, cannot keep up with that demand for long. They will have no chance of meeting the incremental acceleration that will begin in three years, when James Watt patents a new steam engine that supposedly quarters the owner's fuel costs.

In vast numbers, the packhorses populate the highways. They are picking their way slowly around an ancient network of precarious tracks, delivering the steel and crockery and clothing and timber of an industrialising nation. They, with the turnpike roads and the navigable rivers, are at full capacity in 1766. Very soon, they will not be able to keep up.

If I were you, I would allow a week for the fortepiano delivery. You will need to budget for the packhorse carrier and the cart driver, including overnight stabling and fodder; for the turnpike toll; and very probably for someone to screw the legs back on and repair the instrument when it arrives. It's still 1766, and you have finally got your piano to Leeds, but it probably costs twice as much as when it left Liverpool. Well done, and I wish you much joy of it.

To the canals

The Working Boats Project needed an industrial archaeologist. Their HQ was in the most flagrantly English section of English canal, and I barely knew what a canal was. A working boat, you ask? Ah. 'Working boats' is a shorthand for all the boats that used to work the canals, from their beginnings in the 1760s right up to the *de facto* end of canal trading two centuries later – tug boats, maintenance boats, dredgers, floating skips – but in common usage, 'working boats' are canal-based cargo boats. For the purposes of my new job, it meant a collection of ten narrow boats.

On the usual map there isn't much to see at Lapworth in Warwickshire: a pub, a trio of brick bridges, a few houses. But this is not the usual map: this is the water map. The humpbacked bridges carry a minor road over two canals – the Grand Union and the Stratford-upon-Avon. The pub, of course, is called the Navigation[†].

The office where I would be based was close to a large pool, edged with lace and reeds. When I arrived, it was sparkling with dragonflies and patrolled by a pair of bold white swans who protected their new nest like aggressive meringues. Above the pool, nineteen locks climb towards Birmingham. Below it and fed by it are a further sixteen, dropping through a length of green willow-and-kingfisher country to reach Bancroft Basin at Stratford-upon-Avon. A boat travelling down this canal arrives at the threshold of the Royal Shakespeare Theatre, the banks of the Warwickshire Avon and the landing stage where the last

---

† It is always called the Navigation.

chain ferry built in the UK, a little boat called *Malvolio*, takes tourists from one side of the river to the other.

This job was going to be a portal to an alternative England, whose circulating population is the size of a small town. They move around the network of inland waterways, which they call 'the system' at walking pace. They share (literal) landmarks and speak of places like Bumble Hole or Sutton Stop which 'bank people' know by different names. They have a network of news and gossip called the Towpath Telegraph. They drink in pubs called the Navigation. They do not drive, they steer. They do not call themselves sailors. They call themselves boaters.

The project itself was to conserve a small collection of canal boats, restore them to their original appearance as liveaboard vessels which had housed a distinct working population in the post-war years, and to take them around the English Midlands with a crew of volunteers. At schools, festivals and local attractions like the Black Country Museum, we would show visitors a part of their national past that they might never have encountered, and restore the people of the working boats to a history they seldom appeared in.

A narrow boat, you ask? Ah.

from The Book of Nots

What *is* this boat? The book of nots says:
not a barge (that's for the Dutch
and those marooned in Lincolnshire)
not a longboat (Vikings)
not a houseboat (Londoners
and all who think a boat
aspires to the condition of a house).

A narrow boat – please remember this if you want to live a happy life on the canals – is *not a barge*. The clue is in the name. A narrow boat is narrow. It is just under seven feet from side to side, and up to seventy-two feet long. A barge is a wider and more curvaceous creature, belonging usually to the rivers and able to carry a much larger cargo[§]. A barge is voluptuous. A narrow boat is skinny. They are not the same. To confuse them is like mistaking a whippet for a St. Bernard. There are a few places where local dialect makes 'barge' and 'narrow boat' interchangeable, but until you are absorbed by the native population I would err on the side of caution. Saying 'barge' when you mean 'narrow boat' will wind boaters up. Saying 'sailors' when you mean 'boaters' will wind boaters up. Saying 'river' when you mean 'canal' will wind boaters up. Asking 'Is it cold in the winter?' will certainly wind boaters up.

To be fair, almost anything will wind boaters up: but the first of these solecisms was my major sin on my first day as Working Boats Project Officer for British Waterways. I might as well have walked into the office wearing a dunce's cap and a big T-shirt saying 'I KNOW NOTHING, ME'. I am surprised they didn't sack me on the spot. I was a babe in the woods, innocent of the heritage, politics and challenges of conservation that apply to canal boats. The two canny women who hired me had seen me coming.

[§] It follows that since narrow boats are not barges, the people who worked them and now the people who live on them are not and never were 'bargees'. That is another solecism, often used by people who want to be courteous. The men who worked the boats were boatmen. The women who also worked the boats were often thought of as 'boatmen's wives' but this is as much a nonsense as the idea of a 'farmer's wife'. A farmer's wife is a farmer. For that reason, I usually speak of the historic boat community as 'boat people' rather than the usual term, boatmen. People like me who live and travel on modern boats are – as you may have guessed by now – boaters.

As guardians of the waterways, BW had inherited a number of historic working boats; cargo boats, tug boats, icebreakers on which, in a hard winter, men would rock back and forth to clear a passage for water traffic. There were maintenance boats and cabinless 'day boats' that made short trips around the Midlands. Some were still in daily use. Others sat rotting in the quiet corners of boatyards around Birmingham. Most were, as my father would have said, 'neither nowt nor summat'.

The waterways that I was about to experience for the first time would bring together all my work on archaeology, all my studies of infrastructure, and throw into the mix a peculiar industrial alchemy. I walked into that office with a track record of learning quickly about lead mines and textile mills and the manufacture of glass. I expected that the canal system and the boats that worked it would be much the same. They were not.

The boats in my armada of ten were rescued on the same principles as listed buildings; they were either typical or exceptional. The youngest and most endearing was the bright little tug and icebreaker *Nansen II*, whose skipper was as cheerful and workmanlike as the boat. Joe Hollinshead had been in charge of *Nansen* for many years, and it was an unspoken understanding that he would stay with it until one of them fell apart.

The backbone of my fleet was a sextet of lean boats built in the 1930s. Like the animals of Noah's Ark, they came in two by two: *Scorpio* and *Malus*, *Atlas* and *Leo*, *Sagitta* and *Carina*. These 'working pairs' travelled together in their heyday. Each pair has one boat with an engine (the motor) and one without an engine (the butty). The butty is towed on a long rope like a trailer, or on short straps which make the pair a floating juggernaut. Sometimes the boats travel side by side or 'breasted up'. No matter how they were joined, the coupled boats could carry two cargoes with one modest engine. Together they drew around forty tons of cargo over the frictionless waters – that's 183 pack horses' worth.

In the next months I lived, slept and moved on the working boats, marshalling a volunteer task force of 150 enthusiasts. In my archaeology days I always had remnant soil under my nails: now I smelt coal dust and Brasso on my skin, as we kept the tiny range burning in each cabin and polished the brass chimney bands. The volunteers were hardcore boat enthusiasts who worked long hours to keep the boats moving. Most of them knew more than me. Among them was a couple in their thirties called Brian and Anne-Marie, Midlanders for whom the boats were a part of their hinterland as coal and steel were part of mine. Where other people want to start up a company and make a million, they dreamed of a fleet of coal boats. Another regular crew member was Skipper Jon, mischievous and intelligent, a collector of vintage cars and risqué jokes. With these, and surrounded by colleagues who had years of experience with boats, I thrived in the discrete corridor of life, gossip and work.

Boating required a slow, attentive frame of mind, and the ability to always find a little magic in even the most unpromising spot. In a grubby pound behind derelict warehouses in Stoke-on-Trent we were voyeurs as a pair of swans mated in a royal flurry of white. We often moored in the elephant's graveyard of working boats at Icknield Port Loop in Birmingham, a dirty backwater that only boaters could then reach. Retired boats huddled in companionable pairs, keeping company with disused warehouses in a tangle of buddleja and butterflies. On the opposite bank there was a makeshift shelter of corrugated iron furnished with an inexplicable armchair and a brazier. Passing the old works of Armitage Shanks, we saw mountains of freshly made toilet bowls stacked on the bank. In Birmingham we passed the scaffolded facades of Chance, the glass works that supplied the Crystal Palace, and moored under canopies at Bournville Wharf, where Cadbury's unloaded tonnes of chocolate crumb.

These places have never been grand or genteel. Even so, the deep peace of water answered something in me. It did the same for the people on the towpath, wherever we passed them. Dog walkers, joggers, the dodgy urban anglers who always looked as if they ought to be reporting to their probation officer, and the many people who sat quietly on canal-side benches, eating their lunch and thinking through their troubles: to all of them, the water was an aid to thought and – more precious still – to *un*thought, the stillness of mind that so many are looking for. The people who understood that search best were those who had chosen to live as close to water as possible. Some were hirers, some liveaboards, some day trippers or even hauliers; in all their forms, they were boaters.

Wherever we tied up, we were instantly at home. It took a while to fully understand the shift in mindset. Visitors often exclaimed that being on the boats was 'just like camping' and I could see why, but it always brought me a prickle of discomfort. It would feel far worse when people said it of my own boat in later years. Certainly, the pleasure of waking up in a different place each morning had something in common with the transient and light-footed life that most of us only experience on a camping holiday, but doing it full time was a very different thing. As a society we have settled: we live in settlements. This other way of life seemed to be a process of *unsettling*. The very sense of 'home' was different; home was no longer a fixed point, but a moveable feast. A boater could explore their own country as a resident in each of the many counties and villages. This sense of home was something I felt right at home with.

As for boat handling, I did my best. I had instruction from true boatmen with varying degrees of patience. Joe Hollinshead was unflappable. As I scraped one of the heritage boats against a bridge or frantically swung the tiller this way and that with no sense of what it might accomplish, Joe remained serene as a Black Country Buddha. 'Never you mind, her's all right. I been on the water sixty years,' said Joe reassuringly, 'and every time I go out I've made some kind of mistake.' This was not true, but it made me feel better. 'Trick is to mek 'em slowly,' he added – and, crucially – 'try to mek a different mistake each time.' It's a good rule.

I did get better at steering, beginning to feel in my body the relationship between a boat and the water under it. I understood when to cut the engine and let the hull drift under its own weight. I could read the water, spotting a 'cat's paw' of breeze which foretold an unhelpful side wind, or anticipating that a hidden weir would drag the nose of the boat across the canal. I was as capable a lock-wheeler as anyone, walking ahead of our boats to set a lock in advance and hasten the journey. I found that I could touch the back end of the boat softly against the bank to collect a crew member without stopping, and hover mid-channel with perfect control while waiting for a lock.

Thanks to the old hands who taught me, I also knew some things that modern boaters never learn. Born and raised on working boats, my teachers had a repertoire of small movements and long-practised tricks that made boating easy and elegant, and which are the single greatest loss to modern boat culture. They were confident in using the strapping posts and little pieces of lock furniture that help a boat to stop or to start moving again; they knew without thinking how to adjust for the difference in 'swim' between an empty and a loaded vessel. Some of this I learned.

I absorbed some of their prejudices too. If they saw any steerer using his engine to pull away from a mooring, 'proper' boaters like my colleagues closed their eyes in pain. 'It knackers the banks,' they explained, through erosion. Worse, it shows that you are handling a boat as if it were a car. The proper method is to stand on the towpath and push the boat out, step on to the counter as it drifts into the channel, and only then use the engine. It takes a few seconds longer; it looks after the canal; it *feels* right. Their worst scorn was reserved for the bow thruster, a feature of many modern boats. Its distinctive whirr made them all smirk; 'Ah, the girly button!' they would say. The bow thruster is, as you may have guessed, a thruster at the bow. It allows you to simultaneously damage the canal bank and demonstrate that you can't steer your boat around a corner; and it was universally held in contempt by all who had grown up steering a pair of loaded seventy-two-foot boats around the watery slaloms of the Midlands, including the infamous 'Curly Wyrley' as the Wyrley and Essington Canal is called.

Above all, I learned about rope. I learned how to coil it, not in the climber's tight figure of eight, but in a boater's loose O, so that it can immediately be thrown to a crew member without tangling into a serpentine mass; how to clean ropes and keep them soft; how to place them so that the right line is always to hand. I was taught never to tie a knot, which will tighten under tension, but to use a tugman's hitch or a locking turn, which can be swiftly undone even under strain. The greatest sin ever, the sign of utter incompetence, was to cut a rope. The second greatest was to travel, as many boaters now do, with rope hanging over the tiller in a slack loop. This lends an air of jaunty nonchalance to the journey, right up to the moment when it drops into your propeller and brings the engine to a grinding halt.

At last, I could hold my nerve in a tight corner. I could take the boat around smoothly without danger of a bump; and if there was a bump, I learned to blame it loudly on the wind, on another skipper or an underwater obstacle, in the time honoured way. As time went on, Joe began to grin more often: 'We'll mek a boat girl of yow yet!' he vowed.

Brindley

The canals which kick-started a new culture in Britain were not the brainchild of one or two minds, but there were fewer than you might think. They were a handful of charismatic people who came together in the mid-1760s in a single great project born of need, opportunity and ambition. They saw the clogged packhorse trails and rutted turnpike roads, and realised that the solution was not to build or improve highways. Roads would always be worn into ruts by heavy loads; they will always be at the mercy of the weather. The alternative was a network of waterways.

The Staffordshire millwright James Brindley was not alone in seeing this, but it was he who had the idea of connecting England's great navigable rivers in a 'Grand Cross' of water: Trent to Mersey, Humber to Thames. Within three decades of beginning it, the project was largely complete, though Brindley himself did not live to see it. Across the map of Britain there spread a network that would become a conduit for money but also a liquid village; a network which we who live on it now call 'the system'. According to Samuel Smiles writing a century later:

> [Brindley] likened water in a river flowing down a declivity to a furious giant running along and overturning everything; whereas (said he) 'if you lay the giant flat upon his back, he loses all his force, and becomes completely passive, whatever his size may be'.

Canal water has no current. There are exceptions to the rule. You know that you are in one of these spots when your boat suddenly slides left for no apparent reason, as on the Caldon where the river Churnet sneaks into the canal and pins you to the bank just as you approach a lock. On the Llangollen Canal, there is a thin tube of water where you will feel that the engine is losing power and you begin going backwards. In reality, the water is pushing against you and rushing in to the channel from the river Dee at Horseshoe Falls, gently reminding you who is in charge. You recognise your place in the order of things, tug a forelock and throttle up. For the most part, though, canal water is inert and moved to action only when one of these rivers chivvies it along. Canal water is domesticated rather than wild. Sluices, by-weirs and spillways keep the waterway quiet, full and predictable. In fact, that's the very point of a canal. Brindley, as Smiles said, 'laid the giant flat upon his back', making water transport as reliable and unnoticed as a bus route. Brindley's canals were invariably flat, because he didn't like to carry them up or down hills. His was the canal that started 'canal mania'.

Brindley was a Peak District lad whose early working life in the 1750s took him into the mills and mines of a busy and imaginative age. A man of this exact generation, with transferable skills and chutzpah, could dip into all kinds of projects. Brindley had a practical and varied education in the silk mills of Macclesfield, the pot banks of Josiah Wedgwood and the coal mines of Lancashire. 'He is as plain a looking man as one of the Boors of the Peak, or one of his own Carters,' wrote a Brindley stan; 'but when he speaks all ears listen, and every mind is filled with wonder at the things he pronounces to be practicable.'

Everywhere he turned his vivid, instinctive intelligence to the challenges of water: how to limit its danger and exploit its power, use it to turn a mill wheel faster, or use water itself to raise water from flooded coal seams. Famously, in mines near Manchester owned by the Duke of Bridgewater, Brindley and his colleague John Gilbert used a single channel both to drain the sodden coal levels and carry the coal to market. This project of 1760 made his name, and what he learned would change everything. Self-taught, Brindley went on to deliver 360 miles of canal across English fields, valleys and estates 'without written calculations or drawings, leaving no records except the works themselves'. His legacy is the Grand Cross, a giant liquid crucifix with a wonky cross-beam, connecting four big rivers. By 1770 the Trent was hitched to the Mersey, and the Thames to the Humber. Over the next fifty years, scores of capillary waterways were attached to that skewed arterial frame.

In the next generation, a later and very different man would answer the stubborn difficulties of landscape with the full force of late Georgian technology, and with government finance behind him. Thomas Telford could blast his way through a hill, carve multiple locks into bedrock, suspend a bridge over the widest estuary. Brindley, trailblazer of the 1760s, had to work with pick-axe, instinct and a smaller budget. His bridges were sturdy and low-arched, his canals lined with tons of puddled clay. He had a deep understanding of water and its physics – but Brindley had neither the means, the technology nor the budget to lift it above a valley with long embankments, to take it up a steep hill in a lock flight or to carry it across a wide river in a light-weight iron channel. Where there was a hill, Brindley went around it. Where there was a valley, he clung to one low slope, draping the water-way around it at a single level, laying the giant flat on its back.

An age of curiosity

The past, famously, is a foreign country; but we were all born there. We are first-generation immigrants, settling and resettling a new home-land shaped by our point of origin, that land of a few decades ago where we first became ourselves. When we glimpse into the past, we tend to 'other' our countrymen and women, just as we often do with people from a different faith or culture to our own. We like to believe that they were not as clever or as wise as us. They had funny ideas about the movement of the planets, or the mechanics of childbirth, or who should be able to vote. Their cultural norms were a bit weird. Our norms are normal norms.

Brindley, Telford, and their peers lived, as we do, against a backdrop of culture and world events that shaped their fears and expectations. As Brindley surveyed the route of the Harecastle Tunnel, James Cook was 'discovering' Australia and reshaping the map of the world, while William and Caroline Herschel were reimagining the universe it sits in. As Thomas Telford and William Jessop planned the great Pontcysyllte Aqueduct, the French Revolution was as recent for them as the global pandemic is for us, and Horatio Nelson was fighting his last battles.

At the height of the canal-building frenzy there was a slow, private moment of wonder in Hampshire which stands for the novelty and scientific method of the age. On 16 October 1784, naturalist Gilbert

White recorded an unusual event in his famous journal. His normal entries were gentle, precise observations about nature. He noted when the swifts returned each summer, and when Mrs Snooke's tortoise Timothy went into hibernation. One April evening he recorded the first nightingale of the year with a single joyful word, its Latin name: *Luscinia*! But on this day in 1784, the country vicar was hoping to observe something unnatural and wondrous: a man in the sky over Selborne.

White recruited small boys from the local farms and stationed them at intervals across nearby fields. The boys stared towards the smoky smudge of London fifty miles to the north-east. Squinting up towards the sky from their posts, they are a line of curious dots on the time map. Barely able to frame in their minds what they were looking for, they scanned the sky. At quarter to three the first one cried out. The boys began to call out for White. They had seen it: an Icarus over Hampshire. As promised, Monsieur Jean Blanchard had launched his hot-air balloon from Chelsea and was drifting over South East England with a companion. They had the first aerial view of England – its contours, its fields dotted with waving boys and, of course, its rivers. As Blanchard drifted towards touchdown at Romsey he may have seen shallow barges on the River Itchen Navigation, a modest (and never truly successful) waterway connecting Winchester to the coast. Gilbert White, meticulous and awestruck, recorded what he saw:

> *[A] dark blue speck at a most prodigious height, dropping as it were from the sky, and hanging amidst the regions of the upper air, between the weather-cock of the tower and the top of the maypole... and then over the Fox on my great parlour chimney; and then behind my great walnut tree. To my eyes this vast balloon appeared no bigger than a large tea-urn.*

If we stand alongside Gilbert White in his parsonage garden, we can imagine how uncanny it would be to see humans airborne for the first time. White 'felt my heart rebound with fear and joy at the same time...' but he got used to it quickly. 'At last, seeing with what steady composure they moved, I began to consider [the balloonists] as a group of Storks or Cranes intent on the business of emigration.' What astonished him a moment before, was absorbed into a new frame of reference; and he went back to observing Mrs Snooke's tortoise.

There was a lot of this sort of thing going on in the 1780s. The naturalist looking up and the aerialist looking down were both part of a fast-changing Britain. The pace of change was outrageous. The canals themselves were the most visible sign of it, impacting on the landscape as much as a new motorway does now. A previously intact rural landscape would be cut in two by a host of navvies, and once it was filled with water it would quickly be edged with wharves, warehouses, stables and mills. The watermills and pack-horses began to reduce in number, the steam-driven mines and mills began to increase.

If you take a small country with improving roads and canals, a thriving print culture, fast-growing towns and just a few important centres of scholarship or technological development, then it soon becomes an enormous *salon* whose liveliest members can find each other easily. The connections between them would look like one of those posters of band members in the 1990s who spawned one group, drifted into another and survived to influence the next cycle of work. For instance, at the Lunar Society in Birmingham Josiah Wedgwood could discuss his vision of a better-connected Britain with fellow manufacturer Matthew Boulton, and also with his friend Erasmus

Darwin. Darwin's proto-evolutionary ideas were informed by fossils from Wedgwood's canal cuttings. Joseph Priestley would discuss his scientific findings, informing the painter Joseph Wright of Derby in his epic paintings of scientific experiments. Wright was not a Lunar man but another Midlander, as was Doctor Johnson. Johnson would meet Lunar Society members and other friends in London, where they might share news of Joseph Priestley's discovery of oxygen or the revolution in America.

Commerce and philosophy were nourished by these interactions; but so were cruelty and impoverishment on an industrial scale. As we will see, the construction of the canals was underwritten by the abysmal working conditions of the navvies, and the fast-growing towns were underwritten by new concentrations of people, all of them at the mercy of high food prices (between 1798 and 1801 food prices rose by 77 per cent). They were unable either to protest or to lobby for higher wages, since they had no vote and organised labour or striking were illegal; so they rioted. There were plentiful food riots, accompanied by campaigns for a wider vote. The cost of the Napoleonic war, then the release of its veterans onto the streets, added to the visible burden on ordinary people. In West Indian plantations and overseas colonies, the wider economy that the new waterways served was underwritten by enslavement and asset stripping. In this precise period of transformation, there was a feedback loop of technology, curiosity, exploitation and intellect. This book cannot begin to explain the synaptic network of collective thought that connected the thinkers and activists of the time. For that, you need a book like Richard Holmes's *The Age of Wonder*. It shouldn't surprise us that Holmes's age of wonder runs from 1768 to 1831. It coincides almost perfectly with the age of canal building.

Why don't you just turn the engine on?

The split bridges over the locks in the Stratford flight are dainty Georgian structures that look like tiny replicas of Tower Bridge, frozen in a not-quite-closed position. The permanent gap between the two halves was a small time-saving device of sorts, meaning that a horse boat coming out of the lock could drop its tow rope through the bridge without the need for the horse to be unhitched and then hitched again.

However, not all unpowered boats were horse boats. From the 1920s right through to the close of real commerce in the 1960s, the usual formation on the narrow canals was the working pair. Twin boats would be worked together – one with an engine, one without. The boat with an engine is the motor, and the boat without is a butty – the old word for 'mate' which evolved into 'buddy' on the other side of the Atlantic. Sometimes in broader waters the two boats would breast up to travel side by side, lashed together as a single wide vessel, but on narrow canals the motor usually towed the butty behind it like a huge trailer. Together, they formed an articulated vehicle over 140 feet long, hitched together on cross straps (a short flexible coupling of crossed ropes). On a lengthy pound the tow rope might be thirty or forty feet long.

The first appearance of a useful engine on the canals came around 1912, when a distinctive heart-stopping *BOP BOP   BOP* sound was heard on the waterways. This was the Bolinder, a semi-diesel whose eccentric rhythm misses a beat every now and then. It is started by an arcane process involving a blow torch, some courage and, occasionally, a broken leg. Once running, it sounds like an absent-minded man banging a tin tray at the bottom of a long metal tube. There are still a few Bolinders around, and you will know one when you hear it because that popgun sound will bring boaters' heads popping up from their side hatches, peering around like so many meerkats.

The motors in my little fleet were launched in the 1930s, and by my time they each had a Lister HR2 engine whose low, reverberating chuckle made the hull throb with a deep pulse. The motor shudders with life, creating a travelling cocoon of engine noise and exhaust smoke. It drowns out sound and tempers the smells of fresh air, elder-flower or (on the Peak Forest) the delicious smell of Parma Violets as you pass the Swizzels factory.

The steerer of the butty has a very different experience of the journey. She is perhaps a hundred feet behind the churning engine, on a long tow rope, and there is no noise at all from her boat, except the unnameable sound of a steel shape cleaving through still water that never breaks into a wash. The thrush blurting out of the offside bushes is almost riotous. The ghostly heron, lifted from its fishing station by the sound of the engine will settle back into place, miffed, as the butty passes. If a fish splashes into the air or a water vole makes its comical, ungainly *plop* into the channel, the steerer will register it.

The butty, described earlier as a trailer, was actually a bit more independent than that suggests. The butty boat has its own steering mechanism in the form of a person at the back end and a bloody great piece of timber called an ellum. This, you will be told by scholars, is a corruption of 'helm' and so it is, strictly speaking; but 'ellum' is the proper word for the thick, cupboard-door-sized blade of oak that hangs at the back of the butty and directs the vessel.

A competent butty steerer has more agency than you might think. At the height of working boat traffic, the motor would typically be steered by a man, and the butty by his wife or child. If she took a mind to, she could mess him up. The man who had annoyed his wife in the morning might find that he spent the afternoon battling his motor around usually simple corners, as the back half of his articulated vehicle chose to jack-knife him, or simply failed to nudge him around with the considerable leverage of a second full boat. The wife who had annoyed her husband, on the other hand, might find her butty scraping too close to the silted inside of a bend, or veering closer to a river weir than she would like.

There is still a handful of working pairs on the cut. They are a rarity and are often met with bovine stupefaction by other boaters or towpath walkers.

There were three working pairs in my little armada, worked by volunteers with an appetite for long days and for learning skills with no application at all in daily life. Occasionally, it made sense to unhitch the motor on a long flight of locks: the motor would go ahead to the next lock, while the crew bow-hauled the butty from the towpath – that's pulling, in plain English – like overqualified horses. It's not as hard as it sounds. You throw the tow rope over your shoulder and lean into it. The boat gathers momentum, there is no friction from the water, and it keeps going silently until it slides into the lock. At this point, in a perfect world, the butty steerer would effortlessly loop a rope around the strapping post on the lock gate, pulling it closed behind her and braking the boat at the same time, so that it stops under faultless control.

On the Stratford, I was part of a team working *Leo*, our butty, through a remote lock crossed by a split bridge. This elegant, organic process is always rewarding to watch. Tons of stone, coal, or gravel slotting into the lock chamber with a couple of inches to spare on each side: the work of muscle, rope and a mitred gate to collect and release the power of water; the human effort of turning a windlass, that simple bent piece of metal with a hole in one end, to raise the fastened sluices in a *dinkdinkdink* of ratchets and release a bubbling torrent of ozone-scented liquid; and then the silent gliding of the boat as the rope drops through the split bridge, the bow-hauler takes the strain, and the boat gets under way again.

A hire boat drew up behind us, waiting for the lock. *Oh, lucky you,* I thought. *This is why we're here; to show you, the leisure boater, the rich heritage of the waterways. Once in a lifetime you will see this perfect balance of effort and release, with a historic boat worked by experienced crew in the exact way that this canal was designed for. It's almost metaphysical, this exchange of effort and movement.* The hire boat skipper tied up and walked along the towpath to greet us.

'Why don't you turn the fucking engine on?' he said.

Not for the last time, I understood that most canal users are unaware of the motor-and-butty tradition of the early twentieth century. When we told him it did not have an engine, he thought we were joking. The idea that an unpowered boat could exist was entirely new to him. It did not strike him as charming or historic; it was a pain in the bum.

'Why don't you just get it *fixed?*' he said, with absolute incomprehension.

We explained that some boats – most boats, in fact – had never had an engine. We explained that this was a remarkable survival, and that his crew were lucky to see it. They explained that they were trying to finish the Warwickshire ring and get back to the hire boat depot within the allotted week. We were slowing them down.

Hire boaters, who visit the canal for perhaps one week in their lifetimes, can be forgiven this in the same way that I, hopefully, can be forgiven for not knowing everything about the history of the Paris Métro. After all, a year before this exchange I would have been just as innocent of the working pairs. If you want to see them in action, seek them out at a local canal festival or waterways museum. When you see them go by, stop everything. Stand and watch them. Give thanks for the chance to see a unique practice: a dot from an earlier layer of the time map, a dot from the water map, passing smoothly across your own.

The boats in my care were classed as 'large artefacts' in conservation terms. Proletarian as they were, they presented a classic dilemma known to heritage workers as the Ship of Theseus problem. This exalted name refers to the mythical ship which was replaced, plank by plank, until it was no longer the original vessel at all. If you are a fan of the ancient sitcom *Only Fools and Horses*, you'll remember that the same principle applies to Trigger's broom. Trigger, a famously dim street sweeper, is awarded a medal from the council for using the same tool of the trade for twenty years. 'Mind you,' says Trigger thoughtfully, 'the broom has had seventeen new heads and fourteen new 'andles.'

On either the classical or comical model, the motor boat *Atlas* was a good case study. Since her 1935 launch at the Harland and Wolff boatyard, she had been maintained with as little sentimentality as any haulage vehicle. For instance, she began as a 'composite' boat with steel sides and a thick wooden bottom, but like many of her sisters had long since lost her elm planks and acquired a low-maintenance steel baseplate. *Atlas* was a working vehicle whose owner asked the same pragmatic questions as any other cargo fleet operator: what does it need, how cheaply can we do it, and what will last longest?

And then, along comes the archaeologist with her kid gloves. I wanted to preserve the greatest possible percentage of the 1935 boat. If a part of the hull was so rusted that it was about to go through, I would want to weld a tiny patch of new steel on top of it. This made perfect sense to me. We would preserve the original make-up, repair it and keep it floating with minimal intervention. *Ta-dah!*

To anyone who lives and works with boats, it was a nonsense. My clever over-plating solution would be an ugly sticking-plaster and an unhealthy rust trap: any sensible boat builder would just let in a substantial piece of steel. This was explained to me over and over again by perplexed workers at boat maintenance yards around the Midlands. They had fags in their mouths and dismay on their faces. The original boats in the fleet, they told me, would never have been handled in this footling, piecemeal way. To present them reverently as patched relics, which didn't look 'proper' to the people who knew them best, did a disservice to both boat and people.

Atlas was built in the Depression as part of a work creation programme. She worked through the war and the speedy post-war decline of the canals, travelling increasingly derelict waterways and on into an age of leisure craft, finally becoming an attraction for children and museum visitors. Every bit of this life story was a part of her identity. The name *Atlas* describes the story of a boat, as much as it does the plates and planks of a boat. A historic vessel is both itself and a replica of itself. The steel and wood and paint that construct the craft are only half of it. A third part is the water it sits in: this gives it the movement, the float-and-sink tension, the shimmy that makes it boat, not box. The final component is the *idea* of the vessel. Like a human whose cells change, but whose selfhood resides in her experience and memory, every boat carries its own past within it.

A boat, more than any other object made by human hands, loses its meaning once out of the water. The people explaining this to me felt about a 'properly' conserved narrow boat as the tiger feels about taxidermy. I had thought of these vessels as something like farm machinery. In truth, they were more like farm livestock. A working boat is a living thing. We had to take Trigger's approach, replacing whatever was necessary to keep it alive.

Least patient of my tutors as I learned to handle the boats was Richard, the sometime boyfriend who took me out on that magical first trip, as I steered his boat *Cepheus* into the canal basin at Worcester. Soon after our river trip he sold *Cepheus,* got a new job and bought himself a Norwegian fishing boat, a fat little ketch which he kept on a mooring in Gloucester Dock. From here he had a twenty-yard commute to his work as a shipwright in the yard of Tommi Nielsen.

Nielsen's yard was an oak-and-brine oasis which gave me a new experience of life afloat. The historic dock was bounded by high brick warehouses and a cantilever bridge which occasionally raised its two arms to welcome in a new boat. Richard's boat 'looked like melodeon music' as the Norman MacCaig poem 'A Man and A Boat' has it. Her decks were cluttered with ropes and buckets, and she smelt of dead fish, but she kept exalted company. Bobbing alongside her at the old stone wharf were antique sailing ships, freshly arrived for repairs. These are the tall ships that you see on Netflix dramas or in films like *Pirates of the Caribbean.* There were always five or six aristocrats alongside Richard's coarse little ketch; frigates, sloops, brigs and sleek pilot cutters from the high age of sail. Their masts spiked the air like narwhal horns. These were the real Ships of Theseus, their deep cargo holds full of stories.

It was a time of sawdust, pitch and beer. Nielsen's shipwrights were latter-day Vikings, drifting in from Scandinavia to work for a season or two and then drifting away with a heartbroken barmaid in their wake. By day they shaved curls of pine off a bowsprit or caulked the decks of a Nelsonian flagship: by night, we ate together and drank heartily in the bowels of ancient ships. These were dark timbered spaces with low ceilings, scented with ghost cargoes of tobacco, rum or spices and the ghosts of the enslaved people who harvested them. Someone bought a coracle, the round-bottomed rowboat the shape and almost the size of a pudding bowl, used in Britain since the Bronze Age. The shipwrights raced across the dock in it on summer nights, riotous in their laughter as they wobbled over in their water-walnut. The aim was to cross the dock, buy a pint at the waterside bar and bring it back to the wharf without tipping over. At least one sailor fell in every time, and paid the penalty of buying a round.

Boats of all kinds were becoming home. My working weeks passed with the canal volunteers, sleeping in the rose-and-castle, coal-dust cabins of our working boats. At weekends I lived in the twelve-foot square cabin of the ketch. It was no hardship, for I had a long habit of travelling light. I had always moved between archaeological sites in Britain, Turkey and Greece with a small bag of essentials – a toothbrush, clean knickers and Marcus Aurelius' *Meditations*. In my actual home, a tiny low-beamed cottage near the Stratford canal, I began to feel increasingly encumbered by Things. I didn't have much, but it felt like too much. The televisions, furniture, vases and pot plants, drawers full of clothes, cupboards full of seldom-worn shoes; the cycle of buying, cleaning, looking after and replacing these Things felt like physical and mental clutter. The shipwrights had little baggage of any kind, and seemed all the freer for it. I was happiest in the places where I had fewest possessions around me.

My match with Richard was largely based on pheromones, proximity and boat handling. There is much to be said for all three, but it doesn't make for a lifelong commitment. After a few months we found ourselves mysteriously preoccupied with work, and with boats in other places. We were to part company not only amicably, but almost absent mindedly. The phone in the cottage rang one night. It was a booty call.

'Fancy coming down this weekend?' he asked.

'No Rich,' I said. 'I've left you.'

'Have you? Oh.' He sounded slightly put out; but only slightly. 'When did you do that, then?' he asked.

'Six weeks ago. I wondered how long you would take to notice.'

'Right. Well, fair enough then. Cheerio.' I could hear his shipwright friends in the background, getting ready for a night out. Richard, I felt sure, would find consolation in the next hour or two. Clearly this had not been a life-changing relationship for him.

It had for me. By now, I had spent months moving between the cabins of working boat, tall ship, ketch and crabber. It dawned on me that there was a way to stay in motion but to always be at home; to get rid of most of my pesky Things and move to a new place whenever work or romance required and see my own country from the other side of the map; the side where the boaters and the salty sailors lived. I could live like this forever. I could buy a boat.

Buying a boat

A Marriage

The thirteenth boat they show me – *Tinker* –
is the first I know for mine. The pheromones
of hemp and Brasso, varnish, rust – there's always rust –
the base note of warm steel and bilge oils, coal and toast.

It's not called *must* for nothing; that smell,
that rush, that summons back to love. Suck it up;
the cabin chemistry of laundry, chains and diesel
sweat-sweet, signalling our match.

What makes this *boat,* not *box,* is all around. I move
and it replies. With every step the floor shifts underfoot;
my own weight, answered. I step forward
and the boat steps back, recentred.

We shimmy, we judder, we jive. We're learning
how our new-joined self must move. The courtship starts
as courtship starts, with call and gradual response.
The floors are narrow but the drift is part of how we dance.

Where did you meet the love of your life? It's often somewhere unlikely, but you know them when they show up. I met mine near the toilet pump-out at Napton marina.

I had a chaperone on my boat-hunting expeditions. Skipper Jon was one of the working boat volunteers, and a glorious mixture of

wisdom and mischief. His *joie de vivre* and love for old machines –
boats, cars, anything that moved – was surpassed only by his devotion
to his phlegmatic wife Judy. There were two classes of object in Jon's
world; the ones that made him wince, and the ones that made him
half-whistle with appreciation. These – vintage cars, attractive women
or a Bolinder engine with its irregular *BOP BOP BOP*, all fell under
one heading. 'Oh, that's a bolt-shooter. An absolute *bolt-shooter*, darling.'
I didn't like to ask. Jon's bright eye could be surprisingly steely if he
suspected someone of less-than-gentlemanly dealings, and I wanted it
on my side during my search for a home.

Jon and Judy were amphibious, living in a house with two enormous
Great Danes but often taking long trips on their immaculate boat *Ventus*.
The dogs wreaked havoc with their huge silken bodies whenever they
tried to turn around in the confined cabin, and so they had been trained
to walk backwards. Jon and I met on his boat to draw up a wish list for
mine, and the Great Danes moved forward and back like dressage horses.

'Why is your boat called *Ventus*?' I asked. 'Means *fart* in Latin', Jon
replied with a plummy guffaw, throwing his head back in laughter. The
constant joke was that he would eventually persuade Judy to abandon their neat suburban house and live entirely on the boat. 'How
long have you been trying?' 'Oh, about thirty years. But I'll wear her
down, you mark my words.' Judy had very communicative eyebrows.
Not bloody likely, they said.

A modern narrow boat is a steel shoe box with a little house on top.
It's a short floating corridor, seven feet wide and up to seventy-two feet
long. Usually they have a flat bottom of 10mm steel plate, with 6mm sides
and thinner plate of 4mm for the roof. This much they have in common.
After that, they differ just as much as houses do. We drew up a list of non-
negotiables for my ideal boat. 'How big?' asked Jon. 'Big,' I said. Jon looked

at me with a half-smile. He had recently watched me steer a big boat. I had turned the tiller the wrong way at a crucial moment and blocked all the traffic on a bustling junction for ten minutes. What else did I want? 'Light.' The old boats with their portholes looked splendid, but admitted little light. I wanted the big windows of a modern liveaboard.

To this, Jon added practical considerations. A good paint job; a powerful inverter to supply electricity to plug sockets; oh, and a powerful engine. 'Why? I'm not going on any big rivers,' I said with great conviction, remembering my early experience on the Severn.

Jon did his little smile again. 'You never know,' he said.

You find a second-hand boat as you find a second-hand car, by poring over small ads or visiting a broker. We looked over a dozen or so at brokers' yards. Some were Rolls-Royce types with extravagant fripperies, like self-aligning solar panels or dividing walls that slid into place at the touch of a button. They made me break into a sweat. On the working boats our entire water supply was a florid two-gallon can, and our toilet a Porta Potti tucked in the engine room. There was quite enough potential for cock-up on a low-tech vessel, without introducing electronics. Others we saw were floating hovels with mould on every surface. These are the 'project boats' which enthusiastic young men buy in the belief that they can fix them up and turn a profit. You meet them years later, gaunt and harrowed, chewing their nails in canal-side pubs and twitching. 'How's the boat?' you ask, if you're feeling unkind. 'Oh, you know. Coming on,' they say, and swiftly order a whisky.

One or two boats ticked all the boxes on my list. They had a sound hull, a lot of living space, a reliable engine and were made by a good boat builder; yet they were missing something. Like people you meet on a dating site, ticking the boxes isn't enough. There has to be something else. There has to be chemistry. Finally, Jon and I came to a broker at Napton, at the northern end of James Brindley's sinuous Oxford Canal. The woman at the chandlery desk was preoccupied with a hire boater, who was checking in with seventeen children and a dog. She raised an eyebrow and threw me the keys. As always, they were attached to a round cork ball, so that you can watch them floating away when you drop them in the canal. We found the sales mooring where the boat was waiting for us, and had a look.

She was completely unremarkable: functional rather than elegant, bottle green with red coach lines, slightly scuffed and nameless. The hull was long at sixty-seven feet, but smaller than the seventy-two-foot working boats. We stood back and considered her lines, like horse traders looking over an animal. This was not a pedigree racehorse, but neither was it a drab mule. The cabin swept up in a slight curve towards the back, her snub nose was attractively formed and everything about her felt solid.

On paper, she had not one name but two. She was currently *Cariad*, the Welsh for 'darling', but her first name had been *Dream Catcher*. The dual heritage was visible. Jon did his signature wince as he stepped down into the cabin and saw the prints on the walls.

'Oh dear God,' he said. On one side, a serene Native American chieftain gazed philosophically at a dream catcher. On the other was a large map of Wales. Jon was happier as he read the specifications. 'Builder: Graham Reeves. 'Ah!' he said, with the look of a whippet that has just seen a squirrel. Reeves was a good, dependable builder. *Cariad* was not a Lamborghini, but neither was she a Reliant Robin; she was something like a Volvo, not flashy but respectable and not unattractive.

In the kitchen was a mirror-bright steel box the size of a chest freezer. 'Bloody hell,' said Jon, with a half-whistle of approval. 'What even IS that?' I asked. 'It's a Dickinson diesel range, sort of like an Aga. Bloody marvellous piece of kit.' He nodded appreciatively. Above it was a Houdini hatch, a glazed panel that flooded the living space with light.

The range was the only object in the boat that shone. The rest was a Heath Robinson madness of cobbled-together work surfaces, mis-matched pine doors and laminate flooring with unusual stains. 'Cross bed,' shouted Jon from the back end. The double bed lay across the whole width of the boat, blocking access to the engine room and back deck or counter, where I would stand to steer. 'Not ideal', said Jon. He liked constant access to his own vintage engine so that he could drool over it in the middle of the night. 'Well, I won't be steering while I'm in bed,' I retorted. He conceded the point gracefully and propped the bed up on a strut to enter the engine room. Here we found a proper workhorse – a marinised Barras Shire far too big for the space, with barely room to get a spanner on either side. 'Forty-two horse power. Good for rivers,' said Jon, poking its every orifice. I had no intention of going onto a river, thank you very much.

The cabins were dark and slightly damp, the bathroom mouldy and disgusting, but there was the promise of warmth from a double-door log burner and three long radiators. The front doors were solid steel, so I could reassure my mother that no one on the towpath would break in and club me to death. At the very front of the boat was a six-foot-long 'cratch' space with a tent-like green cover and glazed panels.

'Handy for storing firewood in the winter,' I said.

'Bollocks to that,' said Jon, 'it's handy for drinking gin in the summer.'

None of this mattered. I knew as soon as I found her; as soon as I breathed in the sweet wood-and-dirt-and-diesel scent of her cabins. It was chemistry all right, as perfect as any between lovers. I filled my lungs again and again with that pheromone mix of wood, varnish, diesel, the tangs of metal and coal. It was a space made of steel, but with life and warmth in it. There was, too, the way the hull moved. As we walked around opening cupboards and pressing light switches, the boat shifted in response to our moving bodies. They all do this, and they all have a signature; each one carries its build, ballast and fit-out differently. There was something about the way that the weight of this boat moved to meet mine. We began to dance. She was not a remarkable boat, not a rare or elegant or particularly beautiful boat. But she was *my* boat.

We took her out of the marina to see how she handled, working her through a lock in which, for the first and only time, I saw a metre-long grass snake flinch and squiggle by the hull. Had there been any doubt, this test drive would have been the clincher. The 'swim' of a boat, the way it handles in water, is part of its identity. This one sat in the channel like a bulldog, squat and certain. She bit through the water like a plough blade. Most narrow boats don't like to turn; this one hunched down and spun with grace. There was a whole lot that needed fixing, changing or loving. I would fix it, change it and without question, I would love it.

'What do you think, Jon?'

He laughed out loud, seeing that I had already made up my mind. 'I think it's a bolt-shooter. A real *bolt-shooter.*'

River water

Even on a city canal, water sweetens and cleans the breeze: but the freshest of all is river water. I told Skipper Jon that I was staying on the nice dull canals, which were built precisely to be predictable. 'You never know,' he said. You never do. A week later I got a new job and took a mooring on the river Trent. In my first few mornings aboard I would hear not ducks, but seagulls.

The Trent is our third river, after the Severn and Thames. If rivers wore clothes Severn would sweep in wearing the robes of an ancient wizard, bringing mystery and a taste of danger. The Thames would sport a jaunty naval uniform, with the gold of commerce jingling in its pockets. The Trent would roll up in the breeches and woollen coat of an eighteenth-century entrepreneur. It is a Midland river and it means business. Just before it becomes fully tidal, it passes through Newark. Trent is a flooding river and after heavy rain it likes to remind the townspeople who is in charge, but in this ancient market town it slows down to curve placidly between the old warehouses and brewery buildings.

I had decided to rename the boat *Tinker*; I liked the little joke of it with my surname and it was a good word to describe a travelling worker. *Tinker* shared pontoons with narrow boats, wide beams and a handful of white river craft in a Newark marina where I could take delivery of everything including the kitchen sink. The bright range that had so impressed Jon did not work, and was replaced with big cupboards. Shabby carpets were ripped out and my grandmother's wicker-back reading chair brought in. The stove was blacked, burnished and fed with coal until the boat was thoroughly warm and dry. In a corner of the living room, I banged in a nail and hung up a turquoise plaque with a poem I loved, Raymond Carver's 'Late Fragment'.

And did you get what
you wanted from this life, even so?
I did.
And what did you want?
To call myself beloved, to feel myself
beloved on the earth.

And so it began. *Tinker* joined the fresh currents of a living river, and I left the working boats to live among soft-handed boat folk with unnecessary fripperies like curtains and an electric shower[1]. My new job was with the National Trust. One day I was at Calke Abbey inspecting the tunnels that made sure His Lordship would never have his dinner spoiled by the grotesque sight of a working-class person with a wheelbarrow; the next, I was at Woolsthorpe Manor in the quiet chamber where Isaac Newton made his private experiments, splitting light through a prism and throwing rainbows into the minds of his age.

There were no rainbows that first winter. The mornings were opal with mist. The air smelled of beer and smoke and cobbles. My local was, of course, the Navigation, a former warehouse studded with old mooring rings where barges once unloaded grain for the brewers. In those chilly weeks as I wrestled with plumbing and sawdust, the Navigation was (like all the other Navigations) a haven of warmth and raucous good company. Musicians, boaters and renegades gathered to dance and drink beneath the low brick arches, looking out over an elbow of dark water as it slipped past.

On the working boats I had often told visitors that a canal is not a river, and now I remembered that a river is not a canal. Where the canal is domestic, even servile, a river has traction. I remembered Richard's muttered mantra from the Severn: *One rule on the river; the river rules.* But for now, the Trent was kind to me. The stretch between Newark and Nottingham is seagull-and-swan country. Springtime saw the banks blur into green and silver. They hopped with life. Everywhere there was

---

[1] The most recent boater census conducted by the Canal and River Trust found that there are 35,000 boats on the system. By no means all of them are liveaboards, so that doesn't mean 35,000 people. However, those who do live aboard often come in pairs or family units; so let's assume around 30,000 people in our floating town.

a flourish of foliage: white and grey willows, shimmering birches. Grebes partaking in medieval courtship dances and swans conducting their frankly shocking sex lives in plain view. The glassy musculature of the Trent was always there, clenching and unfurling against *Tinker*'s black hull. An upstream journey, pushing against the flow, might take two hours. A downstream journey would take only half as long, borne along like passengers on a travelator. Sometimes the water was wide as a lake and choppy, making *Tinker* wallow a little. Often its surface was corrugated like a ploughed field, each furrow brimming over with sparkling chips of sunlight. After rainfall the grand weirs became waterfalls, foamy and fragrant with the detergent smell of ozone.

The freshness came not just from open air, but from the way I breathed it. As a house-dweller I had often sat in a room for hours without even noticing the weather, but on the boat you stand in it to steer. Even inside, the weather is close and loud. Light rain dropped on the roof like grains of rice on a tin tray. A hot day began with loud cracks as *Tinker*'s steel bones warmed through and stretched in the sun. On a blustery night I would be rocked to sleep by the push-and-pull rhythm of the mooring ropes. Suddenly I was popular among friends with young babies, because newborns are very familiar with the sensation of living in liquid, and they slept like a dream if wedged onto the high bed with pillows. A Molly, a George, a Frank, a William, two Tillies, and numerous other people under the age of one arrived in their parents' arms, and all of them fell sleepily silent on the boat.

Steering with tiller in one hand and a cup of tea in the other, the boater travels a green passageway at one remove from contemporary life – at least, from contemporary *human* life. Even in the inner cities, a waterway attracts what wildlife and vegetation there is. Beyond those urban centres, you are on neighbourly terms with nature, and that isn't always as cute as it sounds. I tied up near Beeston one April evening, and woke up in a slowly brightening cabin full of birdsong. The dawn chorus seemed unbearably loud, as if it were actually playing inside my head. A tiny Pavarotti was belting out his rills and riffs from a scrubby patch of thorn, four or five feet from my pillow. He looked like a feathery olive. At Stoke Bardolph I shared a cobalt twilight with the local blackbird, meticulous and philosophical in his evening song.

As a house-dweller, insulated from your surroundings by thick walls and double glazing, it is easy to feel that nature is a backdrop, a thing that happens outside. A boat-dweller soon grasps that nature is the permanent, enduring world: *Homo Sapiens* is just passing through. It turns out that we are not the centre of the universe. It is a very healthy shift in perspective. On a smoky October evening, the small blue miracle that is a kingfisher shot past me in an unglamorous and littered spot on the Erewash. You never quite *see* a kingfisher; you just miss seeing one as it zips across the surface, low as a tiny Dambuster.

'It's not blue, you know,' my friend Norman told me.

'It is, you know. I just saw one and it was blue.'

'Nah. It just looks blue.'

'If it looks blue, it bloody *is* blue.'

He assured me that it is not. 'It's brown,' he said serenely. 'It just looks blue.' I looked it up. Annoyingly, he was right. The kingfisher 'is a favourite of artists and poets' (guilty as charged) and its feathers are brownish, according to the Game and Wildlife Conservation Trust. Apparently it does something clever with sugar that makes it look blue. I found this difficult to believe. 'If you find this difficult to believe,' the site continues, 'just think that you can see all the colours of the rainbow in an otherwise transparent soapy bubble.' Right. I still think it's blue.

Wherever I was, I was always at home. I had full cupboards, a kettle and all my books to hand. I could stay in one area for days, both tourist and resident. Unlike camping or even travelling in a camper van, there was no furling and unfurling, no putting up the bed or pulling down a table. I could finish breakfast, travel for a dozen miles on the boat, and step inside to find my glass of juice undisturbed on the sideboard. My clothes and saucepans were always in the same place, even if they were in a marginally different latitude. Waterways of all sorts felt like my own territory, and even when travelling conventionally, landmarks I had never seen before were familiar and comfortable; driving over a canal bridge or glimpsing a lock flight from the train, I was in my own parish again. On a country walk, the *dinkdinkdink* of paddle gear told me that I was in my own country.

For most people, being at home and being on the move are two different things. You can't do both at once. It is disarming, and sometimes discomfiting, to have this perfectly normal state of affairs turned on its head. Quite often my guests will almost fall in the canal first thing in the morning, as they try to step off the boat. Not unnaturally, they expect the ground to be where they left it: but perhaps yesterday's mooring had the towpath on our left, and today it lies on the right. *Splosh.* More than once a friend has announced, 'Right, I'll just go and get my walking boots/phone charger from the car,' only to be reminded that we have been on the move for hours since they joined the boat. They might be sitting on the same chair where they ate breakfast, but it is now twenty miles away from their car. They might be looking out of the same kitchen window as yesterday, but today it gives an entirely different view. *That,* I think to myself, *is the whole point.*

The greatest difference between boat life and bank life is not the sense of place, but the sense of time. At a meeting in London I am asked, 'Have you come on your boat, ha ha?' I reply 'No. That would mean a return journey of a month, travelling full time, to attend an hour-long meeting. I came by train. Ha ha.' The glance I get in return is one I already know well. It is the same one you get when you tell people that you are a professional poet. It is a look of complete bafflement. It is the slightly offended look of someone who feels you are playing a trick on them, as if you had turned up for work in a clown suit or announced that you live on Alpha Centauri. Your reply simply does not compute. No one likes to be mocked. Indeed, I am not mocking anyone. How could they know what happens on the other side of the map?

Alongside the steel narrow boats on the Trent, a number of sleek white river craft darted about. Narrowboaters call these plastic cabin cruisers 'Tupperware' or 'yoghurt pots' and are jealous of their light-footed manoeuvrability. They call us 'sewer tubes' and are jealous of the fact that we can stand up. On broad waters like this, they share the giant locks with us and it makes them nervous. Seven tonnes of plastic is a poor match for twenty tonnes of steel. As Terry Darlington says in *Narrow Dog to Carcassonne* – 'If you hit another narrow boat you bounce off, and if you hit a fibreglass cruiser you pass through it, making practically no noise at all.'

The towns and cities at the riverside were different too; not the industrial places supplied by the canal but towns with a longer pedigree. This is true of most old river towns, which began precisely because the river was a natural highway: York, Nottingham, London, and, of course, Newark, whose medieval castle squats on the riverbank like a Lego block. The castle's claim to fame is that in 1216 King John died in it after eating a surfeit of peaches. Everyone was tremendously pleased, and the violent thunderstorm that night was said to be the sound of him being dragged to hell.

The Trent was the best possible place to serve an apprenticeship in solo boating. I learned a lot, and I learned as Joe Hollinshead had told me I would, by making mistakes. I still see the ashen face of the man whose fibreglass cruiser almost came to an end because I briefly forgot that I should moor up facing into the current, not travelling downstream with it. There is a good reason for this. Slow down as you face the current, and the power of the engine allows you to manoeuvre. Slow down as you travel *with* the current, and it makes not a jot of difference; the river will happily sweep you along to crush anything in your path. There was a mooring space next to the little white boat, and *Tinker* bore down on it like a steely missile. The man looked ready to hurl himself aside as I barrelled towards the bank. At the last minute I realised I was about to crush his boat like a plastic bottle; I swung *Tinker* back into the main stream, turned around and came back to moor the right way round, using the engine to bring her in under full control. Cruiser Man was almost breathing again. 'Sorry,' I said. 'Not at all,' he squeaked.

The river cruisers were mostly populated by embittered divorcees with phenomenal alcohol intake, who would tell you at every opportunity that their terrible ex-wife had only left them enough money to buy a boat. They lived in squalid, cold cabins with only a frying pan for company, and disappeared to moor by a riverside pub for days at a time. I could see why. Skipper Jon had warned me, however, to beware the temptation of actually eating in local pubs. 'Too easy. You'll end up skint and fat,' he said. I bore that in mind as I built up a crew of willing friends. Team Tinker grew larger weekly, but I did not. When house-dwelling friends rolled up to crew for me, we drank in the pubs but ate on board. Each visitor brought their own speciality: sausage casserole, Greek salad, Turkish pilafs; German friends brought *lebkuchen*, Scottish friends brought haggis for Burns Night; and in the summer, chickens were roasted and served with little lettuces harvested from the trough on my cabin top. I baked lemon muffins to keep blood sugar up and tempers down. We had towpath barbecues, hearty breakfasts, and always, always biscuits. The evening invariably ended in a pub called the Navigation.

Tinker and I began to work together on these tousled waters of the Trent, travelling long reaches where towns and villages barely approach the river. Even in the populous Midlands, boaters can pass by a town like Beeston or Bridgford without seeing it or being seen. There are steep banks and secret corners thick with greenery which only boaters know about. For miles and miles, we people inside the water map hardly see those on the usual map. The old boat people sometimes acknowledged the difference, saying that a land-dweller came from 'off the bank', especially if they joined the working boat community. It isn't a term of abuse, only a shorthand to distinguish them from native boat families. Mixed marriages between the two populations seldom thrived. As Rolt said in *Narrow Boat*:

> *Few girls not born in a boat cabin can stand the hard conditions of cramped quarters and exposure to all weathers. On still summer days this peaceful gliding through the green heart of the country may seem idyllic, but it is a different tale to stand for hours at the tiller or work a boat through endless locks when cold winter rains come sheeting down, or when a bitter north-easter numbs the fingers, ruffles the water into little breaking waves and makes locksides treacherous with ice.*

Tell me about it. I know of one couple who beat the odds, though she was a born-and-bred boatwoman and he was 'off the bank'. No one expected it to last, but he courted her by leaving roses under the bridges where he knew her boat would pass, and chalking messages under the arches. They lived happily ever after.

The water map

The Slow Machine

City, where do you keep your water and your bulrushes,
your joggers, rent boys, babies in their Sunday pushchairs –
all the things that cost so much to learn
about your clay or cotton or your ruined foundries?
Who's the guardian of your ducks?

Never mind. We know.
You're a dot on *our* system. Birmingham
we'll take, but otherwise your cities
turn their backs on us, and we on them.

What's a canal, to you? An interruption
to dry business – an obstacle that wants a bridge.
To us, the road; the long wet answer
to the only question every day; where to?
The way on. The way through. The water way.

I never understood the meaning of the words 'fresh air' until I woke
up on a boat. Water freshens everything around it. Your neighbours are
feisty robins or hedge sparrows, singing the eternal song that all birds
sing in their different languages, and that young men sing at closing
time: FANCY A SHAG? FIGHT ME! FANCY A SHAG? FIGHT ME!

I never enjoyed a pint of beer so much as when I tied up at The
Unicorn at Gunthorpe, after shooting through the arches of the bridge

there to tie up at a pub populated only by bikers and boaters – a laughing brotherhood of speed freaks and slow travellers. Visiting waterside pubs was a refreshing experience in more ways than one, for when your own bed and cosy living room are a few paces away at the end of the pub garden, and you can nip home to make a bacon sandwich while someone else gets a round in, the pleasures of both home and pub are enhanced. A summer evening at The Plough, Normanton on Soar found my crew sitting in the beer garden for happy hours, the boat at our backs. *Tinker* wobbled in welcome as we stumbled merrily aboard at midnight. The next morning, a friend cured his hangover by jumping into the slow-flowing river, for a brisk swim under the willows with the ducks. Ducks, ever present and comical neighbours, became my soundtrack for that summer. They sat outside the kitchen window whenever I tied up, or walked along squinting into the windows in hopes of a snack. *I wonder if I will remember this summer as the Summer of Ducks?* I thought. Then I realised that from now on, all of my summers would be furnished with the laughter of ducks.

Because our living rooms are too small for much socialising, boaters have a special association with pubs. Some inns which 'bank people' hardly know are secret centres on the water map, where almost everyone in the bar has arrived by boat. One of the most precious is the Anchor at High Offley on the Shropshire Union. I arrived there one summer evening, claimed seventy feet of towpath as my new home and joined friends in the beer garden just as the Mikron Theatre group began a performance of their latest canal-themed work. Mikron is a treasure of the waterways, a company of travelling players who circulate each summer with a new slate of scripts and perform them in the pubs at the heart of the canal system. It is an intimate and ancient way of seeing theatre. One of the players on this evening was Anna Winslet, one of three acting sisters. The most famous is Kate, who had recently been seen at a Mikron performance. At the height of her fame in the aftermath of the blockbuster film *Titanic*, Kate Winslet sat quietly at the back of an English beer garden among boat people. If they noticed her at all, they respected her privacy and let her be. She slipped away before Anna's limelight could be spoiled by her sister's inconvenient fame.

A favourite pub, inevitably called the Navigation, was in the canal basin at Bugsworth. It's a plum-pudding of waterway features, with hidden lime kilns and secluded mooring spots arranged around three short arms of canal. Through the whole nineteenth century and beyond, it was a hectic loading place where limestone from the Peak District hills came down to the canal by tramway. I arranged to meet a friend in the pub there, nursing a shandy as I waited. Half an hour after the appointed time, my phone rang.

'Where are you?' I asked.

'I'm in the pub,' he said indignantly. 'Where are *you*?'

He was not in the pub – at least, not in the same pub as me. Ah, I thought. I think I know what has happened here.

'Jamie,' I asked slowly. 'What town are you in?'

'Marple.'

'Why are you not in Bugsworth?'

'I couldn't find it on the map. This is close by** and I figured it must be the same place. Anyway, it's definitely the right pub. It's called the Navigation and it's right by the canal.'

Of course he couldn't find Bugsworth on the map. It isn't on the map. The place that we know as Bugsworth Basin was named by generations of unlettered boaters. It appears on your satnav or Ordnance

---

** Reader, it is eight miles away.

Survey map as Buxworth. I should perhaps have mentioned this to him earlier. I explained it now, and gave him directions.

'Right,' he said, baffled. 'I'll finish my pint and come and find you. But I mean, it's amazing isn't it?'

'What is?'

'What are the chances of two pubs being called the Navigation?'

Quite high, I thought.

'And both of them by a canal, too!' he said, missing the point entirely. The navigation is, after all, another word for a canal.

From one week to the next I might have a different market or railway station, a different set of shops and streets to discover; but once I stepped into the boat there were my own messy papers, my grandmother's reading chair, my high bed in its nook, my well-equipped kitchen, my dangling plants and warming stove. On the sloping tumblehome walls were the striking linocuts of James Dodds and Eric Gaskell, now fixed beside the enamelled Carver poem and a framed poster with a quote from Jerome K. Jerome's classic *Three Men in a Boat*:

> *Let your boat of life be light, packed with only what you need – a homely home and simple pleasures, one or two friends worth the name, someone to love and someone to love you, a cat, a dog, and a pipe or two, enough to eat and enough to wear, and a little more than enough to drink; for thirst is a dangerous thing.*

Canal travel is time travel. It takes you into two or more layers of the time map at once. The canals connect places that hardly exist any more – or places whose meaning has changed. Where do the canals *go*? Boaters are often asked this. It's a bit like asking where the M1 goes. Strictly speaking, the M1 goes from Edgware in London to Micklefield just outside

Leeds, but if all the traffic on it were going to one or the other, the good people of Edgware and Micklefield would be slightly overwhelmed. The motorway connects all the places between them, and all the places that we reach by branching off it and taking other roads – Oxford, Birmingham, Sheffield and the many smaller settlements where we live, work or build Amazon distribution hubs. Likewise with the canals.

Take as an example the Kennet and Avon, or K&A as it is known to boaters. Where does it go? Strictly speaking, from Reading (on the river Kennet) to Bristol (on the river Avon) but, like the M1, it also connects all the places in between. In 1810 when it was completed, the Kennet and Avon hitched a little timber wharf at Honeystreet to the builders then shaping the great Georgian crescents of Bath and Bristol. It joined all of these to the market towns of Newbury and Hungerford. One ribbon of shallow water linked everyone in that landscape to the greatest trading hubs of the world. East was London, reached by the canal and the Thames. West was Bristol, the sea and the ports of Liverpool or Lancaster, funded by trading and slaving and shipping; also Gloucester, Wales, Ireland, and beyond them the vast promise of New York or the unsettled prairies. Just as the M1 now connects you to any point north or south, the Kennet and Avon connected inland people to a world of trade, news and possibility.

In his poem 'Great Things Have Happened', Alden Nowlan speaks of '... the feeling/you get sometimes in a country you've never visited/ before, where the bread doesn't taste quite the same'. In my process of 'unsettling' I was to rediscover my own country.

Underneath that question about where the canals go is the sense that there is indeed an alternative nation inside your own, a slightly alien country inside the familiar one. For some people the feeling is unsettling, like discovering that the door in your wardrobe leads to

Narnia. True enough, our waterways connect places that don't exist, or that do exist in a very different way. To navigate this nation within a nation, boaters use maps that make sense of it. Most have a strong allegiance either to Nicholson maps or to Pearson maps. I am a Nicholson girl myself; there are seven volumes of these guides to the waterways of England and Wales. They have shiny red covers, spiral bindings and they are surprisingly resilient when dropped into a canal and fished out again. Every one of my Nicholson volumes has deckled pages and handwritten notes – 'Dreadful pub/splendid moorings/secret path to railway station/chicken farm/pub landlord very peculiar'.

The Nicholson maps are disorientating for a bank-dweller, because on every page they show only the canal corridor. Through seven volumes, the thin blue line of the waterway proceeds through lock flights, past boatyards where you can fill up with water or empty your toilet tank, and occasionally touches on villages or historic towns where you can shop for provisions. All of these are faithfully recorded; but anything that falls outside the narrow corridor of canal life is excluded.

My friend Clare was fascinated by the Nicholson maps. They completely reversed her experience of her surroundings. This was the other side of the map she lived on, and the information boaters need meant nothing to her; sanitary stations and water points, dry docks and lock flights. The landmarks she knew, the A-roads and town centres, railway stations and petrol stations, barely appeared at all in the Nicholson guides. Boaters don't care where the motorway junction is; we only need to know where to empty the toilet, and whether the next lock will take us uphill or down. The guides perfectly illustrate the way that many working boat families experienced the world. If it wasn't within quarter of a mile of the canal bank, they hardly knew it was there. They knew the canal-side pubs, the picture houses, the bicycle shops: they lived in straight lines and though their field of vision was narrow, it was 4,000 miles long in its heyday. Clare pushed her finger across the pages, tracing the little black lollipops that mark out the miles and the black V shapes that signify locks.

'What do these little handbags mean?' she asked.

'Handbags?' I said, obviously mimicking Margaret Rutherford in *The Importance of Being Earnest*. I followed her pointing finger and burst out laughing. They did look like old-fashioned handbags, standing on one end, but the travelling boater seldom needs to know where the nearest handbag shop is. They signified something far more important in our linear world.

'They are pint pots!' I said. 'The handled sort. That is where the pubs are.'

Some of these places I had known since childhood, but now saw from the other side of the map. I felt this alien freshness when a muntjac deer the size of a large dog peered out of the trees by the fast-flowing Trent, or when I cruised past a boat stranded in a crop field after floods on the Soar. I certainly felt it when I saw a young couple having sex in broad daylight on a bench in Birmingham – he sitting on it, she straddling him with bouncy enthusiasm. He looked over her shoulder and waved cheerfully, as well he might.

Perhaps I had simply never *noticed* so much. Perhaps trail runners or wild water swimmers feel the same sensation of re-learning their own shape in relation to the elements around them. I had spent much of my life working outdoors and was in every sense weather-worn, but this was new. I felt my animal body occupying space and moving in relationship to air and water more clearly than I had experienced before. I slept better, and not just because of the physical labour and the fresh air. The motion of a narrow boat is barely perceptible – not at all like the sensation of rocking on a sailing boat – but it answers

some requirement in the watery human body, and gives a haptic aware-
ness of the physical world around it. It seemed to me that my body had
been crying out for exactly this kind of movement.

My bed in *Tinker* was set high in the central cabin to accommodate a
chest of drawers underneath, so that the sleeping skipper lay barely three
feet under the ceiling. In a rainstorm, curtains of water swept across the
steel cabin top with the proximity and volume of a car wash. In a hail
storm, one woke up to a sound like lead shot being poured onto the roof
from a bucket. The sensation of being so close to the elements made
my nest of quilt and pillows all the more snug. In an auburn autumn I
tied up in an idyllic (and suspiciously empty) setting at Branston, where
the pickle comes from. There is always a reason why a tempting mooring is empty: at midnight, October storms shook apples from the tree
overhead, so that windfalls landed on the roof like sledgehammer blows.
Best of all was the sound that quickly became familiar; the *THWOP
THWOP THWOP* of webbed feet, as visiting ducks waddle along the
metal thoroughfare, never ceases to make me laugh.

The Houdini hatch, or skylight, in the kitchen ceiling made every
moment of sunlight vividly kinetic. It reminded me of my father's trick
when I couldn't sleep as a toddler. He propped a small mirror at the
side of my bed, so that the strip of light glimpsed under the bedroom
door was reflected onto the wall. It gave a blurry rectangle of comforting light, and kept monsters away long enough for my dad to enjoy
his glass of beer without interruption. He called it a fairy because of
its other-worldly shimmer, and possibly because it worked like magic.
One of the first joys of living afloat was the discovery that on a bright
day, the cabin filled with water fairies. I had never seen them on the
working boats, whose windows were portholes modestly covered with
circles of lace. They were haulage vehicles, not pleasure craft, after all,

and their crew did not sit inside looking at the view. *Tinker* had the broad hopper windows of a modern liveaboard boat. There was ample room for fairies here. I woke on my first bright November morning to find the living room filled with reflections.

Your common house fairy is radiant but static. Its waterborne cousin shimmies, ripples and turns somersaults. In each mooring sunlight struck the boat from a different angle, and the fairies changed character. In river water their movements were smooth and slow, throwing bars of light onto the ceiling. In urban moorings they were triangular, shadowed by buildings. In open countryside they became plaques of light spotted with dandelion seeds, freckled with duckweed or animated with the endless Venn diagrams of rain on water. A passing boat or swan would break the dancing ripples into a new pattern, like the shapes in a shaken kaleidoscope.

One summer morning, awake at dawn to catch an early train, I felt *Tinker* shift lightly in her ropes as she did when another boat passed. In the pink river water outside I saw the widening V of a wake – but I had heard no engine. Curious, I leaned out to glimpse a powerful rower, striking out along the Trent. We were close to the Holme Pierrepont National Water Sports Centre. This sculler in her pod-like boat was part of the national rowing team – knifing through the dawn-fresh water in a solitary rehearsal for the Olympics.

Wedgwood

It makes perfect sense that one of the early advocates for a canal system was Josiah Wedgwood. If moving a piano in 1766 was such a challenge, imagine how many of Wedgwood's fragile jasperware urns would perish on the same journey. Wedgwood, a businessman like the mill owner Richard Arkwright with an eye to the main chance, claimed that half of his fine ceramics were broken in transit when they travelled by road. Bear in mind that he may have been exaggerating: he was looking to fund a canal.

Britain's great ports imported many goods from Europe, rather than bringing them in from mainland Britain on roads unfit for bulky cargoes or fragile goods. With a habit of water transport as old as human civilisation, shipping was often easier, quicker and therefore cheaper. In London, Bristol, Liverpool or Newcastle, merchants were connected to Europe, Africa or North America by the sea; and to inland markets as far as the rivers would carry cargoes. In Stoke-on-Trent, however, they were not.

Wedgwood's factory was deep inland, near the clay fields and the coal fields. His was a luxury product, with a high mark-up value and an immense potential market. Close to his works at Etruria, where the pot bank chimneys stood like giant bottles in a mass of smoke, was the river Trent. It was not very deep at this point around fifteen miles from its source at Biddulph Moor, and it was too small to be navigable by any useful vessels. Meanwhile, the supplies he needed to fuel both his manufacture and ambition were wobbling towards his bottle kilns in a hugely expensive way. Read Samuel Smiles's 1874 description of the materials needed by Wedgwood alone, and the routes they took to get to him: you will begin to see why Wedgwood of all men became the one to imagine a national canal network.

[T]he principal materials used in the manufacture of pottery, especially of the best kinds, were necessarily brought from a great distance.... flint stones

from the south-eastern ports of England and clay from Devonshire and Cornwall. The flints were brought by sea to Hull and the clay to Liverpool. From Hull the materials were brought up the Trent to Willington; and the clay was in like manner brought from Liverpool up the Weaver to Winsford in Cheshire. Considerable quantities of clay were also conveyed in boats from Bristol, up the Severn to Bridgnorth and Bewdley. From these various points the materials were conveyed by land carriage, mostly on the backs of horses, to the towns in the potteries where they were worked up into earthenware and china. The manufactured articles were returned for export in the same rude way. Large crates of pot-ware were slung across horses' backs, and thus conveyed to their respective ports, not only at great risk of breakage and pilferage, but also at heavy cost ... There were no shops in the Potteries, the people being supplied with wares and drapery by packmen and hucksters, or from Newcastle-under-Lyme, which was the only town in the neighbourhood worthy of the name.

Look at these cargoes. Flint, clay, salt – the items needed by Wedgwood himself were bulky, heavy, imperishable and would be immensely reduced in cost if you could load them onto a boat, and deliver it without further transhipment to the door of his warehouse.

Wedgwood was a man of limitless ambition. He was the Elon Musk of crockery. 1766 was an age of possibility. He hired the millwright James Brindley, who had proved himself extremely versatile in his work on Wedgwood family properties and in his canal project for the Duke of Bridgewater. Wedgwood summoned up some friendly investors to meet him at the local pub in Stone, and he set about filling in the water map.

A letter in the *Caledonian Mercury* of 15 July 1765 summed up the novelty and promise of Brindley's canal in Manchester. It was 'the first *still* navigation in England'. It was not a river, subject to tide, flood and drought. Instead, it was placid, predictable, and could deliver goods to the very doors of a warehouse. No packhorses required. The writer grasped its importance and prophesied:

> *It will not be the last, as by this means a communication may be made with most rivers; and trading towns may now have navigations far superior to those of rivers, made by little more than the wastewater that runs from the pumps ...*

The ease of water supply was exaggerated. The ease of use was not.

When I first came to the canals, I had no idea how deep were the waters I was getting into. That was almost literally true. If you ask school children (and indeed many adults) how deep they think the canal is, they will tell you 'sixty feet' or 'ten metres' or 'three metres'. The answer is usually 'about 1.5 metres, if you're lucky'. It's a rather shallow, clay-lined ditch. A canal, I reiterate, is not a river.

A river is entirely natural. Think of a noble one like the Trent or Thames: almost invisible at source, but wide and deep and tidal where they discharge into the sea. They are forces of nature: glorious, moody, muddy, powerful, unpredictable. A river is richly furnished with all kinds of life that requires running water, from willow trees to grebes to caddis flies. Between invisible source and brackish mouth there are shallows and silt banks which change location from year to year. There are spots where the watercourse dries to nothing in a drought. There are places where steep cliffs make access to the shore impossible, and others where the banks slope into the water for many metres so that no boat can get near the sides. A river varies in strength and sometimes in shape from season to season. It winds around contours, following the path of least resistance, not at all concerned with the quickest route between watershed and sea port.

It is a wondrous thing, but it has a number of drawbacks for a person wanting to move twenty tons of coal. Because of this, for many centuries people mucked about with rivers to make them more cargo-friendly. A river thus mucked about is called a 'navigation'. It is improved for boat traffic with interventions (straightened stretches, stone-lined banks, dams or ponds, shortcuts to avoid obstacles like an oxbow, or indeed Oxford) to make it navigable. Navigations have existed in Britain since Arbeia was populated by Roman soldiers. By the mid-eighteenth century they were fairly commonplace. One means of making a river navigable for shallow-draughted craft is to add staunches or flash locks – a simpler and more exciting version of a canal lock. You (or, say, the monks of Abingdon) build a gated dam across a shallow stretch of river, so that the water builds up behind it. Excess water simply flows over the top and carries on regardless. When a boat wants to pass through, it floats up to the gate in the nice deep water you have allowed to gather. Then you release the gate. The flood of liquid, no longer held back, rushes over the dam in a shallow waterfall – carrying the boat with it, in a slightly turbulent and hazardous moment.

A canal, of course, is wholly artificial. Your own local canal was built between 1760 and 1835 to carry cargo. It was financed by private companies and planned by civil engineers who laid out embankments, bridges and aqueducts to slot it into the landscape. It was dug out of the subsoil and bedrock by hundreds of navvies, and filled with water from reservoirs or tributary waterways. The canal is like a national bathtub; when its water level drops, it has to be topped up. When it is too full, it overflows through weirs and channels into the waterways below it. It is always navigable, because it was built for that purpose, and it connects to a nationwide network. On it there circulates a community the size of a small town, on boats of various sizes and types; one of which contains me.

Now that canals are so embedded a part of our map, it's a challenge to imagine the novelty of a perfectly reliable waterway in the 1760s. Most transport in the eighteenth century was at the mercy of nature. Bad weather would cut off high roads for weeks with a snowstorm or flood them into impassable quagmires. Ice would glaze the parish roads, and break the surface into deep ruts. Winter storms could delay or wreck coastal ships. River traffic in the large estuaries ran to tidal rhythms. The new artificial waterways were largely unaffected by all of this. Certainly a bad drought or a hard freeze would make the shallow channels impassable, but for the most part they were calm and dependable. Their reliability through the four seasons set in motion a new set of expectations for transport, which culminated in a culture of pocket watches and railway time.

Humans could overcome nature. Where Providence was careless enough to split the country with a river or drop a mountain across a vital trade route, human labour could even *improve* on nature. The construction of the canals was a pattern for mastery of the landscape. The *Derby Mercury* of 18 September 1767 quoted a letter from Burslem, Stoke, written by an admirer of Brindley. It was not just the engineer's energy that impressed this fan, but the beautiful, cyclical rhythm of the construction then under way at Harecastle. The bedrock dug from one part of the channel travelled ahead to build revetments further down the line. Where the substrate was clay, it went straight into canal-side brickyards, and the bricks were taken by water to the furthest work site. Supply and demand, demand and supply; the canal was the snake fed by its own tail, and the effects brought money pouring in to the Potteries.

'Till our turnpikes were made few people ever saw our manufactories. But now they are gazed at as a novelty. The ladies go to Warburton's to buy the Queen's sets of cream coloured ware; and the gentlemen come to view our Eighth Wonder of the World, the subterranean Navigation, which is cutting by the great Mr Brindley, who handles rocks as easily as you would plum-pyes, and makes the four elements subservient to his will.'

There was a great tunnel building at Harecastle, in Staffordshire. An army of men were cutting north from Staffordshire, and another army cutting south from Cheshire. They hoped to meet in the middle 'by Christmas, when they are to have an ox roasted whole, and an hogshead of ale.' Oh, the promise of this age. The letter is thick with pride, excitement and the sense of possibility. The tunnel would not be completed by Christmas: it would not be completed for another five years.

Boater

'Let you steer?' replied the barge-woman, laughing. 'It takes some practice to steer a barge properly. Besides, it's dull work, and I want you to be happy.'
— The Wind in the Willows, Kenneth Grahame

Sometimes I have trouble with my sciatic nerve. I get up from my chair to make a cup of tea and all at once it seems that my leg is about to fall off. The smallest movement is difficult and painful for days. Then, suddenly, it isn't. I'll be tying a shoelace or taking the bins out when some piece of essential machinery drops into place, and everything is running smoothly again.

It was just like that as I learned to boat. For a long time everything was difficult and anxiety inducing, and there were always three old men watching me with their arms folded when I tried to turn the boat around in a winding hole. (Winding, incidentally, is pronounced as in 'north wind' not as in 'winding a watch'. The wind is supposed to help you around, not that it ever does.) I hated this manoeuvre, which usually ended up with a crew member stuck in a thorn bush as they tried to keep the boat from scraping through undergrowth. Often I felt that it would be simpler to just keep going, abandon the attempt to turn and choose, instead, to travel for the rest of my life in one direction.

I also hated mooring up in a tight space. Parallel parking is an acquired skill even in a car with crisp brakes. It seemed physically impossible in a twenty-tonne boat which kept moving under its own weight when I stopped the engine. It was awkward every time, and of course there was always an old man watching me with his arms folded.

Like sciatica, my learning curve was uncomfortable for me and my crew. Accustomed to working boat people who thought a ten-hour day an easy one, I asked too much of myself and my friends. The eager mates who joined me for a weekend of idyllic gin-drinking on the water were often asked to start early and work me up a flight of sixteen locks. I sent them home weary. It was a tribute to their friendship that they ever came back: but I never intended to spend my boating life alone. Although I made plenty of single-handed trips, longer cruises were always shared. The rhythms of *Tinker* continued the work-play-and-live-together archaeological habit. Crew members arrived in twos and threes, collecting one another from nearby train stations or sorting out car-sharing as they walked down the towpath to meet the boat. They befriended each other as they worked a lock, and chatted in pubs called the Navigation or the Wharf. They took pride in coiling a rope properly or tying a tugman's hitch. When men walking along the toe path approached male crew members with questions about the engine or make of the boat, they loudly said 'Ask the skipper!' and pointed to me. They understood how to move around inside the boat without tripping over each other. None of them called it a barge.

The key to a happy crew is blood sugar. Steering a boat is not arduous but the skipper stands at the tiller for hours. You get chilly and tired. If you lose concentration for a couple of seconds you are hit in the face by an overhanging tree, which will pull your woolly hat off and throw your sunglasses into the water. The crew, meanwhile, are not standing still. They help you to turn the boat by pushing it round with a long shaft (not a barge pole), taking care not to impale themselves. They may work thirty locks in a day, sometimes in freezing rain. Often they walk ahead to set the locks, in that lovely rhythm called lock-wheeling which means they are on their feet and doing mild exercise all day. At about two o'clock they all start to shout at each other and drop things. I had recently learned that if I threw them a biscuit at this exact point, harmony was restored.

I was managing time better now. I had been granted a taste of working boat life and its people, but I did not have to operate like them. I didn't have a cargo to deliver. Boating wasn't my job. *Tinker's* days could be shorter and slower; why, I might even venture to get off every now and then and go for a walk, or spend the afternoon in a nearby town. Eventually, it dawned on me that this was the entire point. For most liveaboard boaters on the living canals, the point is not to get from A to B, but to enjoy the bit in between. Journeys became more leisurely, and my crew more relaxed. We would tie up mid-afternoon in a nice spot to sit on the towpath with a book, chat to neighbouring crews, or sit on the cabin top watching sunsets. We would light a barbecue. Time on *Tinker* became joyful for all of us, rather than exhausting. A great many sausages were eaten.

The nerve-jangling discomfort of learning a new life began to ease, until one late autumn evening in Derbyshire it disappeared entirely. I had spent all day at the tiller, starting on the wide and airy river Trent and crossing the hurly-burly waters of the four-way junction at Trent Lock to join the canal. Like the novice that I was, I had badly misjudged the length of my journey. The sky was a purpling dove-grey as dusk deepened almost to darkness, but *Tinker* was still on the move. I was berating myself: *You're still crap at this. You will never get the hang of it.*

The honeypot village of Willington smelt of apples and woodsmoke. I was tired, hungry and just in time for an arranged meeting with a crew member in the pub, but every mooring space was occupied. The canal bank was an unbroken line of boats: it was a floating village whose residents were perfectly at home here, and who tomorrow would be perfectly at home with a different arrangement of neighbours. My next chance to moor was a mile ahead, and even if there were a space there, it would be fully dark when I reached it. The cabin windows of the moored boats were buttery squares of warmth in the twilight. Woodsmoke and savoury cooking smells drifted over the water. These boaters had been sensible enough to tie up early, before night fell. *Sod them*, I thought. I felt lonely and incompetent. There were no biscuits left.

As *Tinker* crawled along the channel I saw one last mooring space, a slim block of dark water between two boats. It looked about six inches shorter than the boat. *Dammit.* Surely I had no chance of squeezing in. The boat tied up in front of this space, the boat which I would hit hard if I cocked up the entry to a tight space as usual, was an immaculate working boat. Of course it was.

Mek your mistakes slowly, Joe Hollinshead would say. In that November nightfall, it felt as if this move had a great deal riding on it. Was I always going to be an incomer, revving the engine and fumbling every move – or could *Tinker* and I move together, work together, and do the thing gracefully? My long day had not been wasted. On the swirling river waters and the smooth water of the canal, I had finally begun to feel in my bones the slow dance of boat and steerer – this boat, this steerer. *Come on then, let's not cock it up. Tinker's* nose slid gently forward to touch the bank exactly where it needed to, and a touch of the tiller guided the back end in behind it. A half-second of reverse engine brought her gently away from the working boat without so much as a kiss, and we swung into the bank with inches to spare between us and the boat behind. *Tinker* purred quietly as she came to rest. I stepped off nonchalantly to tie up, as if I did this sort of thing all the time. It was the smallest possible victory but a victory all the same, and it was possible.

I caught a trace of cigarette smoke on the autumn air. There was an old man watching me from the back of the working boat, arms folded. I glared at him.

'Nicely done,' he said.

And then it wasn't painful anymore. *Tinker* and I were a single entity when we moved. It wasn't a mystical, new-age revelation but the deep comfort that comes from a learned skill, which became part of my self-hood. Perhaps a toddler feels this when she first becomes a confident walker. I suppose I had simply put in enough hours on *Tinker* to fully feel the interaction of three bodies: her shape, my shape, the water beneath us. At any rate, I no longer had to think about where to put the tiller when manoeuvring between obstacles. It just moved the right way under my hand as the steering wheel does for a driver. I knew when *Tinker* was happy in the water, and when a tangle of weed had clogged the propeller. I knew by the way she swam how much water was left in my domestic water tank. When the canal signalled that we should slow down by throwing up a low breaking wave in our wake, we slowed down. In a tight corner, I recalled the old boater's trick of 'rowing' the tiller a few times to get some extra turning power, rather than holding it steady. The Manchester Central Library frieze had advised me to 'get wisdom, and with all thy getting get understanding'. I laid no claim to wisdom, but I had gained a little understanding. I had become a happy little cog in the slow machine, as I thought of the canal system.

Don't get me wrong, I still haven't got the hang of it entirely. My incompetence, like my sciatica, occasionally flares up. There are many moments when I make a monumental arse of myself, jamming the boat into a tricky angle or allowing the wind to pin me to the bank. I have messed up easier moorings than that one in Willington. I will always make mistakes – I just try to make a new one every time. At those moments, of course, there is always an old man on the bank, watching me with his arms folded. I like to think I make his day a little better.

I went to the pub and met my friend. As we talked about the next bit of our journey, a man at the bar asked us where we were going next. It was a perfectly sensible question, but for a split second I genuinely didn't understand it. 'We're just ... going,' I said. I had forgotten that I was supposed to have a destination. Constant motion had become my constant practice. He raised an eyebrow at his mate as he collected his beer.

'Boaters!' he said.

My crewman caught my eye. 'I'll drink to that,' he grinned.

Is it cold in the winter?

Boat-dwelling isn't just living in a differently shaped space. It is living in a different way. It changes your perspective on many things, including things, as it happens. How many pairs of shoes do you *really* need? Living in a fluid environment, my thinking became more fluid. My sense of 'home' had changed, and my feelings about work changed too. Boats and their people challenged me to be a little less purist and a little more pragmatic. Boats, bridges, locks, sluices, and tunnels are functioning components of a single slow machine, and the sympathetic maintenance they need would make a museum-trained archaeologist's hair stand on end. I had learned to be creative in framing the history of this huge, mobile monument for a wider audience – people like the woman at British Waterways who had no idea when the canals were built. With the National Trust too, my work asked me to be more creative in telling the stories of the past.

As a result, I began to explore a different sort of writing. I had always written poetry as a private hobby. My first degree was in English and History, and so far I had been working with the History part of my brain. Now the pesky Muse seemed to want a little more of my time, and she clawed her way into my workload. Bit by bit, my professional life shifted away from the precarious, poorly paid sector of heritage. With a completely predictable lack of judgment I moved towards the much more precarious, still worse paid sector of creative writing. At first it sat side by side with the archaeology: I began to run small events, to perform and produce, to edit small magazines and be published in them.

It began at the same time as my boating life. To me this seemed like a complete coincidence, but of course it was nothing of the sort. Boating had not only changed my sense of home. It had altered my sense of self, and of possibility; it had convinced me that a life outside the usual rhythms was not only viable, but necessary. If I could do something as unlikely as living on a boat, surely I could do something as unlikely as making a living in poetry. Hanging on the arched bulkhead between *Tinker*'s kitchen and living room was the enamelled turquoise plaque with its poem. It asked me constantly 'And did you get what you wanted from this life, even so?' Almost out of the blue, William Sieghart, the founder of the Forward Prizes for Poetry, offered me the job of running the UK's National Poetry Day. I dithered.

'What's stopping you?' my friend Hannah asked.

'I like the *idea* of being an archaeologist. When you go to parties and people say what do you do, you tell them you're an archaeologist and people think it's really cool.'

'No they don't,' she said. 'They usually think you mean architect. I've heard them asking you about buildings.' She was right. She went on: 'So, the only reason you're not taking this job is that you want to sound cool at parties?'

'I suppose so.' It didn't sound convincing. I don't even like parties. Honestly, I was just afraid to jump.

'You won't ever stop being an archaeologist,' she said. 'God knows we've all heard you talking about Thomas Telford and his roads often enough. Can I recommend,' she said drily, 'that you simply lie at parties?'

So, I became a professional poet and manager of poetry events; a hybrid worker before the term became popular. I did not lie at parties, but soon discovered two eternal truths. The first is that if you say that you are a poet, people move away from you. It is as if you had announced that you were a wizard, or a tax inspector. The second is that when you tell them you live on a boat, everyone – without exception – will ask you one single question.

Is it cold in the winter?

No. Can we move on?

Actually, you deserve a better answer. It is the very first thing that most people want to know about boat-dwelling. If you are one of those who have crunched along a snowy towpath in a woolly hat wondering how we cope, then thank you for asking. *Is* it cold in the winter? It's a fair question – I do, after all, live in a steel box suspended in ice for part of the year – but by the same logic, house-dwellers must be building igloos in the living room when we see snow on their roofs. Next time you walk by a frozen canal look closely at the hulls of the boats. You will usually see an inch or two of clear water around them. They are not perfectly frozen in, but floating in a boat-shaped hole of their own making. Inside there is movement and warmth.

For the most part, not only are we genuinely not cold: we are unbearably hot. We live in a space the size of a large cupboard, with a blazing log burner inside it. It doesn't take long to warm up. The stove is alive from October to April. It sits in the living room, a black box of iron with a red glowing belly, sending its dry heat through the whole boat. On top of mine, a heavy red Japanese kettle is always poised to boil, in a middle-class update of the habit noted by L. T. C. Rolt on the working boats – 'On the stove-top tea is forever brewing, for the boat people are inveterate tea-drinkers.'

Some of us have diesel-powered central heating, of the same kind that long-distance lorry drivers have in their cabs. My four radiators give a gentle heat when I press the button, though I daren't press the button often. It makes the same noise as a jumbo jet taxiing for take-off at Heathrow. My neighbour on the boat next door does not enjoy it, especially at 3 a.m. Other solutions include thick socks, hot-water bottles, neighbours who will light a fire for you if you've been away and (my personal favourite) baked potatoes. If I come home to a freezing boat after a few days away I throw a log on the fire, a potato in the gas oven and go to the pub. So long as I get it the right way round, I come back an hour later to a toasty boat and a jacket potato. What's not to like?

Still, winter *is* hard and some winters harder than others. Older boats with poor insulation can be very cold. Older boaters with poor balance become fearful of slipping as they step in and out of the boat. All of us find it a chore to bring in the coal and firewood we need. All of us try to fill our water tanks on days of thaw, when the hosepipe is not frozen; and all of us fear falling in. Every winter two or three people drown in UK canals. Most are young men taking a short cut back from the pub who stop to relieve themselves under a bridge, lose their balance and find themselves helpless in ice-cold water. Most boaters have fallen in at least once, and we hope to do it in summer.

Like other parts of boat life, winter has its own rhythm. In November we sway and jostle in autumn storms, and begin to take extra care on the white-velvet wooden pontoons or slippery towpaths. At some point late in the year the water turns very clear and begins to look waxy. The first very cold morning brings us 'cat ice', thin as the glaze on a toffee apple. The ducks leave trails in the porridge-like slush, the fairies of light on the living room ceiling go into hibernation, and in

January or February the ice thickens for a few days. Children skim stones across it. The ducks look thoroughly pissed off by now, just as you would if your food supply disappeared and your naked bum was sitting on the ice. They come in to land with their usual comic inelegance and hurtle along the ice for twenty metres like a curling stone. Then they all sit around shouting, hands in their pockets. Watch them on a wintry day and you will see that they have little feathery slots to shelter the bottom of their chilly wings. Ducks on ice beat Disney on Ice every time.

After two winters on the ever-moving Trent, the third was my first winter on a canal. I woke up one January morning with a tingling chill at the end of my nose. The air in the cabin held the pearly silence that comes with snow, and there was an unsettling sensation: the subtle judder and sway of a boat in water was missing. *Tinker* was not moving. She was utterly static, held in a sheet of ice. We were frozen in. I stepped out of bed and as I walked forward, heard a sound like my own feet crunching through deep snow. *Tinker* was a giant snow shoe around me, shifting in the chill and shaking herself free of the ice sheet. I lit the stove, and the day began to warm.

I moved on to Sawley. I got to know the local waters – the gentle river Soar and the substantial Trent, the Nottingham Canal, the Erewash, and the Trent and Mersey Canal. These different waterways converge in a busy set of junctions at Trent Lock.

The broad waters often bristled with miniscule dinghies, handled by miniscule sailors of seven or eight years old (really) who bobbed about near the local sailing club with the learner's mixture of bravado and terror. I recognised it well enough. From time to time the terror was contagious, as their little sails wibbled blithely back and forth in front of my unstoppable boat. One breezy afternoon a dinghy steered by a child barely out of the womb shot with incredible speed into our path. Its fragile sail teetered over and disappeared. At the tiller seventy feet away, I had no sight of what was happening under the bow but my friend Russell, right at the front, went a funny colour and bellowed 'BACK! BACK!' I threw the gear lever full astern, bringing *Tinker* to a momentary, mid-current standstill. No sign of the trembling sail. *Shit, I've killed a child.* Hours seemed to pass in the next few seconds. Then the white triangle shakily righted itself and wobbled back to the bank. 'YOU LITTLE—'

'CHERUB,' supplied Russell.

'How much did we miss him by?' I asked through gritted teeth, when he brought me a cup of tea and some tranquillisers. 'About six inches,' he said.

Adventures like this were small, local and modestly English. Nobody dashed into a burning building or crossed the Antarctic single-handed. My mishaps and successes happened at three miles per hour in the well-populated Midlands of a familiar country. Even so, boating supplied perpetual low-level challenges – the constant working out of how much water is in one tank, how much sewage in another, how many locks you can do before nightfall – and its plea-sures were out of all proportion to them. The small adventures accu-mulated into a single venture of simply being open to surprise. The discovery of a heronry on the Trent, the trick of tying a new knot or the first exploration of the Ashby Canal were fresh and memorable. I was finding my own country one slow mile at a time. Every day I felt more embedded in it, and felt it more embedded in me. In a poem called 'Walking Away', Cecil Day-Lewis wrote of the give and take of nature, and of 'the small, the scorching/Ordeals which fire one's irresolute clay'. Perhaps one's irresolute clay can be fired by small victories too. Nature's give and take included moments of laughter or shared memory that brought my friends and I closer together. We absorbed them with gratitude.

The seasonal cycle of boaters is a little like that of hibernating bears. Spring, when we emerge bleary-eyed into the green world, is a wonder every time. In summer we roam around the network freely, trying out new places, new sources of food and occasionally mating. In autumn we scope out likely sites for hibernation and stock up with roots and berries, or bottles of whisky as the case may be. In winter, like the bear, we hunker down. We take our social lives into the pubs, because there is little room for socialising in a narrow hibernaculum. That winter at Sawley Marina, I often met friends at a pub called the Trent Lock – previously named, of course, the Navigation. I slotted in to a community of narrow boat-dwellers, holiday boaters, and the much-maligned 'shiny boat brigade' who have bought a brand-new boat and become pale whenever they see an overhanging bush that might scratch the paintwork. An outlier among the narrow boats was a curvaceous, broad-bottomed Dutch barge owned by new friends. On Christmas morning I went to check that they were ready for our planned boat trip.

'He's got a new T-shirt. He's not sure about it,' said Phil.

I could not imagine what kind of T-shirt would trigger uncertainty in his partner Luke, a man as confident in his sexuality as Boy George. No one would call him a wallflower, and yet he did look slightly sheepish as he emerged from the cabin. Luke was carrying a large box that obscured his torso. As he dropped it in the bin the T-shirt was revealed in its full glory. A slogan in bold red letters was blazoned across the front: I LOVE ANAL.

'Do you think it's too much?' he said.

'I don't think it will be news to anyone who's met you.'

We agreed that it *might* be a bit much for the public bar of the Trent Lock at lunchtime on Christmas Day. Luke put a jacket on to conceal it.

The substantial box he had been carrying was from the recent purchase of an enormous inflatable snowman, which they had somehow fixed to the roof of their boat. We were about to travel down the river and moor outside the pub for Christmas lunch. The snowman, apparently, was coming with us. They switched on a pump and he slowly reared up from the cabin top, like a terrifying blancmange. He was ten feet tall. *Good job it's not windy.*

We set off down the locks. Sawley has twin locks with a mass of stonework between them. Luke and Phil went to the right, the inflatable snowman wobbling in the slight breeze. I took the left-hand lock. As our boats dropped in the two stone chambers I saw the snowman disappear slowly from view – his wobbly black shoes, his wobbly buttons, his wobbly carrot nose and wobbly top hat. Then there was a peal of laughter. The boys had realised that their blow-up friend wouldn't get under the bridge below the lock. When we emerged, the snowman was slowly melting as they deflated him, pooling into a puddle of disappointed plastic. We slipped under the bridge and out towards Trent Lock, the snowman reinflating as we pushed out into the swirling Trent. By the time we reached the pub he was splendidly tumescent once more, a fine match for the buoyant swans.

'You might want to keep your jacket on,' I said to Luke. We headed for the bar.

How not to work a lock

My latest two crew members, Dave and Shelley, were new to boats, and about to work their first lock. It lay in front of a lively pub called the Stenson Bubble. This bright April afternoon, the beer garden was full of cheerful gongoozlers – the people who watch canal boats go by and ask you if it's cold in the winter. My companions felt rather exposed while working their first lock in front of an audience, so we tied up and watched a few boats pass through it before they had a go.

The most splendid of our little miracles is the canal lock, a combination of wood, water and gravity that allows all canals to function. A lock is a wet elevator. It is the single most essential piece of engineering on the cut, as elegant in its operation today as the day it was invented, by Leonardo da Vinci no less, in 1497. It is an industrialised miracle and like all miracles, it passeth all understanding, but the principle is a simple one. Essentially, it is a sealed box of water with a hole at each end. Let me briefly explain how it works, so that you can understand how this one tried to kill me.

You let water in or out of a lock chamber by 'winding up the paddles'. These are small sliding panels which block water channels. You use a bent metal tool called a windlass (not a lock key, please) to wind them up, as if cranking up an old car like Chitty Chitty Bang Bang. Some of the paddles release water *into* the lock, to fill it and carry your boat uphill. Others drain water *out* of the lock, to empty it and drop your boat downhill. As you wind, the lock gear makes the lovely *dinkdinkdink* sound which is the song of my people. Once the boat reaches the right level, you drop the paddles back into place, sealing the lock once more; and you go on your way.

I explained this to my crew member Dave with unusual care, because Stenson is an unusual lock[††]. It has four paddles at the top end, which gives it an unusual capacity for danger. 'You need to open them in the right order, and slowly,' I told him. Dave was itching to move on. He had not yet dropped into the rhythm of canal time, which is measured in days and miles rather than hours. He was hungry, and wanted to get back on board where the biscuits were.

'What happens if we do it fast?' he asked.

The short answer was that a great spurting waterfall would be cast out through holes in the gates, on to the boat below. Dozens of boats sink in locks each year. This is one way to do it.

'The boat sinks,' I said. 'And I drown.'

'Right,' said Dave. 'We'll do it slowly then.'

We watched a boat called *Kingfisher* going up, for illustration. The skipper steered in to the empty lock. We swung the two heavy oak doors shut behind him. His wife waved her thanks, waited for a nod from her husband and cranked up a paddle to let water in. Slowly. Slowly. She was an old hand, who understood the nature of this particular lock. She worked deliberately and in the right order. Not the usual brisk *dinkdinkdink* this time, but a more cautious tempo; one *dink* every ten seconds. The released water fizzed under the hull like champagne, swirling up from outlets deep in the bottom of the lock. *Kingfisher* began her gradual, swaying rise. The woman walked over to the second paddle and repeated the process, winding it up little by little. She chatted to my crew, but she kept her eye on her skipper.

[††] Not that unusual; many locks in this part of the world have gate paddles, like Stenson. On the system as a whole, they are relatively uncommon. The experienced boater will forgive my lengthy explanation, and revel in the fact that they know this already.

Only when the lock was half full did this boater tackle the two remaining paddles, the ones mounted in the lock gate. High above the boat when it entered the lock, they were now safely submerged. They still gave a bit of a kick, and *Kingfisher* shivered as the fresh streams were opened. The woman worked carefully again. One *dink* every five seconds, perhaps. 'Textbook stuff, this' I said. The lock filled without drama. We pushed the gates open, *Kingfisher* slid out onto the top level. Job done. As soon as the lock was emptied by the next descending boat, we would make the same ten-minute trip ourselves.

Dave and Shelley were ready to test their routine. 'Don't rush', I called up to them, ten feet above me as *Tinker* dawdled in. The doors met with the unhurried clunk that tonnes of wet oak will give when they pivot to greet one another for the thousandth time. My crew walked to the paddles, windlasses in hand, ready to send water spilling into the space underneath *Tinker*; but someone else got there first. The skipper of a nearby holiday boat had run down from his vessel to reach the paddles. He had just begun his week of boat hire. He was ready to travel down in the lock, and could not do so until we had completed our passage. He thought that everyone on the canal was moving with agonising slowness. He wanted us out of his way.

I was checking something in the Nicholson map when he started working the paddles. My head snapped up immediately when I heard a rapid rattle. *Dinkdinkdinkdinkdinkdinkdinkdink* went the ratchets, like machine-gun fire. With the enthusiasm and energy of a man who has just collected a large piece of machinery and wants to prove that he is master of it, the stranger spun the windlass at vast speed, opening the floodgates above me in one swift movement. He ran to the other side and did the same as I shouted. He did not hear me. The water of the Trent and Mersey shot out of the unblocked openings and spurted forth in a thick, tumbling arch. Tons of water reared up and hurled their mass onto *Tinker's* bow in a frothing torrent. A stoneware pot of geraniums sitting on the gas locker was immediately flung over the side, crashing against the lock wall and under the rolling surface. That was nothing to what would come next. Water would soon gush in over the uncovered well-deck at the front of the boat and in through the front door, filling the living room with its black stove, its pink sofa, everything I owned. *Tinker* could fill up in seconds. Her nose would tip down under the vast push of water, she would be pulled down head first and she would sink. If I wasn't fast enough, I could sink with her.

I screamed at the top of my voice, 'DROP THE PADDLES!'

Dave and Shelley met my eye, immediately understood, and leapt for the lock gear. The hire boater actually tried to stop them; he had not grasped what was happening. 'For fuck's sake!' he exclaimed, 'She's over-reacting!' I was not over-reacting. *Tinker* jostled and bucked, unsettled as a fretting horse as the cascade tumbled into the fast-filling pool. I tried to pull her back into the few feet we had available to us but with the water rushing in beneath, pushing against the lock walls, it was drawing her further into the torrent. Dave was already winding down the paddle on one side. A couple of gongoozlers were racing down from the beer garden to help Shelley, but there was nothing they could add to her quick reactions. Shelley pushed the goggling stranger out of the way, racing to the paddle on the other side and knocking off the safety catch or pawl to drop it in a single stroke.

Shelley and Dave stopped winding. The water obediently pulled back. It stopped seething. *Tinker* shook like a wet dog. I ran into the cabin, threw all my bath towels onto the flooded living room floor and shot up the lockside ladder like a rat up a drainpipe, to berate the man who was recorded in that day's log book as 'The Idiot of Stenson Lock'.

It had been the longest minute of my life, and he was about to have his. With a dawning sense that he might have done something stupid, The Idiot leaned against the balance beam and tried to look casual. He had not begun to grasp the danger *Tinker* had been in. His own boat was forty-five feet long. In any lock he passed through, he could pull right back from the gates to lurk in safety at the other end of the lock chamber. *Tinker* was more than twenty feet longer, and had had nowhere to go; she had to face the brunt of the falling water. My boat. My *Tinker*.

'DID YOU NOT HEAR ME SAYING DROP THE PADDLES?' I asked in capital letters.

'Darling,' he said, smiling nervously, 'I think they could hear you in Loughborough. No need to be an idiot about it.' Nobody likes to be told they are an idiot, even when they are. On this occasion, the idiocy was all on the other side. Worse, he had called me darling. His wife was standing nearby looking through her fingers, with an expression that clearly said, 'Oh God, George, not again.' The gongoozlers pulled up a chair.

I don't exactly recall what was said, but I am willing to bet that he does. Seldom have the workings of a large lock been explained so clearly, so quickly, and so very loudly. I explained what had just happened, why my crew had reacted as they did and why he should never, ever do it again. I was magnificent. When I finished, the man burst into flames. His wife had a broad grin on her face. The gongoozlers cheered. We opened the gates, and made our way.

'Blimey,' said Dave. 'Got a biscuit?'

Shardlow, not far from this lock at Stenson, has the air of a well-founded settlement that has put its feet up after a lifetime of good work. In 1770, at the very start of his great canal enterprise, James Brindley hitched it to the nearby Trent with a short artificial cut. It quickly proved its worth as an inland port, and soon stood at the eastern end of the completed Trent and Mersey Canal, which had its head office here. Shardlow's wharves handled coal, timber and iron as well as foodstuffs like grain, cheese and salt. The salt warehouse survives as a low brick heritage centre. Wharves or depots always create a local demand for other services, so here were stables and fodder stores for over 100 horses. There were chandlers, ropewalks, boat builders and housing.

There was also a fly boat company, running fast boats non-stop with relays of horses, for perishable cargoes and occasional passengers. One service advertised in 1772 provided 'regular Passage-boats from Manchester to within 2 miles of Warrington, and other places. Forty, fifty, or sixty people are conveyed above 20 miles, for a shilling a-piece, in a shorter time than they can travel even in a carriage by land,' according to the *Derby Mercury* in October 1772.

Fly boats travelled night and day, reaching the outrageous speed of ten miles per hour. They achieved this by means of a neat trick of physics. It was first noted by the Scottish civil engineer John Scott Russell on a summer day in 1834[#], as he watched a fly boat in motion on the Union Canal. Pulled by a pair of horses in a narrow channel, the boat gathered speed and threw up a kind of 'solitary wave' Russell had not seen before. Happily, he was on a horse himself. He followed the wave

---

[#] Of course it was actually first noted by the canny boaters who understood that they could harness it to shift a boat much more quickly, and create an express route for urgent packages and passengers. But they don't count, because they didn't write a paper about it.

to see what it would do, and gave it a name both romantic and meta-physical. The boat suddenly stopped, he said, but the water did not.

> *[I]t accumulated round the prow of the vessel in a state of violent agitation, then suddenly leaving it behind, rolled forward with great velocity, assuming the form of a large solitary elevation, a rounded, smooth and well-defined heap of water, which continued its course along the channel apparently without change of form or diminution of speed. I followed it on horseback, and overtook it still rolling on at a rate of some eight or nine miles an hour, preserving its original figure some thirty feet long and a foot to a foot and a half in height. Its height gradually diminished, and after a chase of one or two miles I lost it in the windings of the channel. Such, in the month of August 1834, was my first chance interview with that singular and beautiful phenomenon which I have called the Wave of Translation.*

The boat was surfing on that powerful 'heap of water' – a hydraulic roller on which the boat could ride for the rest of the journey with occasional input from the horses. Kept in motion like this, the glassy wave would roll on, giving the boat extra depth of water and never breaking into the messy wash that erodes canal banks. The water wasn't just the passive surface on which the boat moved: it became an active means of propulsion. It is now called Russell's Solitary Wave.

The surviving buildings of Shardlow are still appealing, as Rolt said in *Narrow Boat*: he called them 'the dying spark of that fire which once made the humblest barn a thing of beauty.' Rolt was dismissive of modern architecture, and many people share his feeling that the present generation is hard done by in terms of the built environment. Shardlow's solid buildings were made for people with money, and built for them by people with none. Building was cheap in the canal age because builders were paid very little. The skilled brickwork in a voussoir arch or a tiled frieze, or the massive masonry of a lock chamber, came at a good price. Materials were cheap too, because the people who worked in quarries and brick fields were also paid very little. They worked long hours. Many of them were children. Many of them were women. When labourers of any sort tried to organise, they were punished – like the Tolpuddle Martyrs, farm workers who were transported to Australia for forming a small union in favour of higher wages. The five 'martyrs' arrived in Van Diemen's Land in August 1834.

Only two weeks later, on 2 September, the latest of the great canal builders Thomas Telford died in London of a 'bilious derangement'. He was seventy-seven. The industrial Britain that his own labours had helped to create would do no favours for its workers.

Work is of two kinds: first, altering the position of matter at or near the earth's surface relatively to other such matter; second, telling other people to do so. The first kind is unpleasant and ill paid; the second is pleasant and highly paid.

– Bertrand Russell, *In Praise of Idleness*

If you haven't made a living cutting holes in the ground, you might think it is unskilled work. I *have* made a living cutting holes in the ground, and I can testify that it is not. Russell's 'unpleasant and ill paid' barely touches on the labour or the experience of those who came to be known as navvies.

Archaeology is child's play compared to the work of the 'navigators' who dug Britain's canals out of bedrock and subsoil, but there are some comparisons. We sometimes stood juddering in the freezing rain; wet to the skin, covered in mud, exhausted from digging and gagging for a pint. We were stared at in local shops when we tramped in for a bag of crisps or some rolling tobacco, swathed in scarves and gloves, our boots heavy with clay. Unlike the navvies, however, we clocked off at five. Even when far from home we went back to a dry bed, a full meal and a hot shower. We were paid in money, not in employers' tokens, which would change in value from week to week. We mostly had dry boots and a few changes of clothing. Wherever we worked, we were a source of curiosity for locals, not loathing and violence.

In 1767, the clerk of the Trent and Mersey Canal company, John Sparrow mentioned in an account of the Harecastle Tunnel that 'six hundred men' were typically engaged in the project at one time. Who were they? What was their experience, and what happened when they arrived in a neighbourhood where people had seldom ever seen 600 people at once, to drive a ditch through it?

Whatever they were, they were not yet 'navvies'. The canal age would recruit a new workforce, which got its training, its name and its notorious character through its work on the 'navigations' as a proto-canal age called them. When Sparrow wrote in 1767 there was no navvy class, only an uncoordinated mass of untrained men, but the transformation came soon and quickly. The population was younger than ours, with a vast surfeit of labour and immigration from Ireland making wages low. Mass projects like the canals made work easy to find. Within perhaps a dozen years of the Bridgewater project, there was a cohort of dedicated, itinerant canal builders who moved in gangs from one project to another. Their numbers swelled to as many as 10,000 during the canal mania of the 1790s.

Their skill set was fitted precisely to their task. Even we latter-day earth movers know that there is a world of difference between the rookie who goes home with backache and blistered hands, and a seasoned digger. Trench digging is not simple. It takes skill to slice a straight edge with a spade; to balance a mattock perfectly and shear off a half-inch more from a trench wall; to balance soil in a wheelbarrow so that it doesn't tip over, taking you with it, as you run up a mud-covered plank in the rain. Some navvies did this kind of work. They were muck-shifters, waggon-tippers, barrow-runners. Others had more specific skills. There were timbermen who shored up the trench sides, and tunnel miners or 'tigers' who worked with gunpowder and drill. Puddle gangs chopped and kneaded clay and sand into a thick paste, and trod it into the canal bed with heavy 'puddle boots' to make a watertight lining.

For all of them it was a life of hard labour, hardship and hard welcome, wherever they went. The very fact of their constant movement made them unusual in an age where family and village gave most people their sense of selfhood.

They seem free, fearless ... In reality, isolation was the biggest thing in a navvy's life. They were perpetual outsiders: a people apart. Sub-working class. Sub-the-bottommost-heap of English working society. Sub-all, almost.
                                                  – Dick Sullivan, *Navvyman*

They were killed and disabled at a higher rate than even miners or soldiers. A later scandal made much of the fact that the death rate for railway navvies working the Woodhead Tunnel was higher than for those at the battle of Waterloo. They were killed by landslips, and when tunnel walls or cuttings fell in. During the excavation of the Sapperton tunnel in 1787, a navvy killed his own brother when he dropped the heavy load of spoil he was winding up from the diggings. They were killed by disease – particularly pneumonia and bronchitis, which killed up to a tenth of them in this pre-antibiotic age. They were also killed by alcohol. Proverbially, navvies were hard drinkers.

Sometimes they were killed or maimed by each other, in the tribal camp fights for which they were infamous. Battles between English and Irish navvies were particularly common, though there were not as many Irish among them as we tend to think. According to Sullivan, a fairly constant 10 per cent were Irish. The 1800 Act of Union brought the whole of Ireland into a United Kingdom and gave Telford his Holyhead road contract, to connect the two seats of government. Thereafter, Irish people crossed the water in vast numbers. Long before the potato famine of the 1840s they were driven into Scotland, Wales and England by excruciating poverty and malnourishment. Many skilled Irish went into weaving, mechanics or tradesmen crafts like joinery. Many of the unskilled went into domestic service, construction work and to dig the canals.

Isolated, bored and with no roots in the local area, sometimes the navvies took their violence out of the camps and into the neighbouring country. In April 1811, the *Taunton Courier* reported a navvy riot. The men working on the Grand Western Canal in Devon had 'indulged in inordinate drinking, and committed various excesses at Tiverton' on the previous Saturday. So far, so normal for a gang of labourers who had just been paid. The following Monday, however, the violence escalated. A legion of navvies descended on the annual fair at Sampford Peverell 'for the gratification of their tumultuary disposition'.

Most communities in Britain at this time were rural. The population, eighteen million of them in 1811, had lived for centuries in the quiet rhythms of harvest, holiday and market. Only a quarter of them lived in towns of more than 5,000 people. By the end of the century the proportion was exactly reversed, in an overwhelming cultural and economic shift: but when the navvies arrived in Sampford Peverell, the average Briton could barely even imagine hundreds of people in a single place. Such numbers were reserved for a successful market, church festivals or the annual fair. Even then many of the faces in the crowd would be familiar, drawn from a regional hinterland with shared values. When hundreds of powerful, hard-drinking labourers descended on a village with their strange accents and attitudes, the impact was disruptive and exciting. They brought with them an anarchic shanty town of tents, wagons, rootless families – and an appetite for local food, alcohol and women. When 300 of these workers rolled into Sampford Peverell, a village with a population of 894, the sight of them would have been alarming even if they had come on a Sunday School outing. They had not come on a Sunday School outing. These were 'savage ungovernable banditti'; and by three o'clock they were mostly drunk. They attacked a farmer called Chave and threatened to pull down his house; he shot one of them dead. The neighbourhood was 'kept in a state of the greatest terror and commotion for more than twenty four hours', according to the local paper.

Small wonder that the villagers were terrified. The work of the navvies trained them to a pitch of physical strength that made them famously powerful and fast. Those who survived the conditions of the camps were far stronger than the ordinary labourer, and hugely better fitted for their specialist work. A good muck-shifter on a good day could cut out eighteen tons of soil. (The railway workers, with generations of accumulated training and technique behind them, outdid even this.) 'Theirs was a community in permanent flux, river-like in its constant flow', according to Sullivan.

As a whole, the navvy class included many women. Some ran catering huts or shants – hence 'shanty town'. Others were laundrywomen, sometime prostitutes, chandlers, mothers and partners (if not always wives). A very few of them worked alongside the male diggers. These women must have been preternaturally hardy. It's an idiom among archaeologists that 'absence of evidence is not evidence of absence', but every now and then a female appears in the scant records. In almost any role, at any time in history, there has been a handful of women masquerading as men even in the most unlikely places. By definition, if they did it well the records do not show them as women.

One woman that we know by name was 'Lucky' Logue. She worked on the canal in Edinburgh with her husband and his Irish gang around 1818. Navvies of all kinds were seldom recorded by name unless the law had reason to remember them: one of Logue's navvy gang was a Newry man called Hare who, with his friend Burke, would be remembered as the infamous grave robbers. At least we know where he learned to dig.

The wet network completed, the navvies moved instantly to the dry network of railways, taking with them their filthy reputation. At that exact point, in 1831, a railway engineer called Peter Lecount said of them:

> These banditti, known in some parts of England by the name of 'Navies' [sic] or 'Navigators' and in others that of 'Bankers' are generally the terror of the surrounding country: they are as complete a class by themselves as the Gipsies. Possessed of all the daring recklessness of the Smuggler, without any of his redeeming qualities, their ferocious behaviour can only be equalled by the brutality of their language. It may be truly said, their hand is against every man, and before they have been long located, every man's hand is against them.

People of a certain age or nationalist inclination sometimes ask plaintively, 'Why can't we build big engineering projects cheaply and fast, like *they* did?' Partly because publicly financed projects can no longer get away with settling an army of migrant workers in a shanty town full of cholera, with no provision for welfare or healthcare. Navvies themselves seldom showed any instinct to unionise, but as the nineteenth-century population shifted towards urban living and collective working, others did. The campaign for better working conditions began in earnest there.

Veteran archaeologist Francis Pryor suggests that the Victorian age should be called the Navvian age to honour not a tiny, grumpy, Germanic queen, but the navvies 'whose back-breaking toil built the canals, turnpikes and railways that altered [Britain's] landscape so comprehensively.' Long before Victoria took the throne in 1837 the projects of engineers like Brindley, Telford, Smeaton, Jessop, and others had made them into a well-trained land moving force. For all that, they were still the butt of jokes:

A navvy woman took her son to the surgery. 'H'm, costive bound,' diagnosed the doctor. 'Eh, I don't care if it costs five pound,' said the indignant navvy woman. 'The lad's got to shit.'

– Dick Sullivan, Navvyman

A goose for Christmas

Sixty years before I arrived in Shardlow, a canal village to the southeast of Derby, Tom Rolt reached it by the same route on *Cressy,* the star of his own boating biography, *Narrow Boat.* He crossed the meeting of four waters at Trent Lock, where I nearly killed that tiny sailor many years later, and passed through the double locks at Sawley into the still waters at the eastern extremity of the Trent and Mersey. Rolt described Shardlow as a place 'from the dawn of the new era' when canals were new features in an old landscape. It was the first canal port to stamp its shape on the time map. He admired the waterside buildings, particularly: 'One large, three-storeyed warehouse, which in modern hands would have been a featureless barrack, was miraculously transformed by a combination of detail so subtle that it was difficult to discover why it should be so satisfying to the eye.'

It is still there. One reason for its appeal is that you come upon it without much warning. I slipped through Idle Bridge, enjoying the presence of the working boat *Sweden* moored next to it, and emerged to see a good-looking brick façade, with a low arch. Sign boards with an antique font proclaimed this as 'the Navigation from the Trent to the Mersey' as well they might, since this is its official starting point. The building is now a pub called the Clock Warehouse. It was in the bar of the Clock Warehouse that I first met Digger.

He came in late on a surprisingly warm night in December, a huge man in a long waxed jacket with four sleek black Labradors at his heels. He sat heavily at a table and clicked his fingers. The dogs sat immediately like clockwork creatures, and stayed stock still. They were young, fit and ghostly; shiny as coal and utterly obedient. In that dim corner they were almost invisible, which turned out to be important in their work. Their companion had a silent dog whistle round his neck. He didn't take his coat off, despite sitting by the bright fire.

For some unlikely reason, someone in my group began to talk about woodcock. The large Barbour-clad man sidled up to us. He looked like a cross between Brian Blessed and a grizzly bear. 'Like woodcock, do you?' he said. He opened one side of his waxed coat like a flasher at a county show, and displayed several feathered carcases. Pigeons; woodcock; a few lumpy pockets with a long ear hanging out. This was Digger. Digger was a poacher.

He was passing through Shardlow on a ramshackle boat that looked barely large enough to fit him inside it. Like me, he was tied up at the local marina for a few nights. Digger left the pub shortly before we did. Ten minutes later, as we reached the marina gates, the four ghost dogs poured out to fetch us. Like Lassie in the films, they had something to tell us. They bounded silently down to the water, pacing and circling at the end of a walkway between boats, willing us to come and see what was there. What was there, waist-deep in the cold waters of a midwinter canal, was Digger. He rested his elbows casually on the pontoon as if still in the bar. 'Fell in,' he said helpfully. Weighed down by his coat full of contraband and a thick jumper, he was stuck deep in the mud. It took three of us to haul him out. Digger was better insulated than most of the people who fall into the canals and drown each winter. He seemed unaffected, squelching stoically back to his boat with the immaculate dogs trotting silently behind him. He was lucky that it was the beginning of winter, not February or March when the water has been chilled for months.

Digger wanted to express his gratitude; and he expressed gratitude in the form of dead things. My boyfriend of that time lived on a tiny Springer boat, the size of a large fridge-freezer. Three nights before Christmas as we drowsed by the wood burner, the boat lurched under the weight of a substantial visitor on the counter. We threw open the narrow doors to find Digger, clutching in one huge fist his Christmas gift. He thrust it towards us; it dangled, flaccid as an empty bagpipe.

I am no friend to the Canada goose. To the non-boater they may seem endearing, but when you have them outside your bedroom window playing the trombone at three o'clock in the morning, they lose their charm. They cover the towpaths with unbelievably copious excrement, and hiss at anyone trying to get onto a boat. I would happily wish death on one. I was not, however, keen to eat one. They are vermin; they live on weeds and grass and snails. Shop-bought goose is rich and moist; but shop-bought goose is bred for tenderness and taste, even over-fatty sometimes. This feral bird – spotted in a local field, honking stupidly at the water's edge until Digger hopped off a passing boat and shot it with an air rifle – would not be over-fatty. Not only was it rugged and muscular, but it had been culled in the dead of winter. Even weeds and grass and snails were in short supply. Looking at the drooping carcass, I saw that Digger had not culled a plump young bird in the prime of life but the Albert Steptoe of the flock, a desiccated tribal elder. It was the waterways equivalent of roadkill.

'Thanks, Digger,' I said.

'Brilliant,' said the boyfriend, 'we can have it for Christmas dinner.'

And so we did. There would be five friends at the feast, plus one Border Terrier. For three days, the goose hung from the tiller like a sad hot-water bottle. On Christmas Day, I braced myself and got down to it with a grave sense of foreboding. I salted the saggy carcass, and larded it with bacon. I basted it. I cooked it upside down to maximise what fat there was. I made a rich gravy to moisten it. Some hours later, I drew the roasting tin out of the oven and squinted at it. The carcase of a goose is a different shape to that of a chicken.

'It looks like a toddler,' said one of the gang. It did.

I laid about it with a sharp knife, but it wasn't up to the task. 'Bread knife please,' I said grimly. Someone passed me the bread knife. I hacked at the goose. It squeaked faintly, like polystyrene. It had the texture of the fibreboard used in flatpack furniture. I served it up in large splinters, onto five plates and a dog bowl.

It was vile. It tasted, inevitably, of weeds and grass and snails. The flesh had the texture of wet rope, and much the same flavour. I couldn't eat it; our friends couldn't eat it; even the dog couldn't eat it. We might as well have made a wardrobe out of it. Digger had taken the life of an innocent bird, and that afternoon it took its revenge. Later, after we had cobbled together a Christmas lunch of egg, chips and cooking whisky, Digger silently took the corpse outside and disposed of it. We never spoke of it again.

Everything, everywhere and all at once

What can the England of 1940 have in common with the England of 1840? But then, what have you in common with the child of five whose photograph your mother keeps on the mantelpiece? Nothing, except that you happen to be the same person.

– George Orwell, 'England Your England'

Brindley, working in the late eighteenth century, was the first great engineer of the canals. Thomas Telford, working in the early 1800s, would be the last. In the span of their two lives, the world shifted on its axis; and it did so, in part, because of their work. The canals were both cause and effect of a huge historic cycle. As coal fed the smelters and furnaces, as the furnaces churned out more iron and bricks, as the foundries made their steam engines and the steam engines required more foundries, so there were more and more potential growth areas.

New steam engines drained new mines; new mines produced more coal. All of it had to be moved. The coal, the iron, the bricks, the timber and slate, the steam engines – these heavy, unperishable cargoes were ideal for the canals.

These raw materials built the factories of Wedgwood and the steel foundries of Sheffield, the mills of Halifax and the glassworks of Chance in Birmingham. Once those factories had done their work, hundreds of capillary canals were dug to supply every town with the pottery and cutlery, and broadcloth and windowpanes that they had produced. More canals, more roads, more foundries, more engines – more people. Between Brindley's birth in 1716 and Telford's death in 1834, the English population almost doubled. Workers met in the cities and married earlier; many of them had a waged income. Industry made people socialise differently, eat differently, settle in new places and have different relationships than their parents and grandparents. Industry made people worship differently, as working people grew away from the Church of England and towards the non-conformist faiths that encouraged charity and local action to support the urban poor. More people meant more pots, more pans, more slums, more clothes; more money everywhere, though not of course for everyone.

This society had one word as its steady heartbeat: *more, more, more*. The slow machine that England was became dirtier, greedier, cleverer, bolder and faster. Brindley's generation emboldened the political and commercial giants of the time to feel that they could take over the world. By Telford's time, they felt thoroughly entitled to it; and his cohort built the infrastructure that allowed them to do precisely that.

At the beginning of this great tumbling acceleration, James Brindley had to work *with* the land as he built his canals. When Brindley encountered a hill, he draped his channel around it like a long rope hugging a single contour; no locks, no aqueducts, and certainly no boat lifts. By the time Thomas Telford was laying out canals forty years later, he had available to him the technology, the budgets and the limitless ambition of the last Georgians. When Telford encountered a hill, he reached for the dynamite.

The two men never met. When Brindley died in 1772, Telford was a fifteen-year-old apprentice stonemason in Dumfries and Galloway. There is, though, one place where we can see them side by side. The two great canal-makers encountered the same problem at the same location, in two layers of time fifty years apart. In 1766, Brindley's navvies arrived at the foot of Harecastle Hill, at Kidsgrove near Stoke-on-Trent. In 1824, Telford's navvies arrived at Harecastle Hill. It was probably raining. The two men, each in his own time, looked at the massive obstacle in their path and came to the same conclusion. There was no getting around this hill. They would have to go through.

If you fancy a fight, stick your head into a canal forum on social media and express an opinion on the origins of canal painting. Any opinion will do.

Roses and castles, painted diamonds and other symbols in shining primary colours, are still a signature flourish on older boats. On the working fleets, they were never put there by the boaters themselves but by craftsmen in the company yards. They applied the finishing touches to the cabins and gave each family a water can, the boat name painted around the middle like a vivid cummerbund. A boatman knew which yard a boat came from by its roses: the Braunston type with its dynamic flick of the paintbrush was made by the Nursers, the Polesworth type by the Atkins family. The frillier 'Knobstick roses' are named for the boats they belonged to. The paint style called brightwork belongs only to the Leeds and Liverpool Canal. It was all done quickly, skilfully and with a limited palette, in short time.

The old man excelled at this work. To behold him, as I did, when he sat before the bench in his narrow workshop, the battered bowler firmly planted on the back of his head and a tray of many-coloured paints at his elbow, was to see the past miraculously living in the present. Not a past preserved in a museum or spuriously recreated in an Art and Craft shop, but a vital tradition. Handling his fine camel-hair brushes with wonderful sureness and delicacy, he first of all painted little shaded discs of sepia, ochre and pink on the green ground of the can and surrounded them with a garland of pale green leaves. These were the centres of the roses. When they were dry, the petals, red on sepia, yellow on ochre and white on pink, were superimposed so simply and swiftly that only in the way a mere blob of paint seemed suddenly to blossom forth was the skill revealed. The bright work was completed when the veining of the leaves had been painted in with a very fine brush and a coat of varnish applied to preserve it.

This is Rolt in *Narrow Boat* describing painter George Tooley, working in the 1940s out of a yard in Banbury. He could equally be describing the workshop of Phil Speight, one of the last painters in the lineage of Frank Nurser and Ron Hough, with an MBE for 'services to heritage crafts' to show for it. (He's also my ex, and should perhaps have another one for patience.) He paints water cans, cabin stools, other accoutrements of the working boats, and teaches weekend courses.

People long for a clear-cut origin story which explains these bright shapes, but art forms always have blurry family trees. Some people confidently claim that the roses and castles descend from Romani art, because they resemble the colourful work seen in the vardos and travelling cabins (which they do). Others say with equal confidence that they have nothing to do with Romani art, because they want boat culture to have its own unique painting tradition (which it does).

The first person to pick up a paintbrush and apply it to a canal boat was not working in a vacuum. Phil Speight believes that the cartoonish castle landscapes of the boats stand in a long and wide tradition. It begins, he says, with medieval wall paintings. On a visit to Haddon Hall in Derbyshire, Phil found a conservation team working on fifteenth-century frescoes in the chapel. He was bowled over to see the exact same scrolls and sinuous leaf forms he had been painting on the side of a boat the day before. The landscapes – always with a bridge, a castle, and a distant sailboat made with two or three brush strokes – descend through Italian Renaissance art and Baroque landscapes like those of Claude Lorrain. 'I don't mean that a bloke working in a canal paint shop had actually seen Claude Lorrain paintings', says Phil. The landscapes bled into the craft lineage via popular prints, tea trays, tin ware – and into the workshops of industrial Birmingham, where elegant landscapes were painted onto the faces of grandfather clocks. Phil defers to the acknowledged expert, Tony Lewery, whose book *Flowers Afloat* is still the authoritative source.

Art travels easily. These paintings bear an undeniable family resemblance to the boards of painted farm carts, to Balkan folk art flowers, to Victorian steam-powered fairgrounds with their enticing painted booths, to Romani decorative painting and the long tradition of Anglo-Saxon ornament. My feeling is that the painting of the canals borrowed its colourful clothing from elite and demotic art in many places, picking up a little rubric from each of them. Folk art does not leave a written history; it is what the boat people leave instead of a written history, and it fades.

The paintwork is the brightest and most obvious sign of traditional boat culture. The rest of it may not be where you expect it to be. Take music, for instance. There are plenty of musicians on boats and there is often a squeezebox, guitar or fiddle stowed somewhere, but there isn't a great tradition of music that *derives* from the canals. When a new cut first opened, songs were sometimes commissioned as a kind of Georgian advertising jingle and released as broadside ballad sheets. There are post-war and contemporary folk songs too, but as the custodians of the archive 'Songs of the Inland Waterways' confirm: 'there don't appear to be many 'traditional' canal songs as such, if by that we mean songs sung by the canal workers and boaters from the days when the canals were a working system.'

No doubt the boaters picked up and sang the folk songs of the areas they travelled through, with the mix of sentimentality, wit and innuendo that such music still brings when it is shared in waterside pubs. Rolt found this to be the case in the 1940s. Most boats on the Oxford 'carried a melodeon, a concertina or an accordion. Often of a night-time I would hear the familiar strains of 'Daisy Bell' or 'Two Lovely Black Eyes' floating over the water from the cabin of a moored boat.' Music was constantly played, but not usually written, by the boat people.

There isn't a distinctive cuisine (see Canada goose), or musical tradition for the same reason that miners or engineers didn't have a distinctive cuisine or musical tradition. Everyone was knackered. They often worked sixteen hours, and then lay down to sleep in a space filled with other bodies. It hardly allowed for fiddle practice. If the culture of working boaters does not lie in their songs, their music or their cooking, then where the hell is it?

It's in the boat. The culture of the working boats was in their fabric, and in the ways of working them. It was in the steel and wood and paint of the boat, the language of the boat, the working of the boat, the furnishings and etiquette and equipment and the smell of the boat. It's in the roses and castles of course, and in the hand-lettered name on the side of the boat, and the proper vocabulary that distinguishes a narrow boat from a barge or a Josher from a gas boat. It's in the superstitions that 'scholared' boaters ignore at their peril, and in the folk stories of tunnel boggarts. It's the place names and pubs that only boaters know, and the curious bankside gantries or covered loading bays that only boaters understand. It's in personal nicknames, and traditions of placement on the boat – how the water can and mop sit on the cabin top; how Brasso is stored or cloths folded; the automatic polishing of every piece of brass on a boat to signal that the people are clean, though their cargo might be dirty.

Boating culture lived mainly in actions, not artefacts. Much is now lost to liveaboard boaters on modern vessels. It survives in some things, like the way that ropes are looped – not in a figure of eight like a climber's rope, but in a loose and ready coil. It is there in the etiquette of knocking on the cabin top as you step over someone's boat. Above all, the old culture survives in the gentle choreography of taking a pair of boats through a lock with perfect economy of movement, so that not a calorie of effort is wasted. The sequence of raising and dropping paddles, crossing the lock from one side to the other and setting locks for the approaching boat, so that the gates are opened exactly when needed; these were all part of a dance which is 250 years old. It is the deepest part of the living culture of a canal; and it is a dance that still happens whenever boaters reach a lock flight.

Names

The Book of Nots says:

Not sailors – boaters. Not water gipsies – boaters.
Not primitives or hippies; dropouts; crackheads, dickheads;
                    [sometimes dickheads]
on the run or on the scrounge; not travellers or workshy,
wild or wastrels, dossers, thieves. Not cool and not unkind.

Not bohemians, eccentrics, characters or alcoholics
necessarily; not poets. Not inclined to ask you in
or tell you where the two most perfect pubs are;
                    [Ashleworth; High Offley]
unless they like the look of you. Not going through a phase.

Not named in quite the usual way; Baddie, Digger,
Her Off Cheshire Rose or Shaman Wayne
                    [he's not a shaman, he's a plumber].
Not stopping long. Not certain where they are
as far as B&Q, the ring road or what day the bins go out.

Not all there – but here, today. And not surprised
by what your city does with water.

The culture of boating is also in the place names that canal people used – the Jam'Ole, Sutton Stop and Bugsworth were Rubastic Dock, Hawkesbury Junction and Buxworth, respectively. Birmingham was, and still is for a few older boat people, Brummagem. Boaters themselves have their nicknames too.

> *One day a man, not a navvy, went down to a dam asking for Mr Millwood.*
> *Nobody knew him. 'Hang it,' then said a stringy woman, taking a gum-*
> *bucket pipe from her mouth, 'Tha means my feyther. Why didn't tha ask*
> *for Old Blackbird?'*
>
> *– Navvyman*

I moored up next to a boat in a sunny stretch of the Shropshire Union, painted in what looked like camouflage. It turned out to be overlapping cannabis leaves. Its skipper, emerging in a green cloud, introduced himself as Wayne – 'but people call me Wayne the Shaman.' *I doubt that very much.* A couple of days later his name came up in a local chandlery. 'Shaman my arse,' said the chandler. 'He's a plumber.'

Like the kings of medieval France (Pepin the Short, Louis the Stammerer, Louis the Fat) we have nicknames. Like them, we don't get to choose our own. Those who try to reinvent themselves with an interesting new name will find that it does not stick. I'm always suspicious of those people who introduce themselves with, 'My name is Stephen, but people call me Sven the Well-Hung.' *No, they don't. They call you Fat Steve.*

Sometimes the name is a mystery (as in the case of Chris Shipwreck) but often it distinguishes between people with the same first name. The most popular name for men in the UK is David, so it was no surprise that we had a bundle of Daves, and accordingly a bundle of nicknames to identify which one we were gossiping about. Dusty Dave was a bin man; Electric Dave, an electrician; Deckchair Dave, a sometime actor who liked to sunbathe in a deckchair on his roof. Diesel Dave was a sweet and cackling car mechanic who later, for reasons of sad practicality, became known as Dead Dave[§§].

Equally tasteless was the nickname granted to Dave the Stroke. He had had a stroke. This is, of course, appalling, but Dave the Stroke took it in good heart. It was no surprise to him that he had had a stroke. He knew the name was a description, not an insult. As he recuperated, he struggled to regain his language but he was constantly giggling at his own failures of speech. Cruising along a sunny stretch of canal one day, I saw Dave's boat tied up by the bank ahead of me, and decided to pull in for a cup of tea. 'Get the kettle on,' I shouted. He was trying to communicate something but struggling with his words.

'Careful, it's ... you know.' He pointed to the canal.

'It's what?' I said, nudging the boat towards the bank.

'It's ... it's ... it's ...' he said, struggling for the word. Too late: the boat tilted to one side, and I felt the familiar shudder as she struck into a substantial bank of mud. We were solidly aground.

'Shallow, Dave?' I asked. 'Is the word you were looking for *shallow*?' He was laughing; too hard to answer.

'I see you've got a dog now,' I said when we were finally drinking tea together on the bank. 'What's he called?' There was a thoughtful pause. 'Dog,' said Dave.

'Yes, but what's he actually called?'

[§§] Recently Deckchair Dave passed away too. He immediately became 'the other Dead Dave'.

'He's called Dog,' said Dave. 'Only name I can remember.' He laughed heartily; Dog curled up at his feet. It was as good a name as any other, as far as he was concerned.

Some people, when they hear that you live on a boat, look at you as they would look at a street sleeper – with a bemused pity that you've allowed things to go this far. They ask questions but their interest is polite and baffled, like Boris Johnson on a hospital visit. They assume that present-day boaters are uneducated, poor, limited, and dirty. They see us as people who have failed. We have apparently been unable to get a proper job and buy a house, as grown-ups are supposed to do. 'Where do you do your *shopping?*' they ask, as we live in a parallel universe where our groceries are delivered by unicorns".

There is suspicion too. In some minds, an internal voice pipes up: *These boaters are getting away with something. Why am I breaking my back to pay a mortgage when these water rats are getting away without one? Surely in* some *way they are sponging off me, or failing to pay their way?* To many people, living differently is not just difference, but threat. It is disorientating; it changes their sense of their own environment. They don't live where they thought they did. It turns out the map has two sides, and there are people living on the other side of it.

One friend, whose two children were raised on a boat, had to move on to the bank when her partner fell ill. He was unable to move safely around the canal bank, and they decided to buy a house. With two good jobs, they moved into a pleasant terrace on the outskirts

---

" At the Co-op, as a rule. Their delivery unicorns are marvellous.

of Birmingham; but when her colleagues heard about this they were amazed. ('You could have lived in a house *all along*?') It was inconceivable to them that a person who could afford a house might choose to live on a boat.

Not everyone who lives on a boat does choose to do so. An increasing proportion of people in our slow, mobile, nationwide village would prefer bricks and mortar, but can't afford a house. This is especially true in London, where nobody can afford a house. Some boaters *do* fall into the stereotypes of the narrow-minded: poor, uneducated, parochial, mentally unwell, unorthodox; but then plenty of house-dwellers fit it too. Among boat-dwellers of the UK are millionaires, MPs and thousands of perfectly ordinary working people.

Most of us live afloat not because it's cheaper than a house, but because we find it *better* than a house. It's not a lifestyle. It's a life. There are inconveniences, and compensations. Domestic water is a good example. If you live in a house, your water is supplied by witchcraft. It runs out of the kitchen tap, abundant and endlessly replenished. It is one of the greatest things about civilisation. It also ties you to the mains supply, and can make you a little blasé about how much water you use. On a boat, by contrast, the kitchen tap is fed from a holding tank that you need to fill up every few days. It takes a long hosepipe and five minutes of faffing about. The tap will be jammed, or one of the connecting fixtures broken. It might be snowing. It's a bit of a pain in the neck. Tasks like this are constant, and they are the price for the small freedoms of boat life.

Actually, no freedom is small. The opportunity to wake up tomorrow in the territory of a different blackbird, with a fresh arrangement of trees; or to visit old friends in another mooring and become neighbours for a night or two. The opportunity to take a new footpath on your way to work in the morning, figuring out a fresh route through familiar streets, noticing new buildings and road names – so that your fifteen-minute commute is a refreshment and a surprise – and in all of this slow, local travel, the opportunity to take with you all the comforts of home. For those who enjoy them, these are not inconveniences but pleasures. Perhaps boaters are people with a low boredom threshold, or a high tolerance for change.

It may be that these disruptions to routine don't sound like a pleasure to you, but an inconvenience. Not everybody *wants* to skip through the housing estate by a different route every morning, or work out where to buy a pint of milk now that the usual corner shop is five miles away. If you have a regular job in a single location, if you have a divided family, regular evening commitments, an allotment, a teenager, a yoga class or if you simply cannot be arsed, then fair enough. This book isn't here to convert you to the righteous path of boat dwelling but to show a glimpse of a life with a different rhythm.

Born-and-bred boaters – low in cash and high in resourcefulness – have for decades put up with 'scholars' like me whose education is a badge of incompetence. They have rescued me when I was about to drill an actual hole through the floor of my own boat. They have explained to me that my boat is sinking because I am missing a gasket which any sensible person would have checked straight away. They have taught me the two handy twists of rope that allow me to tie up without ever making a knot. When my useless boat-handling made it impossible to respect me, they waited for me to learn. When I learned, they congratulated me. Eventually they gave me the real badge of acceptance; they ignored me. They are not the salt of the earth; that's something rich people say to patronise poor people. They are just boaters.

Settling

Hall Green

Near the unfortunately named Bleeding Wolf pub in Scholar Green, Staffordshire, a path between suburban bungalows leads straight into the eighteenth century. The walker drops down a flight of steps into a pure and unsuspected corridor of deep leaf, with banks of brambles on the far side of a narrow canal. A white cottage stands by the towpath. Of course, there are rambling roses around its door. The quiet lock next to it is spanned by a cast-iron footbridge with black-and-white roundels like shield bosses. This is Hall Green lock. It marks the beginning of the Macclesfield Canal.

My brother James was squinting at the almost-level lock when a man walked past in full Victorian dress. He was about thirty, wearing a large handlebar moustache and the distinguished waistcoat and trousers of a funeral director, with a brassy watch chain. His outfit was topped with a full-length cape and a silver-topped cane. He had a twinkle in his eye, as any man might who is dressed as Jules Verne on a Thursday lunchtime in the outskirts of Stoke. He walked with purpose, as if expecting a challenge. 'Some sort of re-enactment going on, is there?' asked my brother as he wound up the paddles. 'No, no,' said the gentleman blithely. 'Just going to work.' And he strode off into the featureless countryside. Perhaps there was a penny farthing repair shop around the bend in the towpath.

It was late spring. The blackthorn trees were in a full fizz of blossom, promising a good harvest of sloes later in the year. James, happily for me a natural boatman, had walked ahead to work the lock. I knocked the boat out of gear and drifted towards the gates, realising as I did that Hall Green is a stop lock.

There are very few left: one at Autherley in Staffordshire, one at Dutton on the Trent and Mersey, and another at Sutton Stop (the name used by boaters for Hawkesbury Junction near Coventry). The stop lock is like an ordinary lock, but instead of the usual ten- or twelve-foot drop, it has a drop of about three inches. Why bother? To keep water from moving between two canals. The canal builders were jealous of their water supply, because it cost them a lot of money. All our canals were built by private companies (they were nationalised only in 1948). Imagine yourself as the chairman of one such company, perhaps in the 1780s or 90s. Building your canal is obviously a huge expense: but that is only the beginning. The company must fill the canal with water. It must keep it in water, and the water must be held at a constant level so that loaded boats can navigate. And there's the rub; because every time a boat passes through a lock, at least 80,000 gallons are drained out of the level above that lock*** . An artificial waterway has to be topped up, or it will literally run dry – and so will your company funds. The company can't rely entirely on natural streams to supply the canal, because they dry up in a hot summer and might be blocked by local landowners. You will have to build reservoirs, culverts, sluices and weirs to supply water, and to regulate the level.

Water is as vital to your new canal as tarmac is to a motorway. Unlike tarmac, water does not stay put. Where your canal meets another one (which, after all, is the point of a network) you risk watching it flow into a neighbouring canal, owned by a different company. Why should

***Locks vary of course. This is a typical narrow lock.

your shareholders top up *their* supply? To protect your own water, you build a stop lock. The boaters work it in the usual way, but the boat rises or falls only a couple of inches; and only a tiny amount of liquid passes between the two canals. Clever.

This commercial jealousy was seen at its craziest in central Birmingham. There, beneath the mirrored slabs of the Marriott Hotel, the softer mirror of the canal narrows into a boat-length bottleneck called Worcester Bar. At its construction in 1792 the Bar was an actual barrier: a seven-foot-long section of ground left in place between two canals. It separated the water of the Birmingham Canal Company from the water of the Worcester and Birmingham Canal Company. In this, the capital city of our parallel map, in a time and place of unprecedented industry, every single cargo travelling between these two waterways had to be unloaded from one boat, put piecemeal into barrows and wheeled seven feet along the towpath, to be loaded into another. It was an insane arrangement. It ended in 1815, when the two companies came to their senses and built a stop lock, like the one at Hall Green.

There were two of them at Hall Green originally. The nearby cottage was then a toll station, where skippers were charged for the use of the canal they were about to enter. Nowadays the toll is paid in time. You pause to let the lock rise by a couple of inches; give up two or three peaceful minutes, and move on. In this case it was also a portal for time travel.

It seemed right that we should meet our steampunk passer-by at a stop lock, a place where the present day has to hold its breath for a moment and acknowledge the time when these small, simple mechanical boundaries counted for something. *Funny old world*. Then James opened the gate, and I drifted onto the Macclesfield Canal.

By the time James and I reached Hall Green, I had been in water-proofs for a month. The May Bank Holiday of 2006 was a record-breaking wash-out. It was, of course, raining in Stoke-on-Trent. On the way north to Hall Green, it was raining. After Hall Green on the way to the high cattle pastures of Cheshire, it continued to rain. At Bosley locks near Congleton, James worked me through the twelve narrow chambers, emptying each one ahead of me with the beautiful, ergonomic rhythm of an experienced lock-wheeler so that *Tinker* never had to wait. We rose at last into the long, uninterrupted pound of the upper Macclesfield Canal. It was raining.

It rains a lot here, at the western edge of the Peak District National Park. Rainclouds hit the stubborn Pennine landforms and release their water or snow or hail. Sometimes they stay cloudy, and drape themselves around the bends of the infamous Cat and Fiddle high road to lie in wait for motorcyclists. On this occasion, the weather gave us one short break. The shining fields where Cheshire cheese begins its life were dappled with cow parsley and milky sunshine. Ahead of us was one of the longest pounds in the UK. James put his soggy feet up by the stove and wrote up the log book. 'Many lock-free but extremely pretty miles' he wrote, 'allowing us to race along under very lovely bridges at break-neck speeds.'

By break-neck, he meant three miles per hour; but he was right about the bridges. The Macclesfield Canal's bridges are honest, squat Peak District structures of ash-coloured Keuper sandstone. The arch extends beyond the strictly necessary semi-circle, returning on itself slightly as if to complete a circle just under the water. Some of them are skew bridges, with slanting lines of ashlar which only a skilled mason can make. The late canal builders used these to build bridges at an angle across the cut, rather than realign the road above. Occasionally a 'snake bridge' or roving bridge lifts the towpath from one side, crosses the canal and delivers the path to the other in a curve, which allowed tow horses to cross without the need to unhitch any ropes. It was a practical solution for horse boats, and two centuries later it is still a deeply satisfying arrangement of function and form. The same material was used for milestones and even half-milestones, the slabs rising like grave markers in the towpath edge to mark the distance from Macclesfield or Marple in the heavy serif font of the 1830s.

There was something familiar about these furnishings. The milestones gave the route a distinctive brand identity. The bridges were more beautiful than they needed to be. They reminded me of a long archaeological survey in North Wales, spotting milestones in the rain with a soggy colleague. Consulting the Nicholson canal map, I saw why these way markers rang a bell. The stones, the lovely bridges, the long lock-free pound and its many little aqueducts, all take the form they do because the man who designed the object of that survey, the old Holyhead Road, was also the chief architect of the Macclesfield Canal; my long-dead professional crush. 'Hello Thomas', I said, just at the point where a flying golf ball from the nearby course zoomed across my eyeline. 'Thomas who?' asked my mystified brother. 'Thomas Telford', I said.

Telford

In the early nineteenth century a man dubbed 'The Colossus of Roads' by his waggish mate, the poet Southey, did battle with the very landscape of Snowdonia – and won. He draped a long, solid road across North Wales. In the wettest winter of the twentieth century, myself and a bedraggled co-worker called Pete walked every inch of its ninety-two miles. It took us three weeks, recording every damn milestone and bridge, aqueduct and embankment. The life of an archaeologist is full of surprises, and in this case the main surprise was just how much it rains in Wales in November. 'Oh look, another milestone,' Pete would say. 'Yes,' I would say. 'What a complete surprise that it should appear just here, exactly one mile after the last one.' It was dreary fieldwork: but the research sent me into the archives of museums and record offices, in search of Thomas Telford.

There he was, in his notebooks and accounts; keeping meticulous notes on every bit of his projects, sending instructions to overseers and quarrymen, sketching alternative routes and cross-sections of trackbed which looked very similar to the Roman highways of an earlier Britain. I developed a bit of a crush on him.

I would soon come to know his canals as well as his land routes. Both were part of Telford's conscious, strategic effort to cast a net of safe, reliable transport routes across the United Kingdom. If the nation didn't squeeze every last bit of juice out of its resources – animal, mineral and vegetable – it wouldn't be for a lack of communication between its important nodes of power and commerce.

The Romans had built their roads with cheap labour, centralised government, and a powerful sense of entitlement. Those preconditions for infrastructural success were back in force by the time Telford got the contract for his Holyhead Road. The same methods that the Romans had used to colonise, and to bring home the wealth of its colonies, were in use across a newly United Kingdom. Ireland was hitched, unwilling, to Great Britain in an 1801 Act of Union. With growing political and commercial muscle, the Westminster government was not only stretching into India and Africa, but dominating Scotland, Ireland, Wales and its own English regions to enrich the landowning class and to keep them unassailable.

His temper was not that of the fiery younger genius Isambard Kingdom Brunel, whose letter to a demanding customer I once read in an archive: 'I am, sir, your obedient servant; and if you were mine, I should give you a damn good flogging.' Telford was a lifelong bachelor who roomed for many years above a London coffee house, and later over the Royal Engineering Institute (which he founded). His clerk wrote after his death that 'his laugh was the heartiest I ever heard'. He was born the son of a Dumfriesshire shepherd in 1757, and became a self-taught and voracious scholar with immense skills for engineering and organisation, but his success began with a lucky break: he went to school with William Pulteney, who later married into money and became an immensely helpful sponsor, putting Telford repeatedly in the path of opportunity.

Telford was an experimentalist, a risk-taker who used new materials like hydraulic cement and cast iron to throw canals and roads across the most challenging contours of the nation. In Wales, he used a cast-iron trough, caulked with felted wool, to lift the Llangollen Canal 126 feet above the river Dee at Pontcysyllte. He took the age-old valley roads of North Wales and moved them wholesale, wrapping them around the free-draining slopes of Snowdonia, blasting tunnels through hillsides and building vast embankments with the spoil. At the Menai Straits, where ferry boats had made the perilous journey around the notorious Swillies stones for thousands of years, Telford sunk deep anchors into the rock and strung a high suspension bridge between Anglesey and the mainland.

In each massive project, Telford kept one eye on the budget like the country bridge builder he had once been, and one eye on the next job, like the freelancer he had become. He branded his work with a Telford flourish, so that potential clients would know it was his hand that had written this great feature across the landscape. For the mile markers of the Holyhead Road, that increasingly important route between Westminster and Ireland, he used Anglesey limestone with cast iron plates: for the Macclesfield Canal, the solid local stone with its deeply incised letters.

The committee that met in Macclesfield to agree the need for that canal, and who appointed Telford as its consultant engineer, did not know that they stood right at the cusp of two technologies. Theirs was almost the last narrow canal built in England – only the fourteen-mile Chard Canal, in Somerset, was later. On 11 April 1826, the Act of Parliament authorising the Macclesfield Canal was passed.

By the time it was finished five years later, transport had changed forever; for in the interim, in October 1829, Robert Stephenson's locomotive steam engine *Rocket* had taken part in the Rainhill Trials. It wiped the floor with its rivals, and began a step-change in steam technology. Stephenson's locomotive immediately made railway transport a viable alternative to canals. Railways are laid on top of the landscape, not dug into it like the canal bed: faster to build, cheaper, lighter, easier to take across difficult terrain. Not for many years would they supersede the canals completely, but in the long term, rail freight made the decline of the waterways inevitable. *Rocket's* success at Rainhill lit the touch paper for an industrial explosion and accelerated everything, everywhere, forever. But the construction of the Macclesfield Canal was already underway.

If it came at such a late stage, it wasn't for lack of commerce. This corner of north-western England specialised in fripperies; portable, luxurious, perishable products. Macclesfield, one of the world's first mill towns, specialised in silk-covered buttons and woven jacquard silks using a punch-card technology that anticipated programmable computers. Congleton made ribbons; Stockport, hats. Poynton, just to the north, produced the less luxurious but supremely useful commodity, coal. All of these businesses wanted improved access to the immediate markets of Manchester and Stoke – and beyond them London, Severn, the world. They could get it by linking two existing waterways, joining the Peak Forest Canal to the Trent and Mersey to complete a north-western circuit and graft themselves on to the greatest money-making network in Georgian England.

Before 1826 the Macclesfield project was always rejected by investors because the local hill country required a lot of engineering wizardry. For canal builders, there are three solutions to a hill. Go over it with locks, cut through it with a tunnel or pursue a contour all around the hill. The first engineers had followed the contour and produced notoriously wiggly routes like the Wyrley and Essington, now known to boaters as the 'Curly Wyrley'; but by Telford's time, he had the materials and techniques to propose an affordable route for Macclesfield. There were still some wiggles in his proposed line. Executive engineer William Crossley took it further, adding aqueducts and other tweaks. Reservoirs were built at Bosley and Sutton; cut-and-fill embankments were raised, using spoil from the canal bed. The twelve neat locks that James and I worked through at Bosley were the only ones on the whole route, slotted into a compact two-mile stretch to minimise their impact on travel time. They used side ponds to save water. These mini-reservoirs retained half a lockful of water each time a lock was emptied – so that the next person to fill one could do so with only half a lock of 'fresh' water.

On 9 November 1831, the Macclesfield Canal opened to traffic for the first time. The first working boat passed through Hall Green, which became a meeting place between (almost) the oldest and newest waterways in England; not just a stop lock, but a full stop for the first canal age. In this quiet spot on the county boundary, Telford and Crosley's new canal met a spur of Wedgwood's pioneer waterway.

In the fifty-five years between Wedgwood's start-up and Telford's full stop, landscapes had been split open, production scaled up. The technologies of quarrying, milling, textiles and mining had been advanced; the population was getting used to new ways of working, consuming and being oppressed. The canals brought work, urbanisation and poverty all at once to people who had formerly lived in smaller communities, further apart. A new class of workers was growing in the smoke. A new political framework would be needed to express their experience. Brindley's age set the industrial economy going with the first canals and turnpike roads: Telford's supplied the greater roads, harbours and waterways which further connected Britain's component parts to each other and to the world.

Three years after the completion of the Macclesfield Canal, in September 1834, Telford died. The next generation, that of Stephenson and Brunel, would turbo-charge the existing structures of industrial Britain and bring an unimaginable pace of change which would not slow for a hundred years. It was thanks to Telford, at any rate, that a post-industrial boater in search of pastures new could drift for twenty miles without incident in the rain, drinking tea from a Thermos mug and looking around at the outskirts of a Pennine market town.

Elvis

In his wisdom and his eagerness to save water, Thomas Telford decided that the bed of the Macclesfield Canal should have a V-profile, not the more usual U-profile. It took less time to cut and less water to fill. In the days of regular cargo, this uncommon shape was deeply scoured by the passage of working boats, which were famously loaded to the point where 'a sparrow could drink from the gunnels'. Nowadays boats are lighter, smaller and less frequent. The banks have silted up. Often, eroded by private boaters who ignore the 'no breaking wash' rule and allow a little white-topped wave to run in their wake, great chunks of the bank break off and slip beneath the water so that the canal side is not only shallow and ragged, but studded with great chunks of invisible masonry. There is (usually) just enough water in the middle of the channel, but not much at the edges. In short, it is really bloody difficult to bring a boat in to the bank.

By the time we reached the town moorings, the famous rain was thundering down. I was drenched. My boots, socks and even my knickers were well supplied with rainwater. The canal was not. There were only four official moorings on the towpath side at the time. It was impossible to draw a big boat close to the bank in any of them. *Tinker* dug in like a mule, two feet from the edge. The propeller chewed into shallow silt, throwing up leaf mould and swirls of russet mud behind us. I was forced to jump on to the squelching grass and put down the gangplank, laying a tiny bridge between boat and bank. 'Very disappointed with the Macclesfield bit', I wrote in my logbook. I peeled off my chilly waterproofs, and fell asleep on the sofa. When I woke up, peppercorns of ice were bouncing off the steel roof, making a noise like ball bearings being dropped onto a tray. The boat was already drifting away from the bank, as the pull of passing traffic dragged our mooring pins out of the soupy mud.

This won't do, I thought. I wanted a nice easy mooring for the night. I wanted a place where I could fill the diesel tank, plug in to mains electricity, run the washing machine, dry damp clothes and not worry about the boat floating away from the bank; a place where I wouldn't have to leap off the boat like Errol Flynn across a castle moat, to get to the Co-op.

Right on the other side of the canal was a little boatyard. It lay in the lee of the Hovis Mill, a chimneyed landmark now apparently given over to tiny flats for people with a heavy cannabis habit. *What the hell, let's pay a mooring fee for one night in a boatyard with the luxury of a dry path.* It wasn't much of a manoeuvre to yank out my mooring pin from the sodden towpath and back up slightly to the unsteady guest mooring at this way station. My log book for the day records the fact that I spent the night here, and that I filled up with diesel and water. Oddly, there is no mention of the most remarkable fact about the marina.

The rain stopped. A man came out to see what I wanted. A narrow boat has almost no steer in reverse, so I was preoccupied with pulling back into the diesel station and didn't pay him much attention. Once tied up, I glanced at him. He was a squashy young man, with a dark goatee and shiny black hair; cheerful and friendly as a cartoon character. He was dressed as Elvis Presley. The black hair was styled in a buoyant quiff. The trousers were flared, and a sparkly bootlace tie was held in a neat bow around a white shirt.

Mindful of our recent encounter at Hall Green, where my brother had asked Jules Verne if he was on his way to a fancy-dress party and been dismissed as if *he* were the eccentric, I decided not to mention the fact that my new friend was dressed as 'the King'. Presumably he knew that already. It might be best not to excite him. I walked across the gravelled yard, where a few caravans rested alongside the rubbish skips and a cage full of gas tanks, and into the chandlery shop to pay for my diesel. Behind the counter was a sturdy blond man of about fifty, with rosy cheeks and pale blue eyes. He was dressed as Elvis Presley.

In the car park, a third Elvis – short and balding, but with distinctive 1970s lapels and, if I was not mistaken, rhinestones – was carrying an Elsan toilet cassette across the yard. This was too much. Could it be that they had not noticed, and in a moment they would be mortified to realise that dammit, they had *all* come to work dressed as Elvis?

I paid for the diesel and cleared my throat. 'I can't help noticing,' I said, 'that you are all dressed as Elvis Presley.' 'Eh?' said the blond Elvis. There was a moment of silence. A very large middle-aged woman stepped out of the back office, and joined Elvis Number 2 behind the counter. '*I'm* not dressed as Elvis,' she said. She was quite right. She, a woman in her late fifties and around sixteen stone, was wearing the pigtails and circle skirt of a teddy girl. She had a little pink chiffon scarf tied at her throat. I began to panic slightly, like the policeman in *The Wicker Man* when he realises that the natives are all mad.

The blond man suddenly twigged. 'Oh THAT,' he said. 'Yes, I suppose it does look a bit odd.' His laugh was deep and real. His blue eyes actually twinkled as he stuck a pipe into his mouth. His quiff jiggled slightly as he took a drag. 'We're having a rocktail party. Would you like to join us?'

His name was Ged, and his pigtailed wife was Mal. No, they didn't usually dress like this; yes, they were having a bit of a do and I was very welcome to stay for it, if I had a bottle to bring. I said that I would go and check.

As I left the chandlery, I almost tripped over a young man sitting on the steps outside; a long, lean figure with the dirty blond locks of a Charlie's Angel, and a wicked grin. He had a bottle of champagne in one hand.

'It's my birthday,' he said. 'Would you like a glass of bubbly?' He was not dressed as Elvis. How very odd.

Like many boatyards, this one was formed around an old wharf, with a short arm of water sheltering two dozen boats. It was raggedy and intimate all right. Here were one or two tiny Springers ready for a weekend trip; a colourful day boat for people to hire for birthdays and piss-ups; a few sixty-foot family homes. One was named after the Victorian railway engineer, Sir Daniel Gooch. Some were tied up with a tangle of blue nylon, others with the shipshape knots of a former sailor. There was one large iron boat which I recognised as a survivor of the 1890s, with a young birch tree growing out of it. Behind it was a barely serviceable portacabin with a hand-written sign on the door: SOCIAL CLUB. A boy of about eight was pushing a mouldy kayak into the water, supervised by his father. The cars parked around the yard included a top-of-the-range Range Rover and a clown-style jalopy that looked as if its doors might fall off and a bunch of flowers pop out of the radiator.

'I would like to join you,' I called back to Ged.

I stayed for six years.

On my very first morning in the mill-side canal basin, I made a cup of tea and set up a camp chair outside the boat. I surveyed my new location. The Elvises were all looking a little worse for wear, their quiffs sagging in the breeze. I bestowed upon this place the name I would always know it by – the Macclesfield Home for the Unusual.

I heard a deep, familiar chug. By now the sound of a Lister HR2 would bring my head up like any other geeky meerkat with an ear for a traditional engine. A blue-liveried working boat called *Halsall* was sliding past on the main canal. It sat low and well trimmed in the channel, pushing up smooth furrows of water. Its sixty-foot open hold was loaded with sacks of coal, orange nets of firewood and two large tanks in the middle – one full of red diesel to pump into fuel tanks, the other one empty and ready to pump out toilet tanks. *Halsall* was clearly on a regular delivery round.

The man at the tiller looked familiar. It was Brian McGuigan, the working boat volunteer I had last seen in the Black Country. In the open hold I could see Anne-Marie, hefting bags of coal to the side in preparation for delivery to a nearby boat. Brian had been dreaming of running a coal boat since his first trip to Shardlow in his late teens. He had made it happen. 'Morning Jo!' he shouted, as if it were entirely unremarkable to see me in a new mooring. Which, of course, it was.

Ingenieurs

Brindley was by no means the only creative engineering mind at work on the early canals. He was not even the only creative engineering mind at work on the Duke of Bridgewater's canal. A week after a Staffordshire man celebrated the Harecastle tunnel builder as the man 'who handles rocks as easily as you would plum-pyes,' a newspaper carried a counterblast from the Cheshire side of Harecastle. The Burslem correspondent, sneered the writer:

[M]akes Mr Brindley the Sir Isaac Newton of this age, but seems not to know, that the Duke of Bridgewater, has another ingenious man, viz. Thomas Morris, who has improved upon Mr Brindley and is now raising a valley to the level by 7 double water locks, which enable him to carry

earth and stone as if down steps ... the valley will soon rise to equal the
hills around, and the navigation keep its level.

Brindley's contour-dependent cut was already being adapted by more ingenious minds. Brindley did not reply to Morris's friend: he was no scholar as we know, and in any case he had a tunnel to build. He was less concerned with haters than with progress on the obstinate central stretch of the Trent and Mersey. The pioneer who lays out a national network and persuades people to buy into it is perhaps bolder than those who extend his original, after its worth is proven.

Still, Brindley was only one pioneer. On the Bridgewater he was under instruction from John Gilbert. Even on his own projects he often acted as a remote principal, popping up to advise. He was joined, helped, and rivalled by others in the great national project to make a silver net of water across the trade routes of England. Brindley and his peers were first called 'ingenieurs' and soon began to call themselves civil engineers. They reframed the map (and the possibilities for movement inside it) by constant problem-solving. Every valley was answered with an aqueduct, every steep slope with an embankment or a flight of locks; every hill with a tunnel, every landslip with an abutment. Commercial and personal competition drove them to find new solutions with every mile of canal. Like hip-hop artists today, their reputation is often proportional to their ego and promotional nous. Like them, they often jostled for billing.

Brindley's manager John Gilbert was a dynamic and capable proto-engineer, working on other underground canals and an inclined plane. On the Leeds and Liverpool Canal, John Longbotham met a steep rise and a shallow budget with the Bingley Five Rise, a compact 'staircase' lock which saves space, water and money by emptying one lock directly into the one below. Staircases like this still require a little head-scratching to work. Robert Whitworth crossed the Calder Valley with a fifty-foot-high embankment now called the Straight Mile. Benjamin Outram's work on the Ashton Canal developed the deceptively simple skew-arch bridge. In Wiltshire, John Rennie addressed the long, steep haul between Seend and Devizes with a stunningly ambitious twenty-nine-lock flight at Caen Hill, the water supply protected with a system of side ponds; it tumbles down the hill in a mass of black and white timbers, like a disassembled piano.

Innovators were clearly not in short supply. A perfect storm of appetite, resource and personality converged in Britain. Their collective genius was about more than reducing the price of coal, though it certainly did that (Bridgewater's canal halved it instantly on reaching Manchester). The canals were both cause and effect of a new relationship between humans and their environment.

As the price of coal dropped, the sense that anything was possible crept into the national consciousness. This little island was rich in the resources that the coming technology required: not only coal but water, stone, iron and other minerals: and labour was cheap. The work force was not allowed to organise itself into trades unions, and did not have the vote. The hereditary land owner, the business investor, the talented engineer, the merchant or manufacturer; all would benefit in a seemingly endless cycle of create and consume. The right of the land owner to exploit the land, as a thing to which he or she had literal entitlement, was never questioned. Resources seemed infinite. The appetites and impact of industry on the biosphere could hardly be anticipated by those who set the ball rolling in these middle decades of the eighteenth century.

Learning always costs something, and at this scale lessons were expensive. Pioneers met the occasional disaster as they learned by bitter experience the limitations of their materials and methods. In 1798 Rennie's stone aqueduct at Avoncliff was opened, carrying the Kennet and Avon Canal over the Wiltshire Avon. It immediately began to sag in the middle. The weight of water, stone and dense clay lining was unsupportable at this height. At precisely this time Telford and his colleague William Jessop began to suggest an iron channel for their spectacular Pontcysyllte aqueduct, whose trough would stand 126 feet over the Dee near Llangollen. Rennie's unfortunate experience must surely have been part of their learning curve; innovation walks a tightrope which sometimes lurches into a disaster.

Kevin

The Macclesfield Home for the Unusual was under new management. Ged and Mal retired to a cottage in Suffolk, as far from the canal system as practicable. Our new feudal lord was a substantial, gruff-voiced friend of theirs called Kev. He had the build and temperament of a gorilla. His dietary preferences (bacon at all times) were those of a boater, but he was not one himself. Indeed, this was his proudest boast. He took over the premises with his wife Mel, and commenced his reign with a clear-out of the junk-filled boatyard office. He would rule over us with an iron fist in a rubber glove.

Anyone who runs a small marina fulfils a number of roles, and every one of them makes him unpopular. Kev is not only the landlord of a small village with more than one idiot, but also the policeman arbitrating between disputes. He is a shopkeeper, mechanic, boat fitter, boat salesman, launderette manager, social worker, post master, diesel pump attendant, janitor, dog warden, grounds maintenance man and, essentially, proprietor of a floating mental institution.

The landlord role alone makes him an object of complaint. Nobody lives on a boat because they like authority. Having your rent collector right there on the premises is like having HMRC at the bottom of your garden. The chandlery has the monopoly on coal, electricity, water and basic supplies for a small but captive market – so whatever Kev charges, he gets it in the neck from the customers who live at the bottom of *his* garden. Occasionally he has to intervene in a fight, fish a drunk person out of the canal, get up at 2 a.m. to turn off a car alarm or call the fire brigade because someone's boat is on fire. Very occasionally he is also a funeral organiser. Like any village, we lose someone once in a while.

It's a varied and stressful working life. A sensitive person would soon be reduced to a nervous wreck. Kev, however, is by no means a sensitive person. He is a former bricklayer and right away took a straightforward attitude to his new menagerie. Most boatyard owners dislike boaters, and to be fair it's entirely mutual. Usually the antipathy comes after years of well-deserved grievance, like a gradually increasing sensitivity to solvents or bee stings. Kev, however, hit the ground running. He had decided to pre-empt the gradual process of coming to resent boaters by simply hating them from the start. He hated boats and their many failings. He hated boaters and their many demands. 'Fucking boaters' was his frequent catchphrase.

Anything less than straightforward mystified him. An asymmetrical haircut (like mine) or unusual job (like mine) were a fair target. 'Why don't you let me just straighten that fringe up for you?' he would say with a pair of secateurs in his hand. Customer service was not his strong point. Kev and Mel's arrival coincided with the rising use of smartphones. It was a new thing to see people looking at goods in the shop and checking their screens to see if they could get a better price elsewhere. One man, hoping to haggle, ventured to say 'I could get this cheaper down the road at Miggins & McBlag in Altrincham.' The air tingled with the promise of a punch in the face. 'Fuck off to Altrincham and buy it there then,' said Kev. Once when I texted him about a neighbouring boater running his engine for hours – 'It would be such a shame if I had to club him to death.' Kev's reply came back immediately: 'CLUB THE FUCKER. I NEVER LIKED HIM ANYWAY.'

If Kevin was our sovereign lord, presiding over the battlements from a swivel chair in the chandlery, Mel was the quiet power behind the throne. A small, private person and never talkative, she communicated largely by means of posters. Signs on the gate soon declared NO ACCESS TO THE TOWPATH HERE and PRIVATE YARD, NO ENTRY. Inside the yard, others shouted THESE TOILETS ARE FOR BOAT OWNERS ONLY. NO PUBLIC WATER POINT. One man going into the boatyard toilet found a message, written across the mirror in lipstick: I KNOW YOU HAVE BEEN SMOKING IN HERE PHIL. Once she acquired a laminator, Mel was unstoppable. IT IS VERY UNPLEASANT TO HAVE TO CLEAN WHAT YOU LEAVE UNDER THE SEATS. We started to see alarming placards dotted around in the verges between parts of the marina, like flags to warn of landmines. Each one was planted in a pile of dog poo. THIS IS DISGUSTING, they said. It certainly was. PICK UP AFTER YOUR DOG. It worked. I became slightly nervous whenever I stepped off the boat. Would I find a boater face up in the grass, with a laminated placard sticking out of him? THIS IS WHAT HAPPENS IF YOU DON'T PICK UP AFTER YOUR DOG.

There were many joyful moments of watching Kevin try to keep a straight face as one of the inmates tried to persuade him into some unwanted favour, or as he legislated like a boatyard Solomon between two piles of washing in competition for the tumble dryer. One thing was clear; our new overlord would not be dressing up as Elvis.

Gradually we came to understand that this curmudgeonliness was exaggerated for effect. It would not do to look like a soft touch. There were many occasions when Kev and Mel did good deeds in secret – holding back a bill, keeping a bailiff at bay, seeing off an unwelcome visitor. On sunny evenings, they would fire up the enormous gas barbecue and bring out a bottle of wine, raising Mel's famous toast – 'Bollocks to the world'. Kev professed to hate boaters, but he was chieftain of this ragged tribe and felt a fierce territorial urge to defend us against any threat.

We saw this best during the pandemic. On the first day of the first UK lockdown, he swung shut the big iron gates to the yard and padlocked them, patrolling the boundaries with his rolling silverback gait and glowering at anyone who tried to gain entry. No one came in. Post and deliveries were collected at the gate. We were slightly surprised that he let us out, to buy groceries or go to the doctor.

It seems to me now that we have a sort of national, traumatised amnesia about that warm spring of 2020. Everyone in the country was isolated, bewildered and a little kinder than usual. In some households grief, loneliness and domestic abuse festered with no hope of rescue. In others, marriages thrived or declined in the hothouse atmosphere, and 'coronial' babies were conceived. The marina was a moated settlement, quarantined and quiet behind bars. Even the largest houses felt claustrophobic during the pandemic. Our little corridors of steel felt doubly so for many. Trapped in this new gated community were some very elderly and fragile people.

There were moments of wonder too. Under a sky untroubled by the usual flights from Manchester airport, we heard the hedgerows as a wave of uninterrupted birdsong. The resident ducks were delighted by the tranquillity and brought two broods of ducklings to meet us. Like us, they watched with dismay as the cackling Canada geese nested openly on the untrodden towpaths. Bankside greenery filled out, disappearing the empty benches behind a mass of leaves. Clouds of minnows hovered below the canal surface. In the dead of night, an occasional flurry of water and muscle attested that freshwater predators were enjoying a bonanza of undisturbed food. The otters who had established a holt nearby, and the legendary 23-pound pike we called Moby, were patrolling their underwater parish as diligently as Kevin patrolled his.

Boat traffic on the canals stopped almost entirely. The hire boats with their unpredictable learner drivers, the day boats with their festooned birthday bunting and screaming hen parties, lay empty and silent on their moorings. The continuous cruisers stopped cruising, and sat dotted along the towpath. Like everyone else, we liveaboards were forbidden to travel except to fill our water tanks and empty our toilets. Brick-and-mortar Britons sat in their houses, breathing quietly and crossing their fingers. For the first time in history the other side of the map became static too.

There was one exception. Apart from the few boaters making short necessity trips, there was only one vessel regularly passing by during lockdown. This was Brian and Anne-Marie's work boat *Halsall*. Through bloody-minded persistence and utter reliability, they had built up a tiny fleet in a blue livery which defiantly proclaimed their name – *Renaissance Boats*. By now they were well-established suppliers to the many boats circulating on the local system. They delivered coal and firewood, emptied toilet tanks and filled fuel tanks. In this national emergency, the few working boats still running did have a renaissance. Operated by a handful of reliable crew, they were classed as 'essential services'. They had been needed at the best of times, but now they became the only source of life support for the stricken liveaboard community outside of the marinas.

The boatyards that act as service stations were deserted. Their dry docks and repair shops were silent. Fleets of hire boats lay empty, sleeping in bobbing rafts while the furloughed staff twiddled their thumbs at home. By contrast *Halsall*, crewed by capable renegades Lee and Roberta, was busier than ever. Their volume of trade increased by 50 per cent, but their own suppliers were crippled (like everyone else) by restrictions on movement and low staff levels. The coal boats struggled to get supplies to everyone, but knew they had to. Even when stuck in one place, a liveaboard boat needs diesel to support electricity, hot water and sometimes central heating. No one was more invested in the canal population than Brian, the admiral of Britain's smallest fleet of working boats. This was a life he had wanted since he was a boat-spotting teenager. He felt very keenly the responsibility of looking after the community that he had worked so hard to be part of. Under the stress, and with no chance to get together in the pub to decompress after a long day 'coaling', relationships in his team were strained and sometimes broke. 'How was it?' I asked him afterwards. 'Challenging,' he said with a grimace. I got the feeling I didn't know the half of it.

In the hermetic community of the boatyard, we sometimes felt able to gather in the sunshine and sit outside, together-but-apart. The grassy margins of the car park became a precious country estate, where each boat household took up a picnic table. We sat many feet apart, a half-dozen of us talking in the fresh air. Sometimes a guitar or two would appear. We felt wary about this. We were in full view of the flat-dwellers in the canal-side mill, and the houses on the opposite bank. Would they feel that the dirty good-for-nothing boat people were flouting the rules, though we were being so careful not to endanger each other? Apparently not. After a round of guitar music, we were startled to hear applause from the opposite canal bank. Two or three people had come out to stand in their gardens, overlooking us from thirty feet away. One or two more stood on the balconies of the apartments in the mill. They shouted down to us. 'We enjoyed that. Thank you for sharing it.' We were a long way apart, but never closer than in that moment of extraordinary isolation.

Nigel and Elizabeth

It is to be regretted that domestication has seriously deteriorated the moral character of the duck. In a wild state, he is a faithful husband, desiring but one wife, and devoting himself to her; but no sooner is he domesticated than he becomes polygamous, and makes nothing of owning ten or a dozen wives at a time.

— Mrs Beeton, The Book of Household Management

Some of my best friends are ducks. It strikes me as odd that Mrs Beeton should concern herself with their home life in her famous book. You would think that her main interest is in how to serve them with orange sauce. In any case, her comment on the wild bird is sadly not true in all cases. Canal-dwellers are well acquainted with the sight of a panicky female duck overwhelmed by the attentions of four or five young drakes. They pile on top of her in a feathery scrum: sometimes the female is drowned before she can get away.

The reputation of the species is not lost, however. Mrs Beeton is right to say that there are more gentlemanly drakes out there. Among them is the duck who regularly reports to my side hatch for breakfast with his wife of several years. Nigel and Elizabeth (not their real names) are mallards, the bog standard urban duck. Elizabeth wears the brown tabby feathers of her class. Nigel shows up in morning dress of sleek grey and black, with a sheeny green flash around the head and wings. In the autumn he looks a frazzled mess as he goes into 'eclipse plumage' and refurbishes his feathers for the winter. They often come to share a little conversation in the morning. They are particularly fond of corn flakes.

Nigel is, as Mrs Beeton hoped, a faithful husband. When a male interloper appears, threatening Elizabeth's peace of mind and food supply, she puts her head down and nods at him aggressively: 'Tell him, Nigel,' she says. Nigel sallies off to tell them, and she enjoys all the corn flakes until he comes back.

The sex life of the duck is described by one writer as 'on the border between cartoonish and sadistic'. Nigel's most private organ has a corkscrew shape, and Elizabeth's is similarly curious. You would hope that they both have the same thread, as it were, but some females go counter-clockwise, presenting a new and exciting challenge for the drake. At the end of the mating season, Nigel's corkscrew shrinks to around 10 per cent of its usual size. It sleeps peacefully until required again in the spring, when it reinflates: 'The process generally resembles a cross between using your arm to evert a sweater sleeve that is inside out and unfurling the soft, motorized roof of a convertible sports car with a hydraulic drive' writes expert Richard O. Prum.

Nature has bestowed upon the female duck a similarly thoughtful gift. She has a sort of internal dead end, which she can close off so that mating is purely recreational. It seems like a very useful design.

You may have read advice that you should not feed ducks with bread, and it is broadly right. The street-fighting gangster ducks in the local park, gorging on mouldy Homepride that's lobbed at them by the handful, become bloated and malnourished. Nigel and Elizabeth enjoy the odd scrap of bread, which varies their diet of towpath weeds and invertebrates. I feed them porridge oats and sometimes blueberries that have seen better days, which are processed and returned in the form of violently purple droppings. They forage for other food and are not dependent on me, but what they really want is corn flakes. Corn flakes are like crack for Nigel and Elizabeth. They return season after season, coming to my side hatch like Glastonbury festival-goers returning to a particular food van every summer.

I have read the guidance on what to offer them. I do not feed them bird seed, which they will not eat, nor lettuce leaves, which they also will not eat. I do not throw them peas or scraps of spinach, which they watch with mild curiosity as they float away. Above all I do not, as the Canal and River Trust suggests, feed them halved grapes. They are wild animals, not Marie Antoinette.

Elizabeth disappears for a while in the spring, and returns with a string of fuzzy ducklings, each one the size of a golf ball. She is a useless parent. She wanders off to the far side of the canal while the ducklings career about in the channel like fluffy dodgem cars, their little legs going so fast that sometimes they lift up and scurry across the surface. I try never to count them. Often there will be nine on the first day, six on the second day and one or two left on the third. They are bite-size morsels for all kinds of predator. In the canal itself are the monstrous forms of pike, who will take ducklings from below in a sudden gulp. Herons predate them from above, but worst of all is the newcomer to the duckling banquet; the mink.

My affection for Nigel and Elizabeth was not unrequited. One spring morning, I received a remarkable gift. Opening the side hatch, I was amazed to see an egg on the pontoon right outside it. It was almost white, tinged with a porcelain green. Elizabeth sometimes lays a rehearsal egg or two in the spring, and she had decided to bestow it upon me. I won't record what I did with it, in case vegan readers are shocked: but I was very grateful to Elizabeth, for her own expression of neighbourly gratitude.

It was a bright cold day in April. If this were Orwell, the clocks would be striking thirteen. Orwell, however, was not hosing mink poo out of his well-deck.

I had gone to fill the domestic water tank, lifting the lid of the locker in the front of the boat to fetch out the hosepipe that connects to the boatyard tap. There was an unusual fishy smell. Nobody wants their fresh water supply to smell of fish. In a corner of the locker was a scattering of sequin-like scales. I had suspicions as to the source, but no time on my hands to investigate. I filled the water tank, spent the day working and finished it with a trip to the pub.

Coming back after dark, I found that a small something had visited in my absence. Whatever it was, its diet was piscine and its visiting card unneighbourly. There was a modest heap of droppings in the front of the boat. They were the size and shape of the ash left by an unattended cigarette – and much more pungent. I gathered up the scat in a dustpan, threw it overboard and spent a queasy five minutes googling animal droppings. A couple of disturbing specialist sites confirmed that my unhygienic visitor was a mink.

Don't let the slinky pelt fool you: a mink is nothing but a weasel in a fur coat. It was for its fur that the American mink was first bred in the UK during the 1920s. By the mid-1950s, escapees from mink farms were breeding in the wild. As the market for fur coats diminished, the number 'escaping' into the countryside increased. There are no native mink in the UK, so these lithe and adaptable predators quickly colonised rivers and canals. They are aggressive, bold and sleek. They carry Covid and avian flu; they mark their territory and sexual availability by spraying, and leaving chemical signals like the pile in my well-deck. It was a sort of feral aftershave, not unlike Lynx Africa.

In captivity mink are fed on all sorts of things; out-of-date cheese, eggs, fish, dog food and waste meat, including turkey livers. In the wild, where turkey livers are in short supply, they eat fish, so anglers dislike them. They leave putrid fish heads in our lockers, so boaters dislike them. They compete with otters for the food supply and eat water voles, so otters, water voles and ecologists dislike them. They eat rabbits, so rabbits dislike them.

They also eat ducklings; and that is fighting talk.

On behalf of Nigel and Elizabeth, and in defence of an uncontaminated water supply, battle was joined. I blocked his access point with tinfoil. Cats hate this, and perhaps the mink would hate it too. Hostilities escalated. Next morning, it was clear that the upmarket polecat had returned in the night. Finding his usual access thwarted with the devilish tin foil, he simply came up through another drain hole or scupper, and expressed his feelings with the uninhibited clarity of a TripAdvisor reviewer. A generous pile of scat clogged the wide mesh of my rubber doormat. I would certainly have been in the market for one very small fur coat that morning.

The only virtue of these sharp-toothed predators is that they keep down the population of signal crayfish, another invasive species from North America. Nigel Farage would tell you that the signal crayfish has come over here to steal the jobs of decent British crayfish and put them out of a home. Indeed, it is displacing them all over the UK, but the mink does not discriminate: it will happily eat native crayfish too. That morning, the pontoon was scattered with evidence that one or two substantial crayfish had been dismembered overnight. They crunched under foot as I went to collect my post.

It seemed likely that the locker was being appropriated as a den. Mink are like teenagers – messy eaters, too lazy to build their own burrows, and ready to retreat with a snack to any comfortable nook. On the other side of the marina, Ray's gas locker had already suffered this fate. Now they were coming for me. They would try the gas locker next, because it too has a scupper. I couldn't block that one, because it allows any leaking gas to escape. Instead, reading up on the enemy, I decided to fight fire with fire.

If they were going to leave their 'chemical signals' to entice the lady mink, I would retaliate with an olfactory signal of my own. The adolescent human male uses it as a powerful indication that he is ready to mate: sometimes I get a whiff of it even in the swimming pool. If I can smell it with a nose full of chlorine, surely a mink would be overpowered by it. I crunched down the pontoon to the corner shop and bought a canister of Lynx.

I cleared the well-deck of the kindling and firewood stacked there, swept it out and set about marking my territory. I sprayed the inside of the lockers, the steel floor, even the cratch board with its two glazed triangles at the very front of the boat. In a confined space, it was enough to make my eyes water. I closed the doors and covers, and retired from the field. I patrolled my boundaries for the next few days. Within a week the dead crayfish and their pungent aftermath were no longer seen; Nigel, Elizabeth and my hosepipe had been saved.

Trouble at t'mill

Each spring and summer, I cruised the system: each autumn, I tied up at Macclesfield in the shadow of the Hovis Mill. There was a ready source of good company, coal for the stove and a place to keep the car. I hadn't found anywhere to rival it on my travels. In fact, after a handful of seasons in this rhythm it was disturbingly easy. All the waterways within easy reach were very familiar to me; in fact, it was beginning to be a bit predictable. I began to feel that actually moving the boat was something of an effort. Staying put at the Macclesfield Home for the Unusual became easier and easier.

My mantra had always been that when a boat-dweller stops wanting to move, that's when they really need to move. If you don't start the engine soon, you forget the joyous happenstance of a day out on the canal and become a sucker for comfort. That was certainly happening to me. The daily problems that once felt like a pleasurable challenge – the new route to work, the search for a corner shop – begin to seem inconvenient, and I felt that I was at risk of settling down in one spot. Helen Babb's book *Adrift* confronts the same tension. When she was offered a permanent mooring, she felt that to take it would be 'to give up by rooting down'. I wasn't ready for roots. *Tinker's* engine was hankering for the deeper waters of a big river like the Trent or the Severn.

In short, I began to get itchy feet, and to wish for a slightly larger sphere of motion. I wanted an adventure.

Be careful what you wish for.

When the adventure arrived, he was a tall man with the energy of James Brindley, the chippy self-confidence of Telford and a certain something that was all his own. I met him at an event held in an old mill near Cromford – the same Derbyshire village where Richard Arkwright had set up his water frames in 1771. I knew Calum was trouble. I walked briskly towards it.

Sometimes life takes you to the edge of a cliff, and asks if you want to jump. It was yes to archaeology; yes to poetry; yes when I bought a boat. When life asked me whether to jump into a relationship with Calum, I didn't even wait for it to finish asking the question. You don't need to hear the sordid details. Honestly, you don't. I don't want to tell you the sordid details, because the story is not mine alone. Besides, I don't come out of it very well. But this was the starter motor that got me off my too-comfortable backside, and into a renewed love affair with the inland waterways.

In the Derbyshire valley where Richard Arkwright began a factory system, which became the model for textile mills all over the world, Calum and I began something less edifying. The attraction was strong and inconvenient; he was a maelstrom of a man. In the course of our second conversation I asked how tall he was. He was wise to me at once and laughed out loud. 'Are you *measuring* me? For your little bed?' *Guilty as charged.*

He lived then in one of northern England's most beautiful villages; a hamlet with a river running through it instead of a high street. It was a couple of hours' drive from my mooring at the Macclesfield Home for the Unusual, and far from any navigable waterway. The blood-fizzing endorphins of a new entanglement did their usual mind-altering thing. The year was young: I drove gladly and frequently north, through snowdrop season and into crocus season. The days length-ened. Cold, bright sunlight and fast-moving rainclouds threw shadows across the high pass at Shap, and over the Cumbrian fells. There was anticipation in every drive. There was tension too – a tightrope feeling of sickness and guilt. There were, as Princess Diana almost said, three people in this relationship. I was Camilla.

Very soon, while novelty was still strong enough to negate common sense, there was a further challenge. Calum got a new job, which would winkle him out of his northern stronghold and take him south. *A good thing*. It would lessen the distance between us. Oh, Wiltshire? *That* far south? It was a four-hour drive.

The relationship was still full of promise. It was fuelled by excite-ment, poetry and a fairly enthusiastic suspension of disbelief. It was all very thrilling. On the other hand, I did not want to spend my life driving up and down the M6, a motorway which I dislike at the best of times. Was it all over, just as it began? Privately, neither of us was sure that the other was worth the effort of a long-distance liaison: but we enjoyed feeling irresistible and tragic. An alternative to the four-hour drive began to frame itself in my mind. It was four hours on the road map, but on the other side of the map, the water map, a long series of routes led down to the Kennet and Avon. There glinted the possibility of a grand gesture. The K&A is famously beautiful, and the landscape around it full of world-class archaeology. I lived on a boat, for God's sake. I could make the long, slow journey south myself, to join him and start a new life. It was either a brilliant romantic deed in prospect, or the action of an unusually committed stalker. Was I just looking for drama, or was this the start of something worth fighting for? I decided to sleep on it.

You may well point out that if a man isn't worth driving four hours for, he isn't worth moving house and travelling the length of a nation for. Thank you. I see this now. At the time, what I saw was my fossilising self, settling quietly into a risk-averse life. Secure in my mooring in the shadow of the great brick mill, surrounded by cheerful company, I had begun to perceive the small challenges of boating as an obstacle rather than a gift. It was months since I had made a serious journey on *Tinker*. People knew me in the local pub, and I had a postal address for the first time. I was taking root in exactly the way I had feared. I began to see that I was absolutely on the verge of staying put for years, perhaps forever. *Tinker* would become one of those greening boats that sits in one spot, a sorry landmark as fixed as the village hall. Calum was a temptation, but he was also a pretext for moving. On that pretext I could pin my hungry future.

Wondering what guidance my old mate Marcus Aurelius could offer, I consulted *Meditations*. My eye fell on the convenient epigram:

Accept the things to which fate binds you, and love the people with whom fate brings you together, but do so with all your heart.

I should have kept reading until I reached another maxim: 'A bitter cucumber? Throw it away,' but I had found the answer I wanted at that moment.

I called Calum the next morning with my brilliant idea. 'Why don't I come too?' I asked.

'What?'

This was not the unqualified joy I was hoping for. If there was panic in his voice, I was deaf to it.

'To Wiltshire. I could bring the boat.'

'Erm. How long would it take you?'

I had a look. I leaned over from the sofa to my solitary bookshelf and pulled out the familiar red Nicholson guides, with those beloved linear maps that show only the canal corridor. One after another, I laid open the spiral-bound bibles and traced the long blue line that *Tinker* and I would have to follow on this voyage – a slow, constrained pilgrimage with its terminal point 'Somewhere in Wiltshire'.

We would untie our ropes in the middle of Volume 5, on the Macclesfield Canal, heading south through Telford's lovely snake bridges. We would drop down the twelve familiar locks at Bosley, through the peaceful stop lock at Hall Green where we had met Jules Verne, then slip into the north portal of Harecastle Tunnel and emerge, blinking, in Volume 4. We would keep falling through the grim locks of Stoke, where it would be raining, and on down the Trent and Mersey to 'Brummagem'. The Byzantine loops of the Birmingham system would take us through Volume 3, or possibly Volume 2. At the Napton T-junction where I had first taken the helm of *Tinker*, still *Cariad* in those days, we would slide into Volume 1. At Banbury we would pass Tooley's Yard, where Rolt had watched old George Tooley painting roses on a water can. Attaining Oxford via Brindley's contour canals, we would steer into Volume 7 and join a river for the first time, tasting the waters of the Thames as far as Reading. There we would turn right onto the K&A Canal, and onto the home straight – though it wasn't entirely straight, and I didn't yet know where home would be.

The time map, the cognitive map, the actual map; they all blurred into one. The route went on and on. Nicholson takes seven volumes to cover the navigable canals of England, and I would be inching my way through six of them. At least I could put aside the volume dealing with Nottingham, York and the North East. Nicholson marks each mile with a tiny black lollipop, and each lock with a V. I counted them. Two hundred and fifty lollipops. One hundred and sixty-one V's. At three miles an hour (on a good day), with interruptions to wait for crew or actually do some paid work ... It dawned on me how much of a commitment this was, and how far from my people I would be at the end of it.

I called Calum.

'It will take a month.'

'What?'

It would all be completely fine, honestly.

Calum had a gift for finding beautiful villages. In a moment of impossible good fortune, he found a vacant cottage in the almost comically perfect thatch-and-whitewash hamlet of Avebury. Other people have gnomes at the end of their garden: he had the world's largest prehistoric stone circle, a monumental fixed point in every layer of the time map since before maps existed.

Bully for him. Meanwhile, I was about to travel for a solid month to reach new territory, with no destination in mind. It was hardly the South Pole, but to be in an unfamiliar setting, in a difficult relationship and carving out a new workload as a jobbing writer seemed like insecurity enough. I needed a secure, welcoming spot where I could tie up, find a new boating community and establish my own base independent of Calum. In a perfect world, I would have that mooring nailed down before I left the north.

I wanted a pole star to navigate by. I wanted something on which I could keep a steady fix during the long journey down the country, whenever my internal voice threw me off course with its insistent, nagging question – *Are you sure you're doing the right thing?* It asked that question a lot, and so did my mother. 'Are you going to get hurt?' she asked. 'Yes,' I said. 'I think so.' My mother is a wise and extraordinary woman. She knows that none of her children can be stopped from doing stupid things, because they inherit their wilfulness from her. 'Okay,' she said. 'Come home when you need to.'

I knew Wiltshire and its neighbouring country a little: the White Horse bookshop at Marlborough, the Bell Inn in Bath, the surprisingly rural welcome of Swindon Literature Festival. I knew nothing of its water map, except that it was overpopulated and the moorings expensive. I had no boat friends in that part of the network. It was a little overwhelming.

At exactly this time the world of letters lost one of its funniest, best and most vivacious inhabitants, the poet Ann Atkinson. Her wake was a model of celebration and shared grief. A crowd of mournful, grateful friends gathered at Ann's local, the Maynard Arms, for a few hours of togetherness. We jostled in the bar room to tell stories about our friend. Someone asked about *Tinker's* forthcoming trip – was it all happiness and joyful planning? I grimaced. It would be a lot happier if I knew where I was going. I had no idea where to start looking for my mooring.

'Pewsey,' said the man in front of me at the bar.

He turned around to introduce himself, a pint in each hand. This smiling, round-faced man of about forty was Ann's son-in-law Mike. He lived with Ann's daughter Rosie in Sheffield; but as it happened, he had grown up within spitting distance of the K&A Canal. 'Start looking around Pewsey,' Mike advised. The best setting would be a tiny place called Honeystreet, but that was a fool's errand. 'No chance of getting in there,' he said apologetically. 'But that's the general area.'

The most effective way to secure a boatyard mooring is not to call ahead and ask the owner, but to show up on the doorstep. Phone ahead to ask for a mooring, and a boatyard proprietor – even one less hostile than Kevin – will listen to your request, take down your details patiently and throw them away the moment you hang up. They know too well that boaters have a flexible sense of commitment. They also want to look you over and assess just how alcoholic/haunted/shifty/deranged you are in person. I threw the Nicholson books into the car and drove down to reconnoitre my new parish.

West

It was breathtaking. The earth of Wiltshire is sumptuous, chalk-speckled and pillowed with good soil. The land forms are rounded, with none of the spiky outcrops that poke out of my gritstone homeland. The fields rolled towards the sky in slow contours like the lazy waves of a deep sea, and in them were grand sweeps of wheat or barley. They were bounded not with drystone walls but by hedges, all of them loud with life and thickening in the May sunshine. Even the roofs here are soft – steeply pitched beds of thatch, often with a straw pheasant or fox stalking the ridge. It was like driving through an Eric Ravilious painting. *Welcome to the West Country,* sang the birds. If my future lay somewhere in this rich and rolling county, things could be a lot worse.

Through this countryside runs the K&A, built to hitch those two rivers together with a useful thoroughfare. Its two ends, at Reading and Bristol, began as navigations or 'improved' rivers. By the 1720s each town had extended its navigable water a few miles inland, but it was a big ask to connect those loose ends with a ribbon of water broad and deep enough to accommodate the West Country's native barges. The rivers were finally joined and the cross-country route completed in 1810, when John Rennie's superb twenty-nine-lock flight at Caen Hill opened to traffic. A hundred years later it had lived through its busy commercial period and like other canals was falling derelict. Railways had taken over most inland freight traffic, and within a few more years motor traffic would take the rest. When Rolt saw the K&A in the 1940s it was overgrown, sometimes impassable and was one of two waterways he classed as actively endangered.

It's a stunning waterway now, after years of restoration: a wide, glittering slow road full of characters. Like Conan Doyle's *The Lost World*, this canal is partly cut off by geography. There aren't any pterodactyls or hostile tribes – in fact the local tribe proved uniquely welcoming – but there are mammoth boats, in the form of the buxom widebeams that cruise the channel, almost twice the breadth of *Tinker*. With a big river at both extremities, many K&A boaters choose to stay on the tranquil eighty-seven-mile canal, boating unhurriedly from one end of their long blue parish to the other. Some hover around a favourite patch. The city of Bath and the town of Bradford-on-Avon are honeypots, with sweet yellow stone buildings like blocks of fudge. Another favoured mooring is the narrow gorge at Avoncliff, where Rennie's sagging aqueduct carries the canal over the river, and a fine pub called the Cross Guns holds the steep slope between them. None of these had long-term moorings, though. My mission took me elsewhere.

Despite Mike's recommendation, Pewsey looked on the map like an unpromising little dot in the middle of nowhere, so I went first to the larger towns on either side. At Newbury I found a well-equipped marina, efficient and cheerful but with a neat, corporate feel. It described itself as a 'gated facility', which sounded like a prison or Center Parcs. My appetite was for warmth and ragged edges. Devizes with its busy wharf was not quite right either. I walked west along the towpath with one eye open, and pounced on any boater who had a toilet cassette in one hand or a barrow full of firewood. The liveaboards around here were mostly under forty. Their culture was more dreadlock-and-tie-dye than the northern canals. They gladly recommended their favourite spots. All of them signed off with a laugh, and a comment along these lines: 'Of course, Honeystreet is the ideal. But moorings at Honeystreet are like hen's teeth.'

I took the byroads on purpose – each one 'A reeling road, a rolling road, that rambles round the shire' as Chesterton has it – and tasted the warm air with its subtly foreign flavours. Different rock, different water. The promise of apples to come. This was a land of arable and cider, not hill sheep and ale. To my left, the Ridgeway rose above the rich fields; an old, sentinel trackway through long-occupied downlands. Sometimes I stopped to peer over a canal bridge. I saw a road sign for Honeystreet. *Let's see what all the fuss is about.*

You will have guessed how this story ends but it is still surprising to me. I pulled up at the ridiculously named Honeystreet, expecting to see Miss Marple or a Beatrix Potter mouse carrying a basket of fresh flowers. There were a couple of thatch-roofed cottages and one or two larger houses with outbuildings, including the Old Builder's Wharf. At a different point on its time map, this had been a timber mill. I looked over the humpbacked bridge – a shape that always means home – to the broad strip of pewter below. True enough, there were no moorings to spare at Honeystreet. I stepped down onto the towpath just for the pleasure of being near water.

This is actual barge country. The K&A is a wide navigation, with room for the broad western barges and trows that carried produce more often than products. In the heyday of this place, timber and grain were its mainstays. Now Honeystreet Wharf was a secluded waterfront with perhaps half a dozen boats on it, tied nose to tail at the end of a neat garden. In the scant spaces between them were spikes of iris leaf and sharp blades of arrowhead, wild in its deep spring sheen. Above this populated water rose a steady scarp, with a bright heraldic shape cut into it – the Alton Barnes White Horse. Four or five local hillsides had these strange, cartoonish animals carved across them. It added to the strange sense of Middle Earth otherness. This was a deeply, calmly beautiful spot; warm, ragged and welcoming. I could see why it was so much in demand.

Among the boats were two or three expensive-looking widebeams, available for hire as luxury holiday craft. Clearly it was changeover day. A petite blonde woman was emerging from one of the grand shapes with a load of bedding. She stared at me, as well she might. I had purple hair at the time, and was basically prowling at the end of her garden. 'Hello,' she said with a brilliant smile. 'Hello,' I said. 'I was looking for a mooring, but I see you haven't got one.' A momentary pause. 'Come and say hello properly,' she said, and stepped into a shed.

The shed was the smallest chandlery I had ever seen. A kettle, a couple of Nicholson map books and a landline was about all there was inside it. The woman was the smallest chandler I had ever seen. She was forty-ish, impishly attractive and named Nikki. The phone rang. It was – I kid you not – someone else asking for a mooring. 'Sorry,' said Nikki, 'we have a two-year waiting list.' This was perfectly true. She put the phone down and made me a cup of tea.

We liked each other immediately. I explained why I had appeared in her garden, and asked if she knew of any other moorings nearby. Another pause. 'What size is your boat?' asked Nikki. 'Sixty-seven foot,' I told her. 'Narrow boat.' A half-grin appeared on her lips. She had a disconcerting gaze. 'Come outside,' she said. Since the shed was only big enough for one person, I was already outside. She pointed out one of the boats alongside the wharf. 'You see that one?' she said. 'Sixty-eight-foot long. He just gave me notice that he's leaving at the end of the month. When can you be here?' I thought fast. 'August Bank Holiday', I said, 'but I'll pay from the end of the month.' 'Brilliant. See you in August.' We shook on it.

True to form, she had just turned down an anonymous boater in favour of the one who had turned up on her doorstep. I walked back to the bridge and looked back over the parapet. Two familiar shapes slid into view, steering out of a gentle corner and towards the bridge. It was a working pair, hitched on a short line. Motor and butty slid under the arch beneath me, sleek and purposeful as greyhounds. You couldn't make it up, and I haven't.

I had my pole star, and my first friend. All I had to do now was navigate towards them.

South

The boat cracked its bones loudly in the morning heat as its steel plates expanded. Water fairies shimmered and pulsed across the flanks of the boat. The warmth felt like a good omen as I got ready to leave Macclesfield. For the first day of the long trip to Honeystreet I had a crew of three-and-a-half people. Brother James and his wife Amki were with me already. Amki's pregnancy shifted her centre of gravity as she gingerly walked along the gunnels. Boater and musician Steve had a gift for rolling up at any time when food was about to appear. He arrived just as the bacon butties were ready.

James had been with me during my first days on Macclesfield Canal, and it amused us both that he would be with me as I left it. Today would be a long day, but easy and familiar. Telford's twelve neat locks at Bosley would take no time at all with four of us, and we would drift over the little aqueducts of Congleton to moor with a poetic sense of closure at Hall Green, the stop lock where James and I had once met a Victorian time traveller. I handed my brother the new log book. It was shiny and blank, like the mind of Donald Trump. Each page had spaces for the place and time we set out, the place and time we tied up for the night, the places passed and other boats seen; weather, wildlife and the names of crew members. This summer's voyage would be a modest odyssey, and it needed recording. It would end with a new landscape, a new waterway and a new pattern of life with Calum. 'You can write this up today,' I said to James. 'Responsibility at last,' he said happily.

I stepped into the chandlery to pay my final mooring fee. 'You're actually leaving then,' said Kevin gruffly. He was stacking toilet rolls in a wall designed to form a barrier between him and his customers.

'Yes. I am going to the Deep South to live happily ever after.'

He was beside himself with grief. 'Well, I hope there's someone down there who can give you a proper bloody haircut,' he said.

He came to wave me off as I started the engine up and pulled the ropes out of the mooring rings. Nigel and Elizabeth saw us out of the marina like tugs processing ahead of a royal barge, and we swung out into the channel for the first of thirty-two days of travel.

We slid out through the familiar narrow arch of Bridge 38, along the high contour line where Telford chose to set his highest English canal. James put the kettle on. The crew put their feet up. There was nothing to do for a few hours and we had a phenomenal cargo of biscuits.

On the pink chalk board in the kitchen was an elaborate master-piece of logistics: the long list of names, dates, car swaps, coach and train journeys that would deliver *forty* separate friends and relatives to join *Tinker* on her royal progress southwards. In a decade of boating I had built up a network of crew who saw this folly as a shared enter-prise, and an opportunity to spend a few days in good company. They would work swing bridges, lock-wheel, pick up and drop off spouses, deliver a load of shopping or simply join us for the ride.

Some were old friends who had gradually become eager lock-hands, some were experienced boaters I had met in Newark or Birmingham, and a few were complete innocents, like the pair who would meet me at Harecastle Tunnel. Some, God help me, were poets or novelists who could not be relied on to do anything. A previous literary crew had included crime novelist Helen Cadbury, who spent the day asking me about side ponds – 'How long could you hide a body there undis-turbed, do you think?' – and noting that you could kill someone quite easily with a tiller pin. The other crew member was Hugh Warwick, nature writer and hedgehog fan. He tended to disappear just when he was most needed. As we approached a lock, I looked for him in vain: 'I was just taking pictures of masonry bees.'

For each day of the trip my majestic timetable had a projected start and finish point, a crew who knew roughly where to meet the boat, and a healthy margin of error. I had allowed for sickness, car breakdown, or the confusion that happens when a boat person says 'See you at Bridge 66' and a bank person says 'Is that the A537?' It would be a riot of good company and shared purpose, a ripple of companionship running on liquid lines from the north to the south-west. Calum himself would not be on board for most of the journey. He kept the hours of a regular employee, not a freelance writer. He would be elsewhere.

The timetable was a magnum opus worthy of a military commander. It was also a house of cards. If something happened to throw us off by a day or two, there would be a horrible knock-on effect. Everyone would be in the wrong place at the wrong time. People who had already bought train tickets would be arriving two days ahead of us, and people who expected a lift would be stranded in some rural backwater. If something had to go wrong at all, then the later the better – ideally on the last, not the first day. As it happened, both would apply.

The rain that so often drenches the north-west of England is a sort of wet tax, which pays us back in greenery every summer. It had been raining heavily for days, but now the canal-side gardens were thick with flowers and the banks a green blaze of beech and birch. Blades of reed spiked the shallows as we travelled parallel to the land route rising above the waterway. Between us and the first lock there was nothing for the crew to do but work one swing bridge at Fools Nook. After that it would take a couple of hours to work through the flight of locks, and we would cruise onward to a towpath barbecue with a glass of wine.

That, at least, was the plan.

What actually happened was this. I steered out of the town, through the serpentine roving bridges of Keuper sandstone, past the golf course and the cattle fields of Sutton. An hour later James and Steve hopped off at Bridge 49 to work the swing bridge, grinning broadly as the Range Rovers and BMWs of Cheshire seethed behind beeping barriers. I noted wistfully the little fleet of working boats which Brian McGuigan and Anne-Marie had built up, moored in a shady bend of water; and then I noticed the big sign on the towpath. It was not an official sign of the sort that British Waterways would put up, but a makeshift placard with a piece of board and two words in bold spray paint: CANAL CLOSED.

We had travelled four miles.

There was no difficulty working out why the canal was closed. The heavy rain that had fallen for days had loosened the soil in the steep banks over the canal. A very big tree had fallen right across it. Sometimes this happens in areas with lots of resident boaters, and if no one has been crushed to death someone appears with a chainsaw to claim the booty of free firewood, but there were no boating neighbours here.

'What happens now?' asked James.

The answer came from Steve, a boater himself. 'We call British Waterways and they send a man with a chainsaw.'

'How long will that take?'

It could be days. My immaculate timetable of troop movements was already done for, but that was not the only element of bad timing. This tree had made its shift from vertical to horizontal on the very day that British Waterways became the Canal and River Trust. Would the emergency phone number have changed? Would the bank staff all be grounded until they had new corporate polo shirts? We called; they answered.

'Thank you for letting us know,' they said. 'Someone will be there in the morning,' they said.

Steve raised his eyebrows. We were doubtful. It was, I conceded, a setback: but then again, what is the point of travelling with all that you own, if you can't make yourself at home wherever you stop? *Tinker*'s cupboards were well stocked with food and drink. There was good company. We set up the barbecue, opened the wine and accepted that it might be a long, long wait. We talked, ate and slept safely in the green shade of Fools Nook, something less than four miles from our start point.

I glanced despondently at James's first entry in our new logbook:

Waterway conditions: NOT IDEAL.

Places passed: VERY FEW.

Other boats seen: JUST AS FEW.

Purpose of journey: To reach Hall Green.

Result: TOTAL FAILURE.

Say what you like about the Canal and River Trust (and we do, all the time) but on their first day of existence they rose to the occasion. I woke up at six o'clock in the morning with a sound like a chainsaw in my head. I hadn't drunk that much wine: it was an actual chainsaw. I stepped onto the towpath in my pyjamas, mug of tea in hand. Steve was there already.

'Bloody hell,' he said happily.

A few yards away was a man wearing waders and ear defenders, valiantly disembowelling the fallen tree.

'Prompt work!' I said gratefully as he finished.

'WHAT?' said the man in ear defenders.

'Never mind.' An hour later the tree was gone, and we were on our way.

Tunnel vision

As a rule, all of my crew members get on.

Working a boat together is a good way to bond with people who were strangers a few hours ago. 'Hello Janet, hello John, your mission is to deliver me and my boat to the top of this flight of locks without breaking either boat or crew. Off you go, see you at teatime when we will all get drunk and count our mysterious bruises.'

The crew have a shared physical task, which requires teamwork. The four-woman team who worked me up the Tardebigge flight a few weeks before had been strangers at the start of the day, but covering thirty-four locks in ten hours they soon began to work like a team of Border Collies chivvying sheep into a pen.

Never, however, have I known a crew to bond so quickly and so well as Paul and Jonathan did on the day that we entered the Harecastle Tunnel. It was, you might say, like at first sight. Jonathan, in immaculate slate-grey tweeds, looked like an Edwardian motorist spending his day off by visiting the grubby urchins of the towpath. Paul, in bright red Gore-Tex and a broad grin, was full of Irish charm and the welcoming energy of a *Countryfile* presenter. By the time we reached the north portal of the tunnel they had developed a bond so powerful that mere women could never separate them. It was bromance, and it was a wonderful thing to behold. In one another's company they were giddy as newborn lambs released onto grass for the first time.

The tunnel that we were about to enter is not Brindley's, which has long since subsided to the point of uselessness, but Telford's. Here nineteenth-century engineering meets the worst fears of the cave-dweller. Ahead of us were just under two miles of unimaginable blackness in a tight, constrictive tube barely large enough to admit a single narrow boat. It's like being a very slow bullet in the barrel of a gritstone gun. Following years of slow subsidence, the roof is so low that the skipper is well advised to wear a hard hat. The sense of being penned inside the rock, in a place where you really shouldn't be until you are dead, is almost overpowering. That complete engagement with the earth is normally felt only by miners and cave divers. Occasionally an unseen stream, feeding into the tunnel from one of the underground canal arms that supply it, will knock your vessel off course inexplicably.

Halfway through, some wag once stopped their boat to paint a six-foot skeleton on the rocky wall, which looms at passing crew in case they were feeling cheerful. All the time the engine exhaust reverberates against the tightly enclosing stone, to make a rousing and disorientating envelope of sound which travels with you for the duration. Every so often, I warned the crew, you will see a mysterious pallor ahead on the surface of the canal. That glimmer of light shows that we are about to pass under a ventilation shaft. Don't look up unless you want a face full of cold water, dripping down this stony chimney from the land above.

It is a fairly Gothic way to spend forty-five minutes – and that is roughly the time it takes for a boat, pushing against a body of water in a tight channel, to chug slowly from one side of Harecastle Hill to the other. I'll be honest, I played it up as I briefed the crew. I told them the tragic stories that gather around every such place. One was very recent.

A few months before, the tunnel had been briefly closed because of a fatal accident. A boater steering through it was sitting on an unusually high seat at the back end, and failed to spot the drop in the roof level. His head struck the rock with such force that he was knocked off the counter and died in the icy black water. His boat, still in gear, pushed doggedly on through the tunnel. His wife, unaware, sat in the boat as it bumped unsteered towards the other end.

The other terrible story – and it is terrible – happened in 1975. A young woman called Leslie Whittle was kidnapped by one Donald Neilson, a career criminal known to police as the Black Panther. Researching places where he might keep her while he negotiated a ransom payment, Nielson checked out the tunnel's ventilation shafts.

Folk memory still has it that Leslie was held captive in one of them, though in fact she was kept for days in an underground passage close by – naked and freezing, with a noose around her neck. She died there, aged seventeen and in unbearably tragic circumstances. In local memory, Leslie Whittle's story is often linked to the tunnel.

Thankfully, darkness has other kinds of magic too. Every boat has a large headlamp which gives an arc of warm light. It shows the contours of the stone and gives a glimpse of other boats travelling ahead. On a previous trip, as *Tinker* nosed into the portal with three boats ahead and three astern, my tunnel light failed. For a moment, I understood what blackness is. This is not the blackness you meet on the landing at night. This is blackness that makes you entirely invisible even to yourself; a blackness that makes you lose all sense of your own body, and question whether you are there at all. I couldn't reverse out with three boats behind me; I remembered the tale of the poor man knocked out by the lowering roof. I was feeling rather queasy.

Then I heard singing. My crew at the time, sitting in the front of the boat to marvel at their weird underground setting, were members of an *a capella* choir. They realised what had happened and ran through the boat turning all the lights on so that window-shaped squares of buttery yellow illuminated the tunnel walls. They shone torches onto the roof, so that I could see where it rose or fell. Then, to give the other boats a sense of where we were, they began to sing. The throb of *Tinker's* engine ringing off the stone became the rhythm section for a strange musical performance. They sang African songs with words I couldn't understand – they sang folk songs – and once, wise to the fact that the skippers in front of us would be listening with their mouths open, they sang 'Nearer, My God, to Thee'. Three good singers can fill the air even in a wide space. Here their music brought us all out of the darkness and into the light, smiling serenely, as we reached the tunnel portal and daylight.

It was, inevitably, raining as I approached the tunnel with Paul and Jonathan on board. I was gunning the engine to make it before the tunnel closed at four o'clock. I didn't want to spend the night on the chilly mooring by the tunnel. Far better to reach the south side and the pubs of Stoke.

When the water beneath us turned bright orange, I knew that we were in the iron-rich waters fed by drainage from the nearby mines. In a moment we would encounter the simple traffic control system at the tunnel. Telford's great rabbit-hole is only wide enough for one boat to enter at a time. No one wants a scenario where two boats meet in the middle. To avoid that, at each portal there is a tunnel keeper, who sits in a little kiosk and waits for boats to arrive. They co-ordinate to make sure that boats are only travelling in one direction. If a boat hasn't emerged after an hour and fifteen minutes, it is an emergency and they will send a boat in to look for you.

Mostly, of course, there is no emergency. The tunnel keepers have a lot of time on their hands, and they get bored. This may be why they enjoy putting the fear of God into waiting boaters. It is perfectly sensible to ask 'How many people do you have on board?' because we all want there to be the same number when you arrive at the other end; but I usually get the one who asks, in lugubrious tones, 'How many souls on board?' The tunnel keeper checks that you have no naked flames on board, which might ignite pockets of methane; checks your tunnel light; tells you to stow any elaborate flowerpots on the cabin top which will be crushed by the low roofs and dragged backwards into the skipper's face. They take your licence number and ask if you are claustrophobic. At this point, you sometimes see one wide-eyed crew member step off to begin the slow walk over the top of Harecastle Hill via Boat Horse Lane. Finally, the keeper reminds you that if you get into trouble you should use the emergency signal to attract their attention – six short blasts of the horn, and one long blast. There is a flaw in this instruction.

We reached the tunnel one minute after the official closing time at four o'clock. The northern tunnel keeper was keen to clock off; besides, he remembered me from a recent trip.

'You should wait for tomorrow really,' he said.

'Oh, come on,' I said, 'are there boats in there already?'

'Yes,' he conceded. 'I've just let seven in.'

The maximum number of boats in a train is eight.

'Ah, go on then,' he said. 'You know the drill. How many souls on board?'

We were still moving as he took the licence number. Without even tying up, we nudged *Tinker's* nose into the northern portal of the northern tunnel. As we entered, I saw the keeper heading back to his kiosk, presumably to call the southern tunnel keeper and warn him that one cheeky boat had snuck in at the very last moment of the working day. He should expect not seven boats, but eight. Paul and Jonathan, no longer able to stand on the sides of the boat as we headed into the narrow darkness, went below and got ready to spend a half hour drinking tea in the underworld.

Just for laughs, and in case you have any claustrophobes on board who thought they would chance it, the door of the tunnel slams shut behind you as you enter. There is a roar as they turn on the Guibal fan that drives air up into the ventilation shafts, clearing any methane and exhaust fumes. At first there is plenty of standing room and the tunnel is about ten feet wide; not extravagant, but spacious enough to allow a little movement left or right. Very quickly however, the tunnel roof comes down almost to meet the boat. The brick lining of the portal gives way to rough-hewn sides, gnarly and elemental, cross-hatched with tool marks. It is just wide enough for passage. The boat bumps and scrapes against the walls. I could dimly see the seventh boat in the train, far ahead of us as the tunnel light cast a wedge-shaped beam into the passage like a torch in a cartoon.

What happened, happened suddenly. We were no more than five minutes in when a god-almighty noise of banging metal began under my feet. It sounded as if someone were lying underneath us, striking up with a sledgehammer. In the close black passageway, the sound was amplified. I had never heard a sound like this before. It sounded catastrophic, as if the prop shaft had broken in two or the propeller had fallen off. I turned off the engine immediately.

If it sounded bad to me, the two men inside the boat must have felt as if they were in the clock tower as Big Ben announces the six o'clock news. They shot into the engine room, appearing at floor level as I stood above on the counter, and asked my knees what was happening. In particular, they asked reasonably, 'Why is the engine not running?'

We could hear the drip of rainwater from the land, trickling into the tunnel; we could hear our own hearts beating. I looked at the two pale faces staring up at me from the engine room, like two baby owls on a branch. We were suddenly aware of the methane pockets, the seeping walls and cold black air, the tons and tons of rock surrounding us like a great clenched fist. We all remembered Leslie Whittle, the poor fallen boater and the desperate navvies whose toolmarks we could still see so long as the tunnel light worked. It was a hard, primitive place to be trapped. We were not enjoying it.

I had never sounded the emergency signal before, and haven't done it since. I did it now; six short blasts and one long one. The first time I did it, the Guibal fan was still roaring. I waited a while, in hopes that the tunnel doors would open just a hundred yards behind us, and the tunnel keeper would shout in to see what the trouble was, but realised that he couldn't possibly hear us above the roar of the fan. The second time, the fan had died into silence. I tried twice more; six short blasts and one long one. Then I remembered that the tunnel keeper behind us would have clocked off. He would have locked his little kiosk the moment we were out of sight, and headed home knowing that we were on our way south.

I knew in the back of my mind that if we remained in the tunnel for more than an hour, someone would be sent in to get us. But the emergency team, stationed somewhere else on their work boat, might have to get to the tunnel from some distance away, and come in from the south end. It might take hours. In the back of my mind, I was also thinking of the other tunnel keeper. Had he really been told that we were in the tunnel? Had he also clocked off, unaware that a single boat was still here in the bowels of the hill?

I reminded myself that I was not Captain Smith on the bridge of the *Titanic*. This was an unusual corner of south Staffordshire, not the wide Atlantic, and I did not have hundreds of souls in my care. Nevertheless, I was a skipper, and I did have two souls in my care. Even a grubby, homely boat like *Tinker* is still a boat; and a skipper is still a skipper.

Perhaps something was caught on the propeller. Usually when this happens it is a rope or a binbag, and it will sometimes come off if you spin the propeller backwards. Sometimes it is a mattress, and you have to call on the Canal and River Trust and all the saints to help you. It would be a very determined fly tipper indeed who would travel a hundred yards into the Harecastle tunnel to drop a mattress. Wincing, I started the engine and put it gently into reverse. Immediately the noise of a deranged blacksmith began again; but it was a regular banging. I had once picked up a rubber fender on the propeller. It had made a regular soft *THWOP* under the hull, as if an underwater policeman were coshing me with his truncheon. Something was certainly moving in rhythmic circles, not jiggling about like a broken shaft. It wasn't a nice soft rope, and it wasn't a mattress; but it was spinning on the propeller. An unpleasant half hour might see us clear.

'Get the kettle on,' I said to one of my owl-eyed crew. To the other, I issued the unique and disturbing command: 'Pass me the bread knife.' In this moment of crisis, Jonathan's tweeds were strangely comforting. Surely nothing bad can happen if one's companion is wearing a tweed waistcoat and flat cap.

Underneath the skipper's feet, below the back deck or counter, is the weed hatch which gives access to the propeller. Even in broad daylight, when I can see what I am doing, I do not enjoy opening the hatch and wrangling with the propeller. There is a possibility of getting a rusty fish hook in the wrist, or cutting open your hand with your own knife in the numbingly cold water. I really, really did not relish the thought of getting into it, disentangling whatever we had to deal with, and reassembling it with the perfect seal that it needed in pitch blackness.

Disturbed and obedient, Jonathan brought me the bread knife and a pair of rubber gloves. He held a torch and watched me as I worked – not through curiosity but because I might fall in, working in the dark and overbalancing on the slippy counter. I lifted the heavy metal trapdoor and with a lump hammer, bashed at the great screw fastening which clamps down the lid of the weed hatch. I lifted out the heavy metal casing, careful as a beekeeper lifting out a frame full of live bees. I put it on the counter beside me. Then, with an owl on each leg to make sure I didn't fall in, I stuck my arm into the chilly waters to get a sense of what the hell was going on. Jonathan and Paul were no longer giggling.

I had an answer, and I didn't like it. The metal bashing sound *had* been caused by something on the prop, and that was good news. The something was a thick metal chain, perhaps belonging to a large fender, and that was bad news. There was no chance of cutting through it. I inched forward further and further, exploring the links with my chilly fingers, pushing my arm deeper and deeper – to the wrist, to the elbow, to the shoulder. Just when I could reach no further, I felt a fibrous tangle under my fingers. I traced its twisted shape. It was rope. I couldn't tell what relationship it had to the chain. Had it been picked up as part of the same implacable bundle, or was it by some chance holding links of the chain together? Was there any point in sawing my way through it?

At this point I would like to pay tribute to the magnificent bread knives made by Taylor's Eye Witness of Sheffield. I have never been so grateful for a serrated edge as I was that afternoon. I angled myself in the strange contortions that must have been familiar to Telford's navvies. I leaned in as deeply as I could to the narrow opening of the weed hatch and hacked vigorously at anything that felt like rope. At first we heard only the unyielding sound of steel meeting steel in the water, as the knife met link after link of the chain. After a moment or two, I felt something soft under the blade. I sawed first in one direction and then another, trying to visualise how the rope was tangled around the links and where I might get a purchase on it.

The crew members both offered to have a go. I felt a number of things at this moment, including cramp; but the most unexpected was a deep sense of protectiveness. *Tinker* was wounded; my crew were frightened. My sphere of influence might be small and unimportant, but it was my job to restore it to normality. I kept cutting. A moment later, I felt the fibres of the rope begin to give. As they parted, two links of the chain shifted. Dragging them speculatively one way and then another, I realised that the chain had been held in a figure 8 by the rope. As the rope dropped away, the chain became a large O and it was possible to ease it over the propeller. It dropped, invisibly, to the floor of the tunnel.

Tinker shook slightly, like a wet dog shivering. I heaved the weed hatch back into place and tightened the screw with unnecessary zeal. I dropped the heavy trapdoor, took a deep breath and started the engine. It ran as smooth as a Taylor's Eye Witness knife through butter.

By the time we reached the southern portal, Jonathan's and Paul's eyes had almost reduced to their normal size. As we emerged, I glanced at my watch. We had taken one hour and fifteen minutes. The southern tunnel keeper, a phlegmatic man of Stoke, raised an eyebrow.

'What took you so long? I was about to call in the Flying Squad.'

'Picked something up,' I said.

'That happens. Thought it was going to be a long night.'

In retrospect, it must have been this man or one of his colleagues who first got news of the man that had died in the tunnel earlier that summer. The dramas of the English canal system are not grand, but still they are life changing for an unlucky few each year. Ours had been relatively small, relatively easy to solve, and no one got hurt. We put the kettle on and had a cup of tea on our way to Stoke, mooring above the locks at Etruria.

This is Ground Zero for the canal system. The first sod of the Trent and Mersey Canal was cut a couple of miles away in Burslem. As soon as Brindley got water into the first branch of his Grand Cross, Wedgwood set up a new pottery works alongside it at Etruria. He named it, or rather branded it, Etruria after the Italian district famed for its classical ceramics and it thrived for 180 years, helping to define Stoke-on-Trent as the centre of 'the Potteries'. Stokies still cling to an identity fired in the bottle kilns, as we Sheffielders do to our erstwhile steel foundries.

We did not care a jot for Wedgwood at this moment. We found our way to the welcoming pub which rejoices in the name of the Holy Inadequate, feeling rather as Shackleton and his men must have felt when they first reached South Georgia after their journey of 3,000 miles in a small boat. The barman caught sight of Jonathan, still immaculate in his tailored tweeds and flat cap. '*Peaky Blinders* is over you know.' Jonathan started giggling. Paul followed suit. The bromance was back on.

Scholars

The past is what happened: history is what we write about it. It is not only written by the victors, but by the literate victors – and then again, by the small subset of the literate with the time and inclination to write histories. By definition, history is textual. It doesn't always make space for those who leave no written record. The navvies who built the canals, and the working boat people who made them function had a casual acquaintance with literacy; but then, for 95 per cent of human history *nobody* was literate.

In the mid-eighteenth century, when Brindley kicked off his Grand Cross of canals, the written word was not the information technology of most people. Brindley himself was not a great speller, as you can see in his notebooks. They are not a gripping read, but then neither are my to-do lists.

One in six – that's 8.5 million people – have difficulty reading English in Britain today. For some of them that's because they are more familiar with another alphabet – for all of them it's a huge disadvantage. Among them are some of the last working boat people.

In the 1940s, Rolt described working boat families in *Narrow Boat* as 'a highly individual community who have so far escaped the levelling influence of standardised urban thought and education.' Rolt himself was a product of that thought and education, but he was right that most boat people were not 'scholars', as they would say. Boat children couldn't both attend school and stay with their parents. Until the mid-twentieth century the families usually journeyed together, not widely but far, working their corridor of water. If one family had too many children to squeeze into the cabins, or another crew was short-handed, youngsters were sometimes 'borrowed' for months or years. They would see their family every few weeks as the two boats passed in the channel.

Strictly it was illegal to keep children out of school after 1880, but only after 1944 did they actually have to turn up for set hours. The children might go to a charity school like that at the Brentford Boatman's Institute, where they were taught to love God and the alphabet, but regular school was impractical. After 1944, the families were more often separated as children stayed 'on the bank' or went to canal-side schools. At the same time, road freight was pushing canal traffic into its last decline;

many of the boat families came to the bank. Right up into the 1960s, easy reading was a convenient extra rather than an essential for families afloat. Some of these elders still don't read or write, but functional illiteracy doesn't equate to stupidity. Any dyslexic will tell you this, and so will anyone who has spent time with adults who grew up on the boats.

Among my colleagues during my time on the working boats project was a man who was learning his letters for the first time at the age of sixty-six. I learned a lot, working with intelligent people whose literate culture was small and functional. I learned about boats, about my own snobberies, and came to mourn a little for the vast, tantalising masses of the brilliant but unlettered past; the cultures whose names are not captured on the time map, whose names we don't even know, the pre-literate problem solvers with brains as great as Da Vinci's or Newton's. This boater was no more a Leonardo than I, but on a road journey to meet with a boat crew he spelled out the words on the road signs. He slowly said 'STOKE ... ON ... TRENT'. The written word was a curiosity. Adventures opened up before him. He took ownership of twenty-six ancient symbols with power to challenge and inform, to distort and to transport. We parked up. It was raining.

Harecastle again

Brindley's mix of pragmatism and imagination were matched by his chutzpah. Envisioning the Grand Cross, the rough X at the heart of the English canals, required ambition and project management on an entirely new scale. All the great engineers had to be canny politicians in the boardroom too, persuading investors to risk large sums on speculative canals. The first generation of canal builders had the hardest battle convincing them, but Brindley was a charismatic man who knew his stuff, and knew how to communicate. Faced with a group of parliamentarians who couldn't quite follow his design for the Barton Aqueduct, Brindley took up a knife and made a model of it in Cheshire cheese. The cheesy aqueduct did not survive the evening; but they gave him the money.

In 1767, Brindley had assured Trent and Mersey shareholders that the canal would be completed within five years. He was mistaken. Five years later, Brindley's tunnelling parties were still making their contortions inside Harecastle Hill as the engineer lay dying two miles away. He had been out surveying for a new canal (the Caldon) and was caught in a terrible rainstorm. Unable to dry out properly in the inn where he was staying, he caught a chill, became seriously ill and died in September 1772, in rented rooms at Turnhurst Hall. He was fifty-six.

There would be another five years of candlelit pick-axe work of rubble clearing, coal-black panic and injury, before the last thin wall of rock was broken through and Brindley's 'air castle' opened to traffic. It had taken 600 men and eleven years to drive this tunnel through the hill. When completed it was not just the longest tunnel in the world; it was *twice* the length of any other tunnel in the world. It was 2,880 yards long. There was no towpath inside the tunnel, so boat horses walked over the top of the hill, and the boats were 'legged' through by men lying on the cabin top and walking against the tunnel walls. It took two hours. In later years a single steam tug would pull long strings of up to twenty canal boats through at a time.

Brindley was not there to see the completion of Harecastle, but he had made the establishment of a canal system his life's work. By the time he died, he knew he had done it. His canals are still in water and functioning 250 years after his death. If they fell out of use tomorrow, the earthworks cut by Brindley's regiment of proto-navvies would survive for millennia as visible features in the landscape. They are as immovable as Hadrian's Wall or the Pyramids, and just as grand.

What they are a monument *to* is a moot point. Like Stonehenge or Silbury Hill, they stand for a civilisation that could mobilise masses of people in one gigantic project. Brindley's and Telford's contemporaries charted out that immense schema of channels, dug it, equipped it with sluices, locks, reservoirs, and culverts; they flooded it with water and released onto it thousands of boats, supplying thousands of destinations in an orgy of commerce. Their vast, wobbling silver grid also speaks of the unstoppable power of empire-building greed, colonising robber barons and the destructive impact of men who will literally blast through anything that stands between them and a fortune. It is an irony of the Navvian Age that its mills, factories and great tunnels are the best remaining evidence for the lives of people who would much rather have been somewhere else. The tunnels at Harecastle monumentalise not only Brindley and Telford but the hundreds of navvies who built them, in conditions seldom rivalled before or since for horror.

Tixall Wide

Tinker dropped through five grim locks in the drizzle and slid on past the curious brick flasks which are the remnant bottle kilns of the Potteries. The air cleared and by the time we reached the rural pound above Meaford (pronounced Mefford), we were in a bright corridor of water overhung with low branches. There was that shocking flash of blue that puts other birds to shame; the arrow shot of a kingfisher.

'They're not blue, you know,' I said to my crew casually. 'They just look blue.'

We tied up opposite Roger Fuller's boat yard in Stone, and I went to pay my respects. Roger's yard at Limekiln Wharf is one of a few places where working boats can be properly repaired. There was a boat shed full of hammering noises, and fumes of paint drifted from the workshop where a skilled signwriter applied her circus-style scrolls on cabin sides. A half-dozen slender working boats in the familiar livery of long-extinct carrying companies were moored in the little basin. Around its edge between buildings and fruiting damson trees ran a miniature railway complete with cast iron signs and a tiny points system, for Roger is an industrial magpie who collects anything related to transport in the canal age.

He emerged from the shed, a slight figure in his fifties with the tanned skin of a man who spends most of his time outdoors. He had a battered felt hat on his head as usual. Through the door I glimpsed the shining curves of a new boat, which he was building with the hand measurements and skilful eye of a craftsman. He was on his own today, but in former years had a handful of men working with him. 'I always knew who was working on the boat at any moment,' he said. 'They all had a different rhythm with the hammer and tools.'

There were other boats waiting to be worked on. One was an old friend. It had been taken out of the water, and stood on the bank by the shed. The blue and yellow paintwork was a little battered, but the boat was very familiar. It was *Cepheus*. It was the boat I had first steered some years ago, when my boating L-plates were still firmly affixed.

I turned from Roger for a moment to find that he was also standing behind me. It wasn't a mirror; it was his brother. Roger and Martin Fuller are identical twins. They dress alike, they sound alike, they have the same wry expression and the same style of hat. When they work a pair of boats together, passers-by are baffled to see first the motor boat, then the butty slip past, both apparently steered by the same man. They call themselves the Trilby Crew.

The wharf was a remarkable haven, home to a small community of people who knew and loved working boats. At the far end of it was a tranquil mooring; a long plot with a private lawn covered in daisies, and a solid picnic bench overlooking the rushing top lock. The little piece of land was furnished with the deep purple foliage of an elderflower bush, florid at the moment with great bunches of pink-speckled blossom. I glanced at the mooring with an envious eye. 'If I wasn't on my way south, I'd quite fancy that,' I said. 'I'll put you on the waiting list,' said Roger with a grin.

We were deep in the epicentre of the canal system now, the place where the network had its Big Bang moment in Stone in 1766. Josiah Wedgwood, engineer James Brindley, and the clerk John Sparrow met in the Crown Inn to plan Brindley's ambitious Grand Cross of liquid connections. It happened fast. Quiet villages like Great Haywood and Barlaston were minding their own business when Wedgwood and Co. sent the boys round. Hundreds of people arrived with shovels and picks, cut a channel into the Staffordshire clay and moved on, leaving a snail trail of water that connected England's interior to its great cities, ports and markets. Local brewery Joule's was one beneficiary. It supplied the ships of Liverpool from its warehouse in Stone: in a later century, the passengers of the *Titanic* were drinking Joule's ale on the night she went down.

In 1951 Tom Rolt arrived in to Stone with *Cressy*, bringing his own *Narrow Boat* to the oldest dry dock in the country. As I passed through, another canal couple were in residence, for Skipper Jon and the long-suffering Judy had a house on the edge of the town. We met in the Star Inn for a pint. He was still conducting his dauntless campaign to get Judy living aboard. 'I reckon she's wavering,' he said. 'Good luck with that,' I said.

If I should perish on one of my epic adventures – perhaps overbalancing while sweeping the chimney, or collapsing in surprise at an older man taking my advice – then scatter my ashes at Tixall Wide. A map of the Staffordshire and Worcestershire Canal will show that it writhes like a convulsed snake on its route near Stafford. At a certain point it bulges, like a snake that has eaten an elephant. That bulge is Tixall Wide. It is a sort of artificial lagoon, where nature meets artifice in ways that connect several layers of the time map.

Tom Rolt arrived here in the 1930s. Like many boaters reaching it for the first time, he came around a bend in the canal to an unexpected broadening of water: 'We found ourselves sailing out into a long lake fringed by tall flags [irises] and dotted with hundreds of coot and moorhen.' When I pulled up here with novelist friend Sarah Jasmon and her teenage daughter Hatty, it looked as if nothing had changed. Bees were bumbling, the hedgerows were vibrating with the busy wings of insects and birds. Around this most natural of artificial water features, the wild carrot flowers were covered in tiny beetles. They all seemed to be copulating; we christened them 'shagbugs'.

Rolt found the water was unusually deep and clear. He could see every pebble on the bottom, and the underwater lines of *Cressy*'s hull.

That clarity comes from the natural waterways that replenish the Wide; it is the river Sow, the river Penk, the Sandyford Brook, the Rising Brook, the Ridings Brook and the Saredon Brook that make it so rich an environment and provide a sump for the local meadows in a season of flood. The other thing that Rolt noted is still striking today. He thought it a monstrosity; it is certainly incongruous. In isolation on the far bank is an ornate Elizabethan gatehouse. It's almost square, and was built by someone who really liked windows and cupolas: almost the whole frontage is glazed with small diamond panes of the age, and the pointed turrets at each corner make it look like a miniature of the Royal Pavilion in Brighton.

A gatehouse is normally an understated little building at the entrance to some great house, and this one formerly stood beside Tixall Hall. Mary Queen of Scots was hurried here for safekeeping on the day that the Babington Plot was uncovered. By 1770, when Mary was almost a myth and the canal running through the estate was a too-visible reality, the hall was owned by one Thomas Clifford. Clifford did not wish to gaze upon the grubby industrial traffic of a commercial waterway. Fortunately, he had a garden designer working on some nip-and-tuck landscaping. The designer had already planted a wood to screen the hall from the view of the nearby village.

The man engaged to 'improve' the natural lines of Tixall was Capability Brown, the genius of designed landscapes. The man who put in place the serpentine lines of the canal was, of course, James Brindley. One of them shaped the land for art and leisure, the other for industry and commerce. Brown and Brindley were exact contemporaries, and here at Tixall it seems likely that the two men worked together to create an industrial waterway that looked like a natural water feature, pleasing the Wolverhampton merchants who had financed the canal and the gentleman resident of Tixall Hall. Both worked in a society where it was taken for granted that a person of sufficient means had every right to reshape the world. The making of canals and industry sat inside the maelstrom of high culture, broad aspiration and deep inequity.

The properties that I had worked on with the National Trust are often called 'designed landscapes', a phrase that camouflages breathtaking privilege. The ruling families of the 1770s felt that they had a perfect right to redesign the existing landscape. After all, they owned it. As scores of noble houses redistributed the soil and the people of their estates into a more pleasing arrangement with the help of Capability Brown, the canals reshaped a wider topography for a slightly different class of people. The canal builders carved out their new network for financial backers including aristocrats, merchants, and what we would call 'venture capitalists'. Resources seemed limitless; coal, iron, clean air, the land masses of Australia or Africa. Many of the shackles and iron nails that supplied the slave trade and, later, the buildings of American frontier towns were made in the Black Country and shipped out by canal. The scythes made in the Phoenix Works, at the top of my South Yorkshire village, were used in the fields of Britain to supply the growing towns, and also on the plantations to supply sugar, tobacco and tea.

The Age of Entitlement dug holes, shaped earth and altered the landscape in pursuit of beauty and wealth. It brought home a commercial and cultural treasure chest which still benefits all of us in the UK. It comes with a great many uncomfortable price tags. 'If the sun never sets on the British Empire,' as a wag once said, 'it's because God doesn't trust the British in the dark.'

Both Tixall Hall and the canal suffered a change in their fortunes, and only one survived. When Rolt passed through, the house was gone.

It had been demolished in the previous decade, and it looked to the *Narrow Boat* author as if the canal was going the same way. *Cressy* was the first boat to pass through the nearby lock in six months. The lower gates 'were so decrepit that they looked in imminent danger of collapse' and leaked so badly that the lock almost emptied itself. The navigation had been declining for years, and was almost unfit for purpose. The canal system had lived through its age of commerce, and the age of leisure and liveaboards had not yet come. The British Transport Commission declared their intention to close the navigation in 1959. It was saved, like many other waterways, by the efforts of volunteers.

Sarah, Hatty and I sat on the cabin top with a bottle of wine beside us. The sky seemed a little wider here than elsewhere on the canal, and the water bustled with natural and human life. We listened, but we could not hear the men riding to imprison Mary, Queen of Scots; nor the shovels of the navvies as they cut the channel; nor the voices of Brindley and Brown discussing their broad collaborative 'lake'. We did not hear *Cressy*'s engine coming to a stop as Rolt drove his mooring pins into the bank by the clear waters of Tixall Wide. We did not hear the banter of canal restorers as they dug and cleared and rebuilt. We mostly heard bees. The bees had been there throughout it all. Literary historian Jodie Matthews writes that 'The canal perennially has the waters of other times flowing through it; reading the waterways is always reading across time.' We had a multi-layered time map in front of us, underneath and around us. Floating on the waterway Thomas Clifford didn't want to look at, we looked out at his estate and tried to imagine where his long-demolished hall had stood. We made do with his gatehouse – an ornamental eye-catcher in *our* garden. Our estate may be narrower than his, but it is 2,000 miles long and somebody else cuts the grass.

Sinking: Oxford

At Banbury, the object of my affections – and my journey – made a rare appearance. Calum himself had not joined me often on the long trip south. He was settling into his new job near Avebury, and as the boat crept down the map of England he was able to come and find me more often. We were still getting to know each other, for we had only met a few months before; and he was getting to know the ways of the boat. He joined me on days when I had no crew so that we could enjoy uninterrupted time together. At Banbury we moored opposite Tooley's Yard, the famous old boatyard where Tom and Angela Rolt's boat *Cressy* was fitted out for them. On the wall was a blue plaque:

L. T. C. ROLT 1910–1974.
Engineering historian, champion of inland waterways,
began his historic Cressy cruise
here in 1939.

I took Calum through his paces as he learned to steer *Tinker*. He was not a natural, but certainly not the disaster I had been in my first months of boating. There is no rush. We spent two days of summer rainstorms boating through showers which released the fragrance of ozone, old stone and earth into a long dark corridor of trees. Calum donned a disposable poncho. 'How do I look?' he asked, peering out of its sheeny plastic. 'Like a six-foot-tall condom,' I said. He grinned and walked up to work the lock gear. He was confident, purposeful, enjoying the movements of his own body and the neat tricks of wood and stone that took us through the locks.

I generally took the helm as we approached a lock flight, but occasionally Calum tried his hand, and slid us neatly into the chamber each time. On a narrow canal this is tricky for a learner, with one or two inches to spare on each side of the boat, but on the broad K&A it was a different matter. If *Tinker* was the only boat in sight, we had feet to spare on each side. If we met with another boat, we slid in together, each boat holding the other in place. The familiar *dinkdinkdink* raised the paddles in a centuries-old rhythm, the water tumbled in or out of the lock, the heavy beams pushed the gates open and the two boats nudged out one after the other.

I went on through the Midlands canals that I knew best with the help of a genuinely motley crew. The time map and the water map had permeable boundaries here. We passed the twentieth-century cooling towers of Rugeley, a town described by Rolt as 'a desert of mediocrity', and slid through Polesworth, home to the Jacobean poet Michael Drayton, who left us a long and not very exciting poem called *Poly-Olbion* celebrating England's rivers. Occasionally the crew included youngsters, who revelled in their encounter with an older way of life. One boy of about nine was bowled over by the most extraordinary thing of all – not that my home was a floating metal box, not that he had to work eighteenth-century ratchets and haul ropes to make progress, but the fact that there was no television on board. 'But where is it, really?' he asked, laughing and looking in cupboards. It took us a while to persuade him that there was no TV. 'Wow,' he said. 'You're *analogue*.' I felt like the last dodo, waiting to be stuffed.

Sometimes I travelled alone, refreshed by solitary boating after days of busy conversation and crowded living. One pink-and-pearl August morning I rose early to work unhurried up the five locks at Atherstone, taking pleasure in the methodical task and its mechanical rhythms. Clank, bump and rush; water, iron and oak. The mitred lock invented by Leonardo da Vinci worked its usual spell, lifting *Tinker* up the levels one liquid step at a time. In Rolt's time Atherstone 'manufacture[d] bowler hats in prodigious quantities' and as he left it behind with *Cressy* he also saw evidence of the local granite quarries: 'minute locomotives and rows of tipping wagons appeared in sharp silhouette on their high skyline, and we heard repeatedly the deep, reverberating thud of blasting.' There is still a quarry nearby, owned by Tarmac. There was no sign of tipping wagons, and no explosion to break up the dawn as I turned the windlass and trod the raised brick quadrants of each lock. It was a thoroughly *analogue* sort of morning; and I headed on, in the general direction of the Oxford Canal.

In January 1790 the Oxford Canal was opened with festivities:

The first boat entered the bason [sic] displaying the Union flag, and having on board the band belonging to the Oxfordshire militia. They were received by a vast concourse of people, with loud huzzas, and an ox having been roasted whole on the wharf, on approaching it, the band struck up, the Roast Beef of Old England, a favourite old tune, and well applied. The fifes and drums afterwards paraded through the streets.

That must have been splendid for the merchants of Oxford, who got a still-water navigation to bypass a section of the Thames: but Brindley's contour-hugging methods made for a very wiggly canal. As I joined this one, I was late for a rendezvous with friends Jill and Bob. They didn't know each other, they had both travelled some distance to meet me and I wanted to turn up at our meeting point when I said I would ('Tuesday'): but the North Oxford is not a canal to hurry. On a summer's day there is none more beautiful. The banks are lush with flag iris and many-layered greens like a Gauguin painting. Dragonflies flash in the bulrushes, and the neighbouring fields make up a rich landscape owned by rich people. As I passed through David Cameron's constituency, the fresh smell of cut grass was underlain by the thick fragrance of money. STOP HS2, said placards on the banks. HS2 was offering to do to the current landscape what the canals did to the eighteenth-century one, and the reaction of landowners was similar.

By now attuned to every nuance of *Tinker*'s movement, I knew how far she slipped in a current, how she would respond to the tiller with more or with less water in her holding tank, how a strong wind would affect her. Right now, something was wrong. The back end of the boat seemed just a tad lower in the water than it should be; she seemed – or was I imagining it? – a little sluggish, though there was no Llangollen-style current working against her. I slowed to tick-over pace, and paid close attention. We were not swimming through the water with the usual clean movement. The back end certainly *was* an inch or two lower than usual. The water looked higher up the hull than it should be. The handling was heavy. I ran through the things that make a boat behave like this.

The first culprit is typically something on the propellor, and I briefly thought about getting the bread knife out. Nine times out of ten, the problem disentangles itself and floats away looking for some other boat to bother. It didn't *feel* like something on the prop. At least I wouldn't have to stick my arm in the water and hack off a length of fishing line, complete with hidden hooks. I sped up, my eye on the clock.

There it was again: a sense that the boat was a little down at the back, beneath my feet. I was probably imagining it. I looked over the side to check that the exhaust was well clear of the water. I wasn't imagining it. The little outlet where engine fumes discharge was not as far from the surface as one would like it to be. There were still six inches between it and the water, but not the eight or nine I expected. If your vessel is suddenly heavier mid-journey than it was when you set out, then you are taking on water.

One of the definite things about boating is that you always want to have more water on the outside than on the inside. By the time you've noticed a boat is sitting differently in the canal, there is already a fair amount on the wrong side of the hull. There are two ways that this can happen. Neither of them is great news. The first is that the water inside the boat is *from* the inside of the boat; the engine cooling system is leaking, or the domestic water tank has cracked and is slowly emptying 300 gallons of drinking water into the bilge. (I have had both of these things happen, and both of them are unpleasant and expensive – but at least when the leaky tank is empty, the water will stop coming.)

The second way that a boat can take on water is, of course, from the outside. I found myself perversely hoping that the domestic water tank had indeed split. I poked my head quickly into the engine compartment. The floor was inches deep in water. It was not the clean water of a domestic drinking supply: it was slightly cloudy. It was canal water. It *was* coming from outside the boat, and I had no idea where it was getting in. *Tinker*'s shape under the waterline was a rectangular metal box. Somewhere in those yards of steel, was there a coin-sized hole that would sink my home in the next couple of hours? Had we hit an underwater rock and cracked a faulty weld? Had we scraped a bridge so forcefully that a thin section of steel plate had given way?

For the next two hours I cursed the name of James Brindley. I threw *Tinker* around the unfamiliar turns and sharp corners of his loveliest canal, each manoeuvre forcing water against the hull on a different plane. Anyone who has boated here remembers the Wormleighton windmill, which appears first on the right, then the left, then behind you and then – impossibly – right ahead of you. This is a by-product of Brindley's serpent route and if you're a hire boater with a week to explore it, it's a charming curiosity. I was neither charmed nor curious.

Tinker was wounded. I needed to get to Oxford before she sank, or before the water reached the engine. Like a motorway driver convinced that the fuel won't run out if you go a little faster, I hurtled at the dizzying speed of four miles per hour towards the dreaming spires, and my waiting crew.

Jill and Bob were strangers to one another. They had been walking along the bank separately for half an hour, each of them worrying about the weirdo they could see ambling up the towpath in this isolated area, until they twigged that they were on the same mission. Sensibly, they stopped walking and lurked together under one of Brindley's sturdy bridges, where I could easily collect them as I passed by. They were chatting and looking forward to a relaxing weekend of idyllic boating when they sighted *Tinker*, half a mile away in the green loops of the Oxford. There she was; then she disappeared in an inexplicable Brindley curve, and appeared again. Finally, I stopped the boat under the bridge. It was clear from my face that no one was going to have a relaxing weekend.

I spent a moment depressing the crew, then noticed with relief that the leakage had stopped. *Only when it's moving does the water come in. It's getting in around the propeller.* Any boat with a propeller has a hole in the hull, where the prop shaft pierces it. A thing called the stern gland (really) greases a tight coil of packing around the prop shaft, to keep water out. Sometimes that packing wears down, allowing water into the engine bay. I hung Bob, a mountainous Cockney, upside down in the engine bay, shouting 'TRY AGAIN, MATE!' as I worked the gears. Nope; the propeller was neatly sealed, even when we drove the engine rather fast. The water wasn't getting in there.

It must be a hole. If we make it to Oxford, we'll be in dry dock for a week. If we don't, tell my mother I love her and bury me in my wellingtons at Tixall Wide.

As I pushed off again, Jill used her phone to look up local boat-yards. We found a promising one called Green Boat Mechanics, which closed at 5 p.m.. It was 4.15, and we had at least half an hour to go. The faster we moved, the more water we took on. By the time we pulled in to the first viable mooring in Oxford, *Tinker* was dragging her back end like an itchy dog on a carpet. Along the way, we had parted company with Brindley and the Wormleighton windmill. We had joined the gentle river that public schoolboys call Isis, and which normal people call the Thames.

Bob put the kettle on. I breathed for the first time in four hours. In the shallow reaches just ahead of us, beautiful young men were bathing in the river under weeping willows. Thin white row-boats sculled past us, full of wholesome young people passing time until they could start running the country. It looked like a scene from *Brideshead Revisited*. This was not the moment for revolution, but I would get right back to it once my limping boat was safe again. It was five to five. I texted Green Boat Mechanics, weary and worried. 'YOU DON'T KNOW ME BUT I'VE JUST PULLED IN TO OXFORD AND I THINK I'M SINKING'.

The phone beeped immediately. 'I KNOW. I CAN SEE YOU OUT THE WINDOW'.

Five minutes later, a gangly man made of engine oil stepped onto the counter and introduced himself as Jon Ody. He folded himself into the engine bay, switched the engine on and put it into full forward gear, far faster than I had ever revved it. *Tinker* heaved at her ropes and prac-tically sweated under the strains. Water obligingly poured in around the weed hatch, the steel box which gives access to the propeller.

'See?' said Jon.

I was indignant. 'But I revved the engine to look at that, and it didn't let water in at all!'

'Not enough,' said Jon laconically, unfolding himself and stretching his arms out like a cormorant. 'It will only do it when it's running flat out. Were you piling it on a bit, to get here in time?'

Bob and Jill glanced at one another. Half an hour before, they had been singing 'For Those in Peril on the Sea' as I threw the boat around Brindley's eighteenth-century slalom. I had indeed piled it on a bit.

'Thought so,' grinned Jon.

It was a simple problem, solved by cutting a new gasket from a sheet of cork. 'I'll get you sorted before breakfast tomorrow,' said Jon. 'See you in the Prince of Wales.'

There followed an evening of dappled sun in a beer garden, with jugs of Pimm's and the kind of deep, laughing conversation you can only have with strangers who share a culture and a keen curiosity. We told of landmarks, place names, mechanical disasters and the connections which members of a small, unusual community use to locate one another in their shared landscape.

We left just after breakfast. There was no hole in the hull. The repair bill was £25. *The revolution can wait,* I thought. We headed on for the Thames proper.

An offering

South of Oxford, the Thames was a sweet-natured river, with wide fields and ancient trees bordering the banks. There were seagulls skimming the open water, and the oily silhouette of a cormorant diving for fish. It was easy boating with no locks or shallows, and *Tinker*'s engine revelled in a little proper exercise. On the canals we sometimes get a problem called 'bore glaze' where the engine clogs up with residue because it has been ticking over at three miles per hour for a long time. On the open river, you can travel faster. The engine coughs and clears its throat. The propeller bites deep into the water, relishing the chance to work a little harder.

That summer evening found *Tinker* in one of the loveliest moorings I ever had, with a crew of two writers. Even on the water map, this was an unnamed place. Like a thousand other moorings, I have no idea where it was: it was a nameless *here* where three people lived together for an August evening, wholly enveloped in one watery moment. We looped our ropes around ash trees in a backwater kink of the river, with clouds of tiny gunmetal fish just under the surface and a small stream running into the channel beside us. The river was slow-moving, and so were our thoughts. The local water fairies threw yellow ripples onto the living room ceiling. Dragonflies the size of small helicopters patrolled a patch of water lilies. The water was a jigsaw of green light and shade, patterned by low-hanging trees and the notched leaves of arrowhead.

One of the great pleasures of boating is that it reacquaints you with the art of sitting still. I sat in the front well deck with a cup of tea and the inevitable biscuit, taking the measure of this evening's neighbourhood. 'What's that up there?' I asked crew member Alan. I was looking at a stand of trees on top of a nearby hill, with red kites circling high above it in the warm air. He spoke slowly, as if to a person who is hard of thinking.

'That? That is Wittenham Clumps.'

There was a silent 'obviously' at the end of the sentence. Alan has been an Oxford resident almost his whole life, and this famous stand of beeches is so embedded in his sense of place that he could barely believe I did not know it. Wittenham Clumps is a grouping of beech trees planted in 1740 by landowners with an eye for the 'improved' landscape, and a stake in it which they knew would last for generations. Now, the beeches are an eye-catcher shared by all of the people who live within forty miles of Wittenham. Local people orientate themselves without even knowing it, by glancing up a few times a day at the wiggy topknot of trees that overlooks the oldest English settlements. The artist Paul Nash, who painted it many times, said the clumps had a 'compelling magic'. He described the view from the hilltop as 'a beautiful legendary country haunted by old gods long forgotten'. We lived for a few hours within their orbit, and honoured the old gods by opening another packet of biscuits.

When people ask boaters 'Is it idyllic?' this closeness to nature is what they have in mind: the sense of being rocked to sleep as gently as in a cradle, the blue-grey twilight interrupted by bats, the mindful contemplation, tra-la-la, etc. What they do not have in mind is the extreme closeness to nature I experienced the following day. As *Tinker* ploughed along the centre of a broad silvery reach, the sky suddenly cracked open in a thunderstorm. The gentle landscape became a pointillist grey painting; which is to say, it was wet. It was really wet.

This was unlike any rain I had ever experienced before. It was the sort of rain that you see in a Bengal monsoon, or a bad film. Standing at the tiller in a sunhat and T-shirt that seemed perfectly adequate five minutes before, I was indeed extremely close to nature. Nature fell in stair rods around me, bouncing off the cabin top and back into my face, making the air impenetrable and screening all landmarks as if through a wet dishcloth. I had nature in my socks, in my ears, dribbling off the brim of my hat to run down my neck and between my buttocks. My shoes pooled up with it. In Sheffield we would say it was 'siling down'.

Then the lightning began. I felt like King Lear in an amateur dramatic performance. There were no trees or buildings in this rural washout. It occurred to me that I was the highest thing in the landscape, a little figure sticking up like a lightning conductor at the back of a large metal box. I was alarmed. 'Cup of tea?' said a bright voice at knee level, as friend Sarah stuck her head into the engine room. I put the tea on the slide in front of me and watched it immediately replace itself with rainwater. 'Do you, er, want me to take over steering for a bit?' offered Sarah valiantly. I considered the offer. 'Not much point,' I said. 'No need for two of us to get drenched.' Nature cascaded off my hat in a little runnel, into her face. 'Righto,' she said, and disappeared into the warm living room.

We tied up at Reading, where the barriers of the recent rock festival were still in place along the river bank. Alan, tall and slender to the point of gauntness, had already been joined on the crew by Robbie, a tiny woman (short for Roberta, if you're wondering) with a twinkling eye and quiet wit. We three in our Gore-Tex and jeans were now in glamorous company. As I wrang out my socks, the poet Kate Noakes stepped aboard, looking unfeasibly put-together. She appeared in the well-deck, a vision of hair and cleavage and sparkling eyes.

'We are going to make a votive offering,' she said improbably.

'Of course we are,' I said. I had no idea what she was talking about.

The next stage of the trip would take us across the junction of the river Thames and the river Kennet. Bronze Age people knew how important their rivers were, and Kate told me that the Atrobates people of this region offered precious gifts to the water deities who met and mingled here. At the junction of the two waters, they cast into the river leaf-shaped swords and precious objects of copper and bronze. Some of them have been retrieved from the riverbed during dredging works. They were donated to the town's museum by a local utility company and are known, accurately enough, as the Thames Water Collection.

Kate knew that this day was an important moment in my snail's-pace pilgrimage. *Tinker* and I had been travelling for three weeks, and for the past few days had been steering almost due south. Today we would turn right and west, out of the river channel and onto the Kennet and Avon Canal. It was the very last waterway of a long journey, and the only one I expected to travel for the next few years. Within the week I would be pulling in to my new mooring at Honeystreet.

The whole trip so far had been a tumble of pleasure and shared purpose. Dozens of friends had already joined me on *Tinker* for a short spell of close company, eating and talking together, working locks together, inching across the water map. They were poets and boaters and engineers, teachers and bankers and archaeologists. All of them were a little invested in my happiness, and my success in the West Country. Notably, not one of them uttered the words, 'Are you sure this is a good idea?' They knew me better. The gesture of following Calum south was a tightrope-tense experiment, but I was full of appetite for it. So far, our time together had not been long, but deep and intensely physical. It was a strong match of two personalities, and the start of a joint project. Soon we would have new, favoured places that would become as familiar to us as the Wittenham Clumps were to Alan.

As *Tinker* approached the river junction I had an instinct that in times ahead, this moment would be rich in nostalgia. A future self would look back to the instant when my present self turned away from the river, and nosed into the K&A. *Bring it on*. I would be a floating resident of many parishes; of Newbury, Bath and Bristol; of the little town of Pewsey recommended to me by a stranger at a funeral; above all of the thatched hamlet of Honeystreet, where Nikki and her secluded mooring awaited me. So, if the gods of the Bronze Age met and mingled at the junction of the Kennet and the Thames, it would do no harm to say hello and ask for their assistance. I had no gods but local gods. I was all for offering up a prayer.

'What do you have to offer?' Kate asked.

It was a good question. What sacrifice could I make that was fit for the old gods? I did not have a leaf-shaped bronze sword or a thick gold necklet. We made do with a bunch of slightly tired roses. Kate and I were laughing as we leaned over the side of the boat with Alan and Robbie; but then again, we were four poets, and enjoyed the ritual.

Poetry is often about acknowledging the real desires beneath our daily behaviours. I summoned up all my hopes for a new homeland and a new tribe of friends; I asked for a good life in the territory of the Atrobates. I gave thanks for Kate's good wishes, and for all the companions who had joined me on the journey so far, bringing their bodies and their biscuits to help me along. I cast a handful of peach-coloured roses on the swirling surface where two rivers meet, and tugged a forelock.

Then I pushed the tiller over and felt *Tinker* swing away from Father Thames, out of the strong river current and into the reassuringly tranquil waters of the K&A. There was no sacred architecture, only a distinctly earthly bridge which almost knocked my hat off. I was back on the canal system. My crew hopped off to work the first lock, on a waterway that none of us knew.

Gods will be gods, however. In a couple of days I would come to wish that I had made a better offering.

The Oracle

The K&A was uniformly delicious; or rather, delicious but not at all uniform. As we headed west, every lock was different. Some had enormous bollards that looked as if they had been salvaged from a shipyard, some had idiosyncratic hinges or ironwork on the lock gates which suggested they had been cobbled together in someone's shed by a hippy with a welding torch. In all likelihood, they had. The K&A was a pioneering canal restoration project, saved from absolute dereliction by a particularly dedicated band of campaigners. The restorers used whatever they could get their hands on to re-equip it.

Most bewildering of all, though, was the very modern fixture we encountered as we left a lock in Reading. As I steered, I could see the small figure of crew member Robbie in the front of the boat, peering at something ahead of us with a puzzled air. 'What is it?' I asked. She took a moment longer to digest what she was looking at. 'It's a traffic light!' she called back with an air of delighted novelty, as if she had seen a unicorn.

Traffic lights are not unknown on the system. You sometimes see them at tunnels, where they work either on demand or on a timer system, so that boats never meet each other travelling in opposite directions inside a narrow tunnel. This was the first time I had ever seen one actually regulating passage in the main waterway. *Tinker* hovered in the channel as best she could, for a river is never entirely tamed; the Kennet had a sly current which wanted to nudge the nose of the boat away from the traffic light. Robbie gamely extended her arm, pointing hopefully in the direction of the faraway button.

Like a very slow horse entering the tiltyard, with a very small knight in place for the joust, *Tinker* inched towards the mysterious traffic light. It was not a perfectly straightforward manoeuvre. I had the boat hook at the ready, for if Robbie should topple into the water I would have to fish her out as she bobbed past the back end. However, she reached the button, pressed it and the light turned from red to green. Filled with foreboding, we proceeded on our way. Why on earth did we *need* a traffic light in this well-maintained, open-air section of water?

What followed was a surreal few moments of boating. This, I realised, was a slalom. It was a slalom with a strong current, and it ran – could this be true? – through a shopping centre. In their wisdom, the town planners of Reading built a mall called The Oracle around the local navigation. To add to the amusement of onlookers, they sited it on a tight and winding reach formerly called the Brewery Gut. The current of the Kennet was surprisingly strong after the downpours which my socks remembered so well, and it was a small challenge to swing *Tinker*'s front end round the bends without a little bump and grind at the tiller. I grimaced as we wound our way between the chrome-and-glass cliffs of metropolitan shop fronts. FatFace and Next loomed above us, and a handful of curious shoppers leaned out from the walkways above us to wave ice creams in encouragement. We had become a sort of living log flume for the entertainment of Reading's consumers.

It was obvious now why there was a traffic light. Every river has its own style and Kennet was a trickster; we were heading upstream, and it wanted to amuse itself a little by pushing hard against us. Had another boat come in the opposite direction, with the current behind it, we would have struggled to turn our two boats in the bending channel and avoid one another.

It was at this moment that my phone rang. I answered it to find Judith Palmer, the director of the Poetry Society on the other end.

'Would you like to be the canal poet laureate?' she asked.

'Erm,' I said, leaning hard on the tiller as a small child goggled down at us from the walkway. 'I didn't know there was one.'

'There isn't,' she said. 'Would you like to be the first?'

Why not? It's already a fairly weird day. 'That would be lovely,' I said. 'Can I call you back?'

As we crept closer to Honeystreet, my new neighbourhood rolled out the blue carpet. The water was clear, with trails of weed waving beneath the hull, and the surroundings continued to surprise and delight. The August sunshine made every day a postcard. The villages were each charming in a different way. Their old-school English names came in a string of hams and tons: Aldermaston, Woolhampton, Benham, Thatcham. Boating happens at walking pace, so we passed through them in a human timescale. Village cricket matches, country pubs and cottages slid by. We floated through a Rudyard Kipling vision of England, lush and gentle with no sharp corners. The old market towns had kept much of their character. It was county-and-country life that we saw dotted around the close-hedged lanes, in a mix of old money, new money and age-old rural precarity. I was completely enchanted with every inch of it.

The canal ran through a crease between chalk downs. Properly speaking, the two ends of the K&A are rivers (the Kennet at this eastern end, the Avon at the other). Both were improved for navigation in the 1720s, and later connected with a stretch of entirely man-made canal in the middle, to cut out the rampant wiggles of the natural watercourses. Nowadays the K&A is usually taken to mean the whole length. The Kennet proper meandered across the land to our left as we took the straighter, artificial line. The chalk makes for a rich ecology, and a rare one; 85 per cent of the world's chalk streams are located in England. Even an artificial water channel makes a rich habitat in this context: former gravel pits had been flooded to make them into nature reserves, and the banks of both river and navigation hummed with the nameless creatures of the water's edge.

I remembered sharing a flat years before with a caddis fly expert, who would bring home trays of black dots and pore over them with tweezers in hand. 'What are you doing?' I asked her once as I tried to move a tray of dead insects from the dining room table.

'Sexing beetles.'

'I see. How do you do that?'

'You get one of these' – she proffered a microdot-sized corpse, peering at it over her glasses – 'and you pull its willy out.'

'What if it hasn't got one?'

'Then it's a girl.'

The living creatures were far more interesting. Damselflies chased across the water and sometimes settled on the tiller. Their slender bodies gleamed like foil in blues and blacks. They have brilliant, descriptive names: Hawkers, Chasers, Darters and Skimmers. Kingfishers scooted across the channel ahead of us, their determined low-and-fast flight patterns smearing the air with blue. ('They're not blue, you know', I said to the crew member passing up a cup of tea. 'Shut up,' he said.)

We worked through swing bridges, stopping road traffic with glee, and through dozens of locks. The locks were all broad ones, for we were in true barge country now: stately wide-beam vessels had carried grain, gravel or timber out of the West Country here and brought commodities back, including Indian cotton, Black Country metalware and Wedgwood's pottery.

At Thatcham we came to something odder and earlier than the usual locks. I had seen nothing like it. Monkey Marsh Lock is a relic of the navigation built here around 1720, predating true canals by half a century. At this end of the waterway, the proto-industrial engineer who made the river navigable was local man John Hore. Like James Brindley, his first work was as a millwright and like Brindley, he drew on his knowledge of both water and mechanics to improve his local waterways. Compared to the solid-walled stone chambers we knew, this lock looked organic and fragile, with no walls but a bare fretwork of timbers holding back a mass of reeds. It was a small, deep pool with a gate at each end.

We dropped quietly through it, moored below and set up a barbecue on the towpath. My crew filled their glasses with beer, and held paper lanterns over the grill to fill with hot air. Forgive us, Reader, for we did not know at the time that the lanterns cause all sorts of problems for livestock and the land. They rose glowing into the sky as a steam train whistled past on the nearby track, sending pillars of steam into the cobalt air. These August hours had a feeling of Narnian foreignness, time travel and magic. We settled in canvas chairs with a glass of wine, the ducks muttering in the rushes nearby. As ever, there was a feeling of residency – temporary, but complete. Wherever you strike a couple of mooring pins into the bank, that's your home.

Newbury seemed like a heaving metropolis by contrast. The next day we slinked through the town like guilty lurchers, glancing back at the clean and populous town marina that I had seen earlier in the year. I didn't regret my choice of mooring; the marina had all the amenities, but I was headed for buttercups and thatch. I met with them both at the village of Kintbury.

I met Calum there too. After almost a month of boating, *Tinker* and I were now within commuting distance for him, and getting closer.

'I'll come and meet you after work,' he said. 'Where are you?' *Here we go.* When the people of boat and bank try to arrange a meeting point, it's always a challenge to locate each other. 'Are you near Marlborough?' I had no idea. If it was more than six feet from the canal, it did not appear on the linear Nicholson map.

'I'm near lock 52,' I said helpfully.

'Not helpful,' he said.

Happily, one sort of landmark is always known to both tribes. We would meet at the Dundas Arms. I was tired and joyful, fizzing with pride in my tribe of crew and the new friends I had begun to gather through poetry contacts. I tied up near the pub and saw a long, lean figure walking towards me. The hot day had just been damped down with a summer shower, and Calum pointed up at the sky behind me: 'Look up!' A double rainbow was printed on the sky, the two arches perfect and impossibly bright. We stood together beaming at it.

We barely heard the engine of another boat chuckling towards us. When I turned, a narrow boat was approaching and I saw for the first time the place name 'HONEYSTREET' written on the side of a boat. The skipper glanced at *Tinker* and her place of origin: HIGH PEAK. He leaned towards me as we passed: 'Are you Jo?' he called.

'I am!'

'Thought so,' he said. 'We're going to be neighbours! See you in a couple of days. I'll let them know you're close.'

The Towpath Telegraph was doing its work; my soon-to-be neighbours knew that I was on my way.

Mrs Rolt

Inconveniently, I sometimes had to interrupt my boating to do some actual work. As Canal Laureate, my reception was mixed. Sometimes I was welcomed as a boater who happened to write poetry. More often, the greeting reminded me of my ex-partner's attitude to macaroni cheese. Given a dish speckled with unfamiliar herbs, he wrinkled his nose. 'Have you done something ... *middle-class* with this?' he asked suspiciously. Reader, I had done something middle-class with it. I had added spinach. I expect no sympathy.

A lot of boaters shared that same suspicion of middle-class intervention, in what has always been a fundamentally working-class environment. The appointment of a poet was often seen as a well-meaning daub of high culture in a place where it had no business. There were many encounters with people who felt that the money spent on me could be better spent on dredging the canal. The laureate post was funded by the Arts Council, who oddly enough have no budget at all for dredging, and by the new Canal and River Trust, who wanted to attract new people and new income to the waterways.

Naturally, I thought my appointment was a jolly good idea. Art has its place in the weaponry we deploy to protect the canals. At last I could claim something in common with Rolt's *Narrow Boat,* as a creative voice in an ongoing campaign. It seemed like a blessing to be invited to the Hay Literary Festival for a panel discussion of Rolt's work. The loved-and-loathed book had recently been reprinted, and I had written the foreword. I arrived at Hay feeling very pleased with myself. I was greeted by Tony Hales, the dapper and mischievous chief executive of the Canal and River Trust. He looked very pleased with himself too.

'There's someone I would like you to meet after the event,' he said.

'Of course, who is it?'

'Sonia Rolt.' Pause. Tom Rolt's widow, apparently, would be sitting in the front row. *Oh great.* 'No pressure,' chortled Tony.

When she first met Rolt in 1945, Sonia South was twenty-six. She was middle class, convent-educated, profoundly independent – and not at all the sort of person usually associated with working boats at that time. The war, which changed the trajectory of so many lives, had brought her to the canals. At its outbreak, Sonia was living in a Knightsbridge flat with four girlfriends – 'It wasn't at all smart in those days,' she later claimed, but she protested too much. It was practically next door to Harrods. Soon, however, she joined the war effort. As Tom Rolt and his first wife Angela sat cooped up on *Cressy* at Tardebigge top lock, Sonia was soldering the wiring for Lancaster bombers in a factory in west London. It was a hotbed of communism, and her openly left-wing views led to an interview with Special Branch.

It can't have made for a comfortable working environment: so soon afterwards, Sonia replied to an advert from the Ministry of Transport, calling for women to work on the Grand Union Canal. She had barely seen a canal at the time. Attracted by the promise of outdoor work and (tellingly) minimal management, she signed up with her flatmates. They joined a handful of women who crewed working boats to supplement a wartime workforce much depleted of men. The waterborne equivalent of the agricultural 'land girls', they were famously nicknamed the 'Idle Women' after the initials of the Inland Waterways authorities. Sonia was assigned to the working pair *Moon* and *Phobos*.

It was natural that Sonia was among those invited to the premiere of a new film called *Painted Boats* in September 1945. It was about canal life, and its scriptwriter had just had an unexpected success with his book *Narrow Boat*. Tom Rolt attended the premiere with his then-wife, Angela. His first impression of Sonia was underwhelming. He noted her flat sandals (eminently practical for boat wear) and peasant skirt: he dismissed her as 'a rather frightening left-wing blue-stocking'. It was the word that men used then to describe intelligent women; nowadays they call us 'woke' or 'strident'. The underwhelm was mutual. Sonia was engaged to a boatman called George Smith, whom she married a few weeks later.

The war was over; a Labour government had just been elected; thousands of people were being released from war service, ready to turn their energies to new projects. Sonia was a born activist. Like Rolt, she belonged to a generation with little money but much discipline, and a willingness to rebuild their battered nation. As their two marriages deteriorated, they were drawn together in the campaign to restore the declining waterways, which had been overtaken by rail and road traffic. By 1951 they were living together. It was at this time that Tom took *Cressy* to the venerable dry dock in Stone, and left his eponymous narrow boat behind for good. The bulk of Sonia's activism would be done as the second Mrs Rolt.

Sonia went on to work with several institutions – the National Trust, the Landmark Trust, the Society for the Preservation of Ancient Buildings and others – to preserve 'large artefacts' throughout her lifetime. Her efforts put mine distinctly in the shade. As I stepped onto the stage at Hay, I no longer felt like an authority on *Narrow Boat*.

In the front row was a very small, very old woman. She was ninety-four, and beautifully dressed in a white skirt suit. She listened attentively to the words of every panel member. I tried to speak respectfully about the working boats and the people who worked them. About Rolt, I said what I've said in these pages; that he may have taken a romantic view of the canals, and he was one of many who advocated for them: but that nonetheless, it was his book that signalled the beginning of a meaningful campaign to restore them.

At the end of the event, Sonia and I were introduced. I wanted to know if I had done justice to Tom Rolt. 'You got it *exactly* right,' said Sonia. 'Exactly.' She fixed me with the same amused glance I imagined she had directed at her Special Branch inquisitors. 'You're not at all how I expected you to be,' she said. I met her eye, enjoying her appraisal.

'How did you expect me to be?'

'I thought you'd be rougher,' she said mischievously. 'With tattoos.'

I raised my hand to show the little boat tattooed on my wrist. 'Ah well', she said, and giggled.

I met her only once more, when we both featured in an episode of Tim West and Prunella Scales' programme *Great Canal Journeys*. We were filming at a site near Stanley Pontlarge, the Gloucestershire village where the Rolts had lived. She looked like a character from an Agatha Christie story; a dainty, alert figure tucked up in a chair with a blanket over her knees.

'You look like a little old lady,' I said, taking a seat beside her.

'I *am* a little old lady,' she said with a giveaway twinkle.

'Hmmm. Only in the chronological sense,' I said.

She died six weeks later. For a brief moment, Sonia Rolt's time map overlapped with my own. She travelled in disguise as a little old lady, but like many others who do the same, she was a lifelong member of the Awkward Squad, that bunch of people who are always unwelcome to the authorities because they get things done.

In the post-war decades, as the untrafficked waterways collapsed and fell silent, thousands of volunteers rolled up their sleeves and pulled on their wellingtons to 'dig for victory' once more – this time not in their allotments, but in the silt and infill of an unloved and decaying canal system. These people belonged to local canal societies, to the pressure group called the Inland Waterways Association, or later to the Waterways Restoration Group; an army of muddy enthusiasts who cleared out locks full of rubble, cut down overgrowing trees and rebuilt collapsing walls. Campaigning, fundraising and execution of such grand works is painfully slow, and the work is ongoing. The Rochdale Canal, for instance, opened to navigation in 2002 after a restoration that required twelve new road bridges and the cutting of a new channel under the M62. The Cromford Canal in Derbyshire, cut off from the rest of the network by the M1, continues to campaign for a link back to the national system.

Little by little, unpaid activists rescued what was about to become a dying system of ditches, and created the nationwide linear village we now have. They made a home for boaters like me, of course; but the canal system is also an industrial monument which deserves as much reverence as Blenheim Palace and Chatsworth House, and did more than either of them to make the Britain we live in now. It is a living corridor for wildlife, and a ready-made national network of flat, accessible paths used by everyone in the neighbourhood to walk the dog, to exercise, to fish, to get a glimpse of nature even in the inmost inner city. The people who benefit from it most are the disadvantaged, the urban, the poor. They are in need of a little peace, and at the canal bank they

can get it for nothing. Where there is a canal, there is often regenera-
tion too. Towns like Hebden Bridge and Bradford-on-Avon depend on
canal-side businesses; the cafés and housing plots at the water's edge,
the hire boat companies, the tourist income brought in by boaters and
all who enjoy watching them.

Hurrah for the canal restorers, then. And now, the bad news.
Astonishingly, every bit of their work is in jeopardy again. The hard
labour of the Rolts, their many allies and all their fellow travellers is
being eroded. The way of life described in these pages is in clear and
present danger. Unless we act, the canal network will begin to shut
down once more, and for good, in the next decade. It isn't a sudden
decline; successive governments have reduced funding for the canals,
and maintenance had already reached a critical point when, on New
Year's Day 2025, a sudden catastrophe happened on the outskirts of
Manchester.

The north-west of England is used to rain, as I know all too well;
but in the last days of 2024, an exceptional 90mm of rainfall drenched
the region. For the most part, the canals coped with the extra water,
discharging the excess as they are designed to do; but the most venerable of them all could stand no more pressure. Near Dunham Massey,
one side of Brindley and Gilbert's great, straight Bridgewater Canal
collapsed. Thousands of tonnes of water rushed out to flood fields and
a nearby sewage works. A major incident was declared. Almost 1,000
people had to be evacuated from their homes.

We call this a breach, and it is not unheard of. Even the youngest
parts of the canal system are almost 200 years old, and once in a blue
moon there is bound to be a breach: but this one is special, and its
implications serious. The Bridgewater Canal is one of the rare waterways not curated by the Canal and River Trust. It is privately owned by

a development company. Boaters are a suspicious lot, and many have expressed fears that this particular owner will choose not to repair the canal, but to infill and develop the land. That remains to be seen; but even if a full repair is undertaken, it will likely take years. As it is, the inevitable, temporary closure cuts off a crucial link in our water map. It is in the nature of a network that all parts feed traffic to the other parts. The Bridgewater is a part of the Cheshire Ring, a circular route that many hire boats travel. It links the Leeds and Liverpool Canal to the Trent and Mersey, and also gives access to the recently completed Rochdale Canal. In our liquid, circulatory system, all of these neighbouring waterways will be atrophied to some extent.

At best, the Bridgewater breach draws attention to the need for constant maintenance in every part of the system, and to the impact of climate change on a historic structure built to hold water. Increased rainfall, hard winters and dry summers all affect the water supply and the structural integrity of the canals.

A chain is only as strong as its weakest link; we boaters are endangered animals, watching our habitat begin to shrink. What the canals need is a regular input of money for maintenance; money to dredge the channel and maintain the reservoirs, to keep bridges from falling in, to maintain the taps and toilet pumps that boaters use. It is not a vast amount, in the grand scheme of things: the canals give astonishingly good value for tourism, health and wellness, access to nature and heritage. The Canal and River Trust warns that a huge slash in their budgets (over £300 million in coming years) threatens the whole system.

Without it, the canals will become eyesores, safety risks, dumping grounds and health hazards. Decay happens much more quickly than recovery. If we don't stop it happening now, we will have a lot more work to save them in future. If you are moved to do something about this, then visit the Canal and River Trust and use their form to contact your MP. Visit the Fund Britain's Waterways Campaign, give them a tenner and sign their petitions. I beg you to help us, and to preserve your own heritage. The next decade may be the most vital yet, in the history of the canals. The legacy of the canal restorers is in our hands; let's see if this generation can rise to the call as they did.

The last lock

Two hundred and fifty miles: 161 locks. Back in March, I had pored over a pile of Nicholson guides, counting up the markers for each. Now, in late August, we had passed 243 of those imaginary mile posts and worked our way up and down 160 locks, tootling through England's canals and rivers at the pace of a walker with sore feet. There were seven miles left, and only one lock. Honeystreet was now only an afternoon's walk away, had we chosen to cover it on foot. This morning, with drizzle freshening our skin, we would work our way through a final, familiar obstacle and drift into my new parish.

The poet in me enjoyed waking up that morning at a literal watershed. We had been working our way gradually uphill since Reading. One slow-filling lock at a time, we had risen 210 feet since Newbury. The previous afternoon, we had reached the summit level of the K&A and I had tickled my industrial archaeology fetish with a quick visit to the Crofton Pumping Station and its stately beam engine. Now we were approaching the 161st lock, which would take us downhill for a change. *Tinker* would be dropping sedately towards the catchment of the Bristol Avon, and pastures new.

My crew and I leafed through the log book as we ate breakfast. The first entry was in my brother James's handwriting: 'CANAL CLOSED!!!' it said, recording our anticlimactic first day. I flicked past the drama of Harecastle Tunnel and the quiet basin full of old boats at Fuller's yard in Stone; past the summer bliss of Tixall Wide, with its invisible stately home; past the near-sinking at Oxford and the weird log flume of Reading's Oracle. I turned to the next blank page. *Day 29,* I wrote. *Weather: grey and drizzly. Crew: Lucy, Martin, Calum.* Lucy English is a funny and wise performance poet, blonde and brilliant. She and her partner were joining us by way of welcome to their part of the country.

Calum was showing up too. Together we could tick off the last short distance, and then glide smugly into the mooring at Honeystreet. I expected a brass band, small children waving handkerchiefs; perhaps tearful news reporters ready to congratulate me on my heroic efforts. Actually, what I expected was a hot shower and a pint at my new local, The Barge Inn. I looked around me. This area would be a taken-for-granted homeland soon, and I wanted to fix every image in my mind. As it turned out, every image would indeed be very clearly fixed in my mind.

Calum met my eye as we approached the lock. 'Can I?' he asked. *Why the hell not,* I thought. It was fitting that he should steer this afternoon, and I could at last relinquish the tiller to enjoy the more physical work of opening gates. After all, that summer he had taken *Tinker* through a dozen or more locks. I realised too late that in every one of them, the boat had been ascending. Calum had never taken the boat through a lock going downhill.

Dozens of boats sink in locks every year, and most of them do it travelling downhill, by catching the boat on the cill (not 'sill', don't ask me why). The cill is a deep stone shelf in the base of the lock chamber; the massive gateposts are embedded in it, so it needs to be a substantial chunk of bedrock. Imagine perching your bottom on the very edge of such a step. If someone magically pulled the floor away in front of you, you would fall flat on your face and break your nose. *Oof.* Hanging a boat on the cill is the same gravitational nightmare on a bigger scale, and the medical bill is far higher. The cill looks like a huge doorstep, with a typical drop of about four feet. As the water level falls, the cill emerges like a mossy little cliff behind the boat.

At least, that's where it should emerge. If the boat is right above that small cliff as the water level drops, then the back end, like your own back end on the stone step, will come to rest on the cill, but the front end continues to fall. The vessel tilts forward like a little *Titanic*. Revving the engine will not get you anywhere, because the business end is high and dry as the front end goes under. You must act like lightning. Your crew must drop all the paddles so that the supportive water stops draining away; then you open the paddles at the top end, so that water refills the lock. If you're lucky the boat recovers, the right way up and in one piece.

As Calum steered *Tinker* smoothly in, we both felt the sense of near-relief you have as you come to the end of a long journey. I felt foolishly proud of the boat: she was not a 'large artefact' but a carapace, furnished like the caddis fly's shell with the ramshackle evidence of my daily life, and about to begin a fresh journey with Calum. We three crew members set ourselves to working the paddles and gates.

In every single one of the previous 160 locks, I had made sure that crew and skipper made eye contact before the lock was worked.

I drilled it into every friend or stranger who joined my crew: 'Take a second; get eye contact; get a thumbs up from the skipper.' Now, for the first time, I did not glance back to get a thumbs-up from the man at the helm. He surely knew what he was doing by now. In that small failure, I failed to look after both Calum and the boat.

In the locks he had encountered so far, Calum had always kept the boat right back in the chamber as it filled. Going uphill, that was helpful: we did not want a repeat of the episode at Stenson Lock. Going downhill, it was exactly the wrong thing to do. As she descended, *Tinker*'s stern was slowly dropping towards the great stone shelf. I did not notice, because I was winding a paddle, or chatting to Martin and Lucy as we worked. I don't remember how the familiar tasks of the lock had been divided; but I will never forget the telltale scrape of steel against stone as *Tinker*'s hull made contact with the cill. She was about to lower her whole weight onto the stone shelf, and tip forward in a heaving catastrophe. There was an unnatural shift in her movement; she began to settle at the back, with a sickening grind.

Calum knew in a flash what was happening. His eyes were wide with shock; he looked up at me, and we worked together with split-second timing. I am not a mother, but I thought like a person running to get their child out of a burning building. '*Gun it!*' I yelled. Calum was ahead of me; he threw the gear lever hard forward, to give the big engine a blast of motion while there was still a little water under the hull. For the second time in my life, I screamed 'DROP THE PADDLES'; and for the second time, a novice crew rose to the challenge. Lucy and Martin dropped their paddles in a single clean movement, staunching the escape of water out of the lock; I flew to the top end of the lock and raised the paddles there, letting water flood back in to refill and lift the boat.

Tinker lurched forward, shook herself and floated free. She shuddered along her whole length, and so did I. Calum's instant reaction had thrown *Tinker* off the stone shelf, with seconds to spare before she was stuck, but that metallic screech signalled something bad below the waterline. I looked down at Calum as the lock filled again: 'Are you okay?'

He was white as a marshmallow: we all were. 'Okay, folks, let's get her down safely and have a look,' I said. I stepped to the tiller and took over, my hand shaking as it curved around the worn wooden handle. The others worked the lock again. As the level dropped, this time without incident, I tried to imagine what damage was done. For a few seconds, the rudder had held twenty tonnes of weight. Had it been bent, or knocked entirely out of alignment? Worse still, had we jarred the engine on its mounts or done other harm? As the black oak gates heaved open, I waited to see how *Tinker* handled.

As we slid forward my stomach churned. The steering was wobbly and erratic. The rudder flapped about like a broken limb. I no longer sensed the familiar, clean response of a boat steering as instructed. *Tinker* careened to the left, then the right in a patternless judder, like a blindfolded child in a game of Blind Man's Buff. We hauled her into the side, poked the rudder with the boat hook and discussed what to do next. It was impossible to judge exactly how much damage had been done until she was out of the water, and there was no dry dock for miles.

A boat called *New Era* came down the lock as we drank tea in a state of self-pity, looking like four Eeyores on the towpath. Its skipper came to see why we all looked so bloody miserable. His name was John, and he quickly understood.

'Shall I try towing you?' he asked.

I considered. 'No, thank you,' I answered wearily. 'We'll see how we go.'

'I'll let them know as I pass through Honeystreet,' he said with a condoling gesture – and headed on, a messenger bearing bad news on the Towpath Telegraph. My mind went back to the votive offerings we had cast upon the waters a few days before, at the junction of the Kennet with the Thames. The little gods must have had better offerings than my drooping florist's roses: but then, I was probably the first to make any offerings at all for several centuries. It seemed mean to take it out on *Tinker*.

The Other Way

Arrival

It was not a great way to begin a new life.

Calum was mortified, and ready to commit *hara-kiri* on the towpath in front of me. I was ready to let him. He knew full well what the boat meant to me, and how far we had come. Truthfully, the failure was mine. I should have checked in on him as he entered the lock.

Marcus Aurelius, who died in 180 CE, presumably never found himself in this situation. If his narrow boat had been hung up on the cill, he might have said (as he does, somewhere), 'It's all in how you perceive it. You're in control ... serenity, total calm, safe anchorage.' He was right, as usual. We were not stranded far from Honeystreet in Birmingham or rural Oxfordshire, but seven short miles from our end point. If it came right down to it, I had plenty of experience bow-hauling working boats. Above all, we had plenty of biscuits.

'What's bow-hauling?' asked Lucy as I started the engine.

'Pulling the boat ourselves, along the towpath.'

'I thought it might be,' she said gloomily.

We did not need to bow-haul. *Tinker* ploughed on gamely through the drizzle, making way in a painful zig-zag through the little market town of Pewsey. As we travelled, we checked for water coming in or inexplicable jiggles. Jiggles there were none: the sturdy hull was intact. However bad the damage, it would be fixable in time.

As for safe anchorage, that came soon enough. We glimpsed the longed-for bridge, the Georgian brick building and the line of boats at Nikki's neat wharf, alongside the little chandlery shed. Her petite figure stood on the misty bank, her arms extended in welcome, calling 'Oh, WELL DONE!' Our harbinger, John, had filled her in on our accident. Nikki took a rope, tied us up and then plugged us in to the electricity supply. We stood together under the little trees that would now be my view from the kitchen, and hugged. She went 'to fetch something,' allowing me time to strip off my waterproofs, burst into tears and take some headache tablets. Ten minutes later Nikki reappeared with a box of tissues and a bottle of champagne. There were no brass bands, but there was at least a handkerchief.

No doubt the champagne helped, but taking stock I saw that things could be a lot worse. I was exactly where I needed to be. There was no immediate need to go anywhere at all. At a pinch, I could even leave repairs until the next spring, and take the autumn and winter as an enforced period of work and neighbourhood-building.

'You've made it!' said Nikki, beaming. I looked at Calum.

'You have,' he said, emerging from his cloud of guilt with a wolfish grin. *I bloody have. And* Tinker *will be healed, in time.*

'Welcome home,' said Nikki, and poured another glass.

I did leave repairs till spring. *Tinker* had a safe mooring, and my priority was to make friends, find work and make some money. Calum and I clicked neatly into a circle of half-familiar acquaintances and new friends, writers and boaters.

The wharf proved to be a floating hamlet full of laughter, where Nikki and her husband, Duncan, bustled around their hire fleet, keeping us all supplied with coal and water. My neighbours were few but characterful. One looked like Santa Claus on a good hair day; there was a married couple or two, and just one troubled divorcee who was, of course, called Dave. As boats called in to the wharf for coal or gossip, the circle of boaters expanded. Even if *Tinker* was unable to move for the moment, she was a part of a floating village once more.

This corner of the West Country was so fruitful it would make a damsel blush; the hedgerows rich with sloes and rose hips; the gardens with pear trees and damsons. I walked the chalk ridges above the wharf, often visiting the Alton Barnes White Horse which overlooked it, and learned the local folds of hill and valley. One warm afternoon I was taken aback by a new shape in the stubble below a familiar slope. Spiralling across the fields were the fractal curves of a crop circle. It looked right at home in this land of monuments and stories. I got to know Bradford-on-Avon, where the medieval Tithe Barn and the village cricket pitch added to the tender Englishness of the creamy stone buildings. I stood underneath the epic arches of the Dundas Aqueduct, listening to sea shanties drifting from the Cross Guns pub; I met up with the boaters whom I had talked to in those first trips to check out the likely moorings.

These boaters converged, as ever, in the pub: and this pub was special. My local at Honeystreet was renowned on the whole system. It was not called the Navigation. In this terrain of wide canals and wide boats, it was called The Barge. It is a joyously peculiar pub, frequented by joyous and peculiar people. The ceiling was painted with a psychedelic scene of alien visitors, green men, and crop circles, and the bar is often propped up by 'croppies' who mysteriously appear at exactly the same time as the crop circles. It is either a way station for alien visitors, or a playground for hippies with a plank and a piece of string. The Barge served a green beer called Ale-ien Abduction, and from time to time the field behind it became a colourful mini-festival with tents, braziers and wild music.

The croppies see several time maps at once, travelling between the weird and half-understood monuments of prehistory, and the modern-day villages that stand around them. There were many such intersections here: Silbury Hill, the Long Barrow at West Kennet, and Stonehenge attracted them. So, of course, did Avebury where Calum's little cottage was. He squinted out of his bedroom window one morning. 'Is it a solstice?' he asked sleepily.

'Erm, I think so, yes. Something celestial anyway,' I yawned.

'Thought so. The streets are full of Druids.'

There is only one street in Avebury, and it wasn't entirely full of Druids, but there were certainly more Druids than usual. A few hairy people were roaming about in heavy woollen capes or Peruvian knitwear. The village shop had stocked up on mead, and was now selling dowsing rods alongside Walkers crisps and pork pies. The Barge was full of dreadlocks and Druids that evening, as well as the boaters moored right outside the beer garden. It felt like a scene from Middle Earth, and I was as happy as Bilbo before the trouble with the dragons and orcs began.

As winter came in, the ochres and deep silt-browns of Wiltshire turned to pale, frosted ash colours. The wildlife around my mooring fell quiet. The insects and songbirds saved their energy for the business of staying alive in a cold season, and I did the same, hunkering down with my books and red kettle, keeping the fire stoked. Outside, the water was flinty and windblown around the rush beds. Inside, the patterned quilts of my Princess-and-the-Pea bed met a milky midwinter light from the bull's-eye glass overhead. The glass door of the stove glowed with heat. *Is it cold in the winter?* I thought to myself, smiling.

Calum and I lived our life between two habitats, one of us on land and one on the water. At his Avebury hideout, two kinds of bird kept us company in these monochrome months. Rooks stalked the pastures around the village, pecking between the frosty stones of the henge. They crowded the bare trees, shouting like drunkards at closing time. The other presence was silent and solitary; a ghostly barn owl that we regularly saw on our twilight journeys between my boat and his house. It seemed to patrol exactly the same stretch as us. Racing towards Calum and the bright kitchen of his old, oak-scented cottage, I often kept company with the soft muscled shape of the owl, a purposeful killer scanning the dark fields. It felt ominous in the true sense, a properly mythical inhabitant of other worlds and other priorities. The Irish speak of 'the thin places' where the spirit world meets the physical. Avebury is one of the thinnest. The cottage, though, was a little totem of hearth and home, thick with hope and enrichment. There was cooking, lovemaking, argument and talk; all the business of building a new life.

Meanwhile on the water, I was discovering that the K&A was just a little feral. Against the backdrop of henges, hillside figures and crop circles, the boaters were very different to the ones I had known in the mill towns and city centres of the north. There were fewer middle aged couples, fewer people in traditional jobs at the Post Office or supermarket; there were more dreadlocks, more New Agers, more alternative-lifestyle pioneers, their faces bright and dirty. Many were liveaboards on shoestring budgets. Their small boats were held together with sealing wax and string, and they travelled in a circuit of short journeys, moving frequently but not far. They were artists, wood turners, freelancers, musicians, and mechanics; people carving a life in the irregular spaces left by regular society.

Like the owl, they patrolled the same stretch over and over again, travelling between Devizes and Newbury for instance. The twenty-nine locks of Caen Hill, if not exactly a barrier between the upper and lower K&A, are a real deterrent from moving regularly between the two[†††]. People would cruise on either the top or bottom level for weeks at a time, only occasionally venturing up or down the hill with windlass in hand. This canal is suspended between two rivers and two cities – at one end the Thames and Reading, at the other the Avon and Bristol. Many boat-dwellers sensibly chose not to bother with the current at either end and stayed on the canal, an eighty-seven-mile high street of interwoven and intimate friendships.

It was a picturesque season, but a bloody cold one. On New Year's Eve the snow lay all about, deep and crisp and inconvenient. Calum and I would not be seeing in the new year together. He was elsewhere. I sat on the boat alone, telling myself that there was nothing special about this evening. Why should sitting alone on 31 December feel tragic, when sitting alone on 30 December was perfectly normal? Ten o'clock came. I put my pyjamas on. Eleven o'clock came. I decided to go to bed and see the new year in with a dram of whisky and a book.

At 11.25, I finally came to my senses. *What the hell am I thinking of?* Calum might be elsewhere, but I was right here. I would not be held hostage by circumstance. I would doll up, go out and have a ball. I would meet the new year with a shout, and in good company. I wriggled out of my pyjamas, into a pair of jeans and a sparkling backless top. I put on lip gloss and wildly impractical boots, stepped out into the vivid air and sashayed up the slushy tow path to The Barge. It was a

---

[†††] Yes, I know that only sixteen are officially Caen Hill locks. There are seven at Foxhangers, and six at the Devizes end of the flight – but 'Caen Hill' generally signifies the full twenty-nine.

clear night. The boats lining the canal were wearing ermine coats, and the water was hammered silver.

I was at the bar with fifteen minutes to spare before the chimes of Big Ben rang out. I ordered my drink and looked around me. There was a slightly peculiar atmosphere. To be fair there was always a slightly peculiar atmosphere in The Barge, but it struck me that with fifteen minutes of the old year to go, most of the people here seemed to be sober. There was warm chatter and the usual feeling of companionable excitement, but most of the young people gathered were drinking water. They were strangers, but they seemed delighted to see me and dragged me into the circle of dancers. I decided that they were probably fairies just visiting from the other world. That would explain the far away look in their eyes and the fact that they didn't seem to have quite the usual number of teeth. If fairies drank anywhere, it would surely be in The Barge. Then again, perhaps the reason was less otherworldly – and more narcotic.

The chimes rang out, there was a clamour of 'Auld Lang Syne', and the gaggle of youngsters began to drift away. One of them turned to me: 'Come back with us, eh?' *Why the hell not; it's not as if I have anywhere else to be.* We slithered and laughed our way down a snowy lane to a small house. I stepped inside, accepted a drink, took my coat off and realised with a sense of mild surprise that I had been kidnapped by friendly crackheads.

I am not complaining. They were friendly indeed, and they had planned their after party with as much forethought as any wedding planner. There seemed to be three separate areas of entertainment in the house. Downstairs was an *ad hoc* dance floor, which belonged to ravers full of MDMA. From upstairs was a swirl of slower, darker music. I had a suspicion that this was the Intravenous Zone. The third area was for soft play, in the widest sense; beanbag chairs, gangly weed

smokers and a very large sofa occupied by two women in their for-
ties. They were full of the milk of human kindness, or possibly cider.
Alcohol seemed very old-school in this company. I felt like a child on
a scooter among Hell's Angels. I settled in with my bottle of beer and
was welcomed.

That evening, I was lonely and in need of good company. They
sensed it, and understood. Some people in that room had habits and
deep troubles that I knew nothing of. For all they knew, I was a member
of the drug squad; but they took me in and showed me a raucously
good evening. We talked politics, music, and boats.

At about three o'clock I stepped outside for fresh air, since the air
in the living room was heavy with smoke. I gasped as I opened the
door; the air was fresh indeed, and the sky was clear as vodka. Above
the glittering water of the canal, the first stars of the new year were
bright. I half-remembered that in some ancient cultures the stars were
thought to be campfires around which the dead or the gods would
gather. I liked that idea of warm companionship in the cold sky. I
leaned against the gate in the lane, my head empty of anything but
stars. A young man, practised in the accidents that can happen to
intoxicated canal people late at night, came out to check on me. He
was barely twenty. He stood quietly next to me at the gate and together
we filled our eyes with starlight.

'You all right?' he asked in broad Somerset tones.

'I am,' I said. 'Thank you.'

'Glad you came?'

'Yes. I really am. Thank you for letting me share your New Year's
Eve. I'm going to head back now,' I said, nodding down the towpath.

'I'll walk you home,' he said. 'You never know what kind of people
you might meet out here in the middle of the night.'

You never do. He walked me to the gate of Honeystreet Wharf and looked down on the boats.

'Is it cold in the winter?' he asked.

The gods looked down on us from their campfires in the cold sky. We exchanged a handshake and a hug. I walked into the boat yard, and the young man picked his way back along the icy towpath; he walking into his New Year, and I into mine.

Elsewhere

If you have to fall badly ill, I can recommend doing it in a seventeenth-century cottage with low beams, floral curtains, and deep snow in the lane outside. That's how I did it. On Valentine's Day I lay in bed at Calum's cottage. Alone. He was, of course, elsewhere.

I had been taken sick. The sheets were drenched with sweat. I was clammy and unable to rest, but full of fever dreams. I felt like a Jane Austen character – the plain and ailing sister, suffering with consumption to show some haughty suitor the error of his ways while the housekeeper heats bone broth to build up the invalid's strength. I dozed and woke, snoozed and ached into the night, trying to make sense of a collapsing relationship and my own future.

A few doors away was the church of St James, built over the walls and bones of its Saxon predecessor. At the end of the street the giant stones of Avebury stood sentinel in their always-and-forever circle. I still didn't think they looked like sheep. A scant mile in the other direction, the monumental pudding-bowl of Silbury Hill stood proud and peculiar in the dark fields. The scope of human time represented within a five-minute walk of my sickbed was immeasurable. It dwarfed any event that might overturn the personal life of one sweaty woman. *Whatever bad decisions I make, time rolls on.* Just as well. If I could stop time with my bad decisions, we'd all be up shit creek.

All of the time maps I had ever known were swirling in my unquiet head. They blurred into the water map, into the real maps of north and south, into the whole cloth map of my life spattered with the small events of family, love, and work. I've always taken comfort from my own insignificance as a dot with a limited lifespan. I felt the immense and unlikely good fortune of being in this magical place, at this moment. I gave thanks for the epic journey (in canal terms) and the leap of faith that had brought me here, but I understood now that the faith was misplaced. I loved the country and the people here, but felt unexpectedly alien; and I did not love the man.

What did Marcus Aurelius have to say in this time of turmoil? 'Neither player-king nor prostitute'. He isn't always helpful, to be honest. I tried again and he did better: 'So other people hurt me? That's their problem. Their character and actions are not mine. What is done to me is ordained by nature, what I do by my own.'

You know what it's like. When your relationship is in a turbulent phase full of tension and drama, it sometimes turns out to be a passing storm that ends in a better understanding of one another. You can batten down the hatches and wait it out. At other times it is what boaters call a sinker: the end. Nothing to do but run for the lifeboats. When you're in the middle of it, thinking in circles, it's impossible to know which is which. They both feel like drowning. I was in that frantic pattern of thought which is both traumatic and boring: *What if/but then/and yet/why did I/why don't I/why should I?*

You will have your own way of working through the dramatic moments of life. Mine is poetry. I sat down in the kitchen of that tiny house, swathed myself in blankets and began to write. Poetry is what I think with. It clarifies thought, and it does the same sort of work that patient excavation used to do on the archaeological sites where I spent my twenties. You expose the bones of your own thinking, look at them with a little detachment, and try to work out what is really going on. You never know where to begin a poem, and I often bring to mind the fine advice of Arthur Ashe, the tennis player. It applies to almost any confusion in life, and certainly to poems. 'Start where you are. Use what you have. Do what you can.' *Start where you are*: I was in Avebury. *Use what you have*: that would be sadness, desperation, a wish for peace of mind. *Do what you can*: write. I wrote.

Writing a poem is like laying an egg. Each time I do it (writing a poem, that is) I remember that I am as unqualified to write a poem as I am to lay an egg. There are peculiar and unglamorous contractions, followed by a final squeeze to produce a new object. The words formed themselves on the page with the usual inky clots and crossings out, half-formed phrases and substitutions. I frisked myself for dishonesty. What came through, I hope, was a mystified love of this fairytale village mixed with a sense that I did not belong in it. The Red Lion pub, the manor house owned by the National Trust, the vicarage that I could see out of the window as I wrote the poem: all were beautiful, blameless and welcoming, but I was an upland girl in a lowland place. No gritstone here, no tall brick chimneys; a soft and forgiving prospect, not the pit-pocked landscape of extraction which, for all its faults, I belonged to.

I swear to God, until I wrote the last line of that poem I had no idea what the problem was: and until I wrote the last four words, I had no idea what the solution was. I stabbed a full stop onto the paper and looked at the ending of my poem. *Decision made.*

Behind these high red walls are gardens, pear trees. I am ravenous for limestone. I am coming home.

– from 'A diet rich in birdsong', *Kith*

All of our exes have one thing in common: they are terrible people and we can't imagine what we saw in them. You didn't need the sordid details of how the affair with Calum began, and I'll spare you the sordid details of how it ended. It involves sadness and sex, and you probably need to be drunk to get the best out of it, as I do to tell it. By the time I made up my mind to leave, it was almost exactly a year since I had decided to follow him to Wiltshire. Now, having decided to go, I had to tell him that I was going.

I would like to tell you that we did this with dignity. We did not. It was a scene. Neither of us came out of it at all well. There was melodrama, manipulation, skullduggery: I was not free with a single bound, but with a bloody thump. The blood, gratifyingly, was his: he left it on the door frame as he stormed out of the boat. He cracked his head so hard he almost fainted. Calum wobbled off down the towpath, mildly concussed. I sat on my little pink sofa and snuffled dolefully.

You're allowed a little self-pity at a moment like this. Mine wasn't solely about the loss of the man, which already felt like a net gain. It was about where to go next, personally and geographically. Was I really going to just return to the mooring I had left a year before? After careful consideration I decided that I'd rather bang nails into my own head. It wasn't just that I would have to repeat the dreary logistics of crew and boat movements; it was the horrible sensation that disappointment had won the day. I would have to start with lock 161 , remembering the lurching panic of that moment a few months before when the boat crunched against the cill; and that would be only the first of a hundred places where the landmarks of the canal would taunt me. As I worked the solitary traffic light in Reading, as I headed through Oxford past Jon Ody's workshop, as I nosed into Telford's tunnel at Harecastle – each one would be a horrible reiteration of failure. After all of that I would end up right back where I started, with my tail between my legs. *Dammit*. I wanted to make a journey, not a retreat.

My self-pity was interrupted by a thick scraping sound from the canal. The Kennet and Avon is heavily trafficked by hire boats. On this mid-March afternoon a little day boat, of the sort often hired for stag parties or family birthdays, had got stuck in the mud about fifty yards away from *Tinker*. Its hapless crew of half a dozen young (and very drunk) men were doing what new boaters often do when they go aground. They revved the engine like a motorboat and drove flat out at the underwater obstacle, hoping that with enough horsepower and optimism it would disappear. This band of brothers was digging itself deeper and deeper into trouble. The boat was hard aground – 'stemmed up' as the old boaters would say. They were leaning over the sides, wasted and jovial and likely to fall in. Groups like this can hurt themselves and cause real damage. A few years ago, a stag party on a hire boat like this one careered into a liveaboard boat close to this spot and sank it. I was really not in the mood for conversation, but I could not resume my own wallowing until they got out of theirs. I leaned out of the side hatch.

One of their number – the designated sober person for the day – caught my eye. It wasn't easy to do, since my eyes were inflated with crying and practically invisible. He was not to know that his Carry On Up The Canal crew had interrupted a moment of anguish. I must have looked like a demented owl.

'Would you like some help?' I said wearily.

'Please,' he said. He looked long suffering, like a wise man trapped in a cage with monkeys.

'Stop revving,' I said. 'Put it in reverse gently, and back off a bit.'

'Right.' He tried to do it, but the monkeys were not having it. They pushed him away from the gear lever, hooted with laughter, and stumbled precariously on the counter. In a moment their merrymaking might end with someone's leg tangled in the propeller.

'Lads!' I called. 'You need to go back a bit, then you'll be able to crack on.' More cackling, now with added finger-pointing. Someone may have said 'darling'. The wise man winced. The monkeys cavorted. I watched them for a moment longer, and then snapped. Reader, forgive me. I was heartbroken and angry and in no mood for jokes. I had not an ounce of courtesy left in me.

'Fuck you then!'

I slammed the hatch shut, fell on the sofa and burst into tears again. For some reason this cartoonish gang of louts had made the personal catastrophe a little harder, a little more isolating. The monkeys fell silent. I heard a brisk word or two exchanged. They reversed, got out of trouble, carried on. The silence was worse than the revving.

Five minutes later, there was a gentle knock at the window. It was the single clear-headed member of the party, come to apologise for his friends' foolishness. I have no idea where he had found a bunch of flowers on his short trip down the towpath, but he had. Even as I write this I find myself tearing up. He was about twenty-two and had no reason to expect a warm welcome from the hysterical middle-aged woman who had just screamed at him, but he knew distress when he saw it. It was a small act of kindness to bring me a handful of colour, on a day when I was sorely in need of it.

'I'm sorry for shouting.' I said. 'It's not been a good day. You weren't to know.'

'It's fine,' he said. 'Hope things get better.'

And they did. They began to get better within the next half hour.

Calum's footprints and those of the flower-bearer were still visible on the muddy towpath when the phone rang. *Why*, I asked myself, *is Roger Fuller ringing me from his famous little boatyard in Staffordshire?* I cannot imagine now why I picked up at that moment. I must have sounded like an advert for Lemsip, muffled and hoarse.

'Is this a good time to call?' said a Midlands voice on the other end.

'Not really, no, Roger.'

'Right-oh,' he said, not listening. 'Do you still want that mooring in Stone?'

'Er ... Well, I did a year ago. I'm in Wiltshire now on the Kennet and Avon.'

'Right. Well, do you want the mooring or not?' Roger was being joyfully obtuse. He was probably measuring a piece of steel plate at the time, and still not listening.

Pause.

I had decided to leave Calum, but I hadn't decided where I was going next. Returning to Macclesfield was out of the question. Much as I had loved it, I couldn't face the shame of drifting into the same mooring with the same neighbours, as if nothing had happened. It would have felt like a horrible joke at my own expense.

'Are you still there, Jo?'

'Yes, Roger. Yes. I do want the mooring. I'll be there—' *Oh, what the hell. For the sake of symmetry, it might as well be ...* 'August Bank Holiday, Roger. I'll see you then.'

I hung up, sat down, and wrote Roger a cheque. I pulled Nicholson's Volume 7 from the bookshelf by the stove. Then I walked to The Barge Inn. I had some thinking to do.

The bottom inspector

According to the Chinese philosopher Lao Tzu, the journey of a thousand miles begins with a single step. It was easy for him to be philosophical; he had been dead for 2,000 years and he didn't have a broken narrow boat. *Tinker* was still in bad shape. The damage done in the very last lock of our southward journey had wounded her. The engine would start and she would make a valiant attempt to move, but she steered like a supermarket trolley with a piece of chewing gum stuck to its wheel. The first step in my own journey – rather less than a thousand miles – was to find a boatyard. I explained to a non-boating friend that I needed to get the boat out of the water and see the hull to assess damage. 'Ah,' she said sagely. 'You need your bottom inspected.' I did. I poured a whisky to help my meditations and consulted Nicholson in search of a bottom inspector.

The nearest dry dock was at Semington, fifteen miles away. There were two obstacles between me and it, though the first was only a minor inconvenience: a seasonal stoppage. In winter the canal authorities often stop canal traffic to do repairs, and these stoppages block the navigation just as roadworks block a road. It was a seasonal part of boating life and would be lifted in a few weeks. The second obstacle was Caen Hill.

Caen Hill is one of the UK's most famous lock flights. It is famous because there are twenty-nine of the damned things. The longest continuous lock flight in the UK tumbles down the slope in a colossal ladder of black and white beams, as if a gigantic piano had fallen downhill shedding keys as it went. It was very beautiful at this time of year; lambs' tail blossoms dangled over the growing water pepper and the side ponds, built as mini-reservoirs to conserve water, were jellied with frogspawn. To a tourist the scene looks charming and picturesque. To a solo boater with no local crew, and with a deranged boat that wants only to travel in circles, it looks like a pain in the bum. I was disheartened. I had made the decision to leave Calum and head north again, but I couldn't see a way to do either without feeling humiliated. The additional burden of a famously long lock flight with no help seemed like another obstacle. I consulted my usual source of inspiration: 'The obstacle is the way,' said Marcus Aurelius serenely. *Oh, do shut up Marcus.*

A broad lock, as you may have guessed, takes two narrow boats side by side. It can be a companionable affair, if you meet another boat travelling in the same direction as yourself. Your boats slide in side by side, and you travel together, sharing locks all the way up or down a hill. You drink tea with your fellow skipper and watch serenely as your crews run around like terriers far above you, doing the hard work. The single-handed boater has a less relaxing experience. I had not yet built up a gang of local boaters who could help me with locks in return for the usual currency of biscuits and bacon. How then would I get to the bottom inspectors of Semington? Why, I would tweet my way there.

At that time, Twitter was not bedogged with conversations about fascism and/or Elon Musk. It was a new-fangled extension to the Towpath Telegraph. Twitter meant that you could quickly pass on news of an obstruction or a stoppage, typing a message with one hand while waiting for a lock to fill. It was worth a try as a means of recruitment. I typed this message in, tagging a local canal group: *Hey @KACanalTimes – anyone free to help me down Caen Hill on 26 March, and a few more to Semington the day after that? Tea/biscuits and gratitude.* Radio silence. It turned out that canal time operates even on social media. The first reply came six days later. *Can offer two people – what time start and where ... and boat name?*

By the time I arrived at the top lock, those two people had become nine. They included not only the two strangers who had replied to my Twitter message but one young poet who had never worked a lock in his life, two trans women for whom boating life was the least of their adventures, my Honeystreet friend Nikki, and two smiling musicians who had come along for the ride. These people were indeed going to be the core of a new boating family.

Some of the crew were on bicycles, some were old hands with long-standing experience of lock wheeling, and others were total novices who patiently absorbed instruction. *Tinker* made her wounded, zig-zag path along the canal to the top lock, and with my new allies the boat dropped down the lock flight in a companionable rush of activity. By the time we got to the bottom of the hill, the trainees had served a full apprenticeship and were rather disappointed to find that the twenty-ninth lock was the last one. We tied up on an unseasonably warm March afternoon and cracked open a crate of cheap beer. The crew were lively and full of their little achievements. It seemed that if I only asked, there would be assistance and community galore to help me through any small or large trials. Perhaps the old emperor knew what he was talking about. The obstacle, as it turned out, was indeed the way.

As *Tinker* crawled towards the dry dock for repairs, I passed many of the boats that had called in to Honeystreet for supplies in the cold months. Winter had been a chilly white corridor, with occasional glimpses of neighbours wheeling firewood down the towpath in a haze of chimney smoke. We had hunkered down; each boater withdrawing to a floating burrow, with the stove burning bright and the air a little stuffy. A thin layer of coal dust and remnant ash settled on shelves and furniture, and we pined for fresh air. In my high nest of bedding, there was an ongoing battle against the condensation caused by sleepy warm breath.

Now, everyone on the canal was enjoying the great unfurling that happens in spring. Moored boats threw open their windows and side hatches. People were rolling up canvas covers and wiping panes of glass to let in the light. A sweep of air and movement rushed through our slender living spaces, and we began again to live a semi-outdoor life. The relief was all the greater, because it had been a particularly *wintry* winter; thick snow on the towpaths, glassy icicles hanging from the thatched eaves in every village, and the old stones of Avebury ringing out with the stark calls of rooks. Avebury was behind me; Calum was behind me. As *Tinker* limped into Semington, both she and I were licking our wounds.

Some places are special because of their situation, others because of pleasing architecture and some because the people who live there make it special. Semington Dock had all three qualities. It was one of the pocket-sized canal settlements where a couple of houses, a bonfire, and a gaggle of unorthodox people make every day a memorable one, full of laughter and sensation.

Tinker and I made our wobbly way towards the twin dry docks, each with a pitched roof like a big shed. I heard boisterous conversation from under one of them: 'FUCKING HELL JASON!' There was a burst of masculine laughter. Jason had evidently done something amusing. Banter was part of the soundtrack of Semington, as the regular employees threw insults and jokes across the dock. The other parts in the orchestra were performed by songbirds, chickens, two floppy-eared spotted pigs, and the Kennet and Avon itself – a constant presence as it ran in and out of a great lock. I tied up opposite a solid yellow stone house which sat like a block of butter at the lock side. In it lived the boatyard proprietors Ian and Liz, though Liz had a side hustle as a full-time GP. I went in to see them, dodging ginger-feathered chickens and meeting two small girls in flowing dresses.

'Ah, fairies!' I said.

'We are PRINCESSES', scowled the smaller girl, brandishing what I now understood to be a regal mace. Chastened, I scooted into the house. Liz and Ian were transparently genuine people who welcomed a constantly shifting population of boaters. There was always something simmering in their kitchen; stew, a pan of jam, a pot of coffee. I explained what had happened. I was sure that in her brief contact with the stone cill, *Tinker* had taken a serious knock to the rudder or even (impossibly) the propeller. She was steering like a bike with a bent wheel. Ian stroked his greying goatee and listened patiently. 'Right,' he said. 'Let's get you into the dry dock and have a look.'

The boatyard was the tidiest I've ever seen, which is to say it was the only tidy boatyard I have ever seen. Jason, who elicited the comical shout as I pulled in to Semington, was a thirty-something mechanic whose freckles and perpetual smile made him look like a choirboy in overalls. The other men of the yard were both boaters, so different to one another that they fitted like jigsaw pieces into a strong and solid friendship. Tony was a stocky merchant sailor, immaculately shaven-headed, with a big heart and a loud mouth. His boat, moored at the end of Liz and Ian's garden, was spotless. His neighbour Geoff was a slight, resourceful man of Traveller stock, rarely seen without a spanner in one hand and a spliff in the other. Geoff's boat was extraordinary. A former lifeboat with additions of his own, it was a silver creation which was almost spherical. It had the air of a Martian pudding-bowl. It looked as if he had made it himself out of colanders, which, after meeting him, seemed very likely. Geoff was a mix of naughty resourcefulness and open-handed joy.

They swung into action as *Tinker* limped into a narrow dock full of water. A gate was dropped, a pump switched on and slowly the water began to drain away. Within half an hour, the boat was sitting on bostocks, the blocks which held her off the bottom. Her sway and shimmy were gone: she was as helpless as a car held up on bricks. I climbed up a ladder to fetch a few things as the last water fell away, and felt the utter strangeness of a boat out of its element. *Tinker* was inanimate, corpse-like; as solid and immoveable as a house. This was the moment of truth, when we could assess the damage. The bottom inspectors set to work.

There was the bash of a heavy hammer, a jangle of chains, and soon the rudder was hanging in mid-air above the boat. It was a dark piece of thick metal, the size of a laptop. It was visibly bent, like a car door after a smash. *Tinker*'s back end looked naked and disabled. I couldn't see underneath her, but one of the lads was sliding underneath to see if there were serious dents or scrapes in various important bits of metal. They have wonderful names: skeg, stock, pintle. They sound like a progressive rock band. No mechanic likes to have the vehicle owner hovering over him, so I was dispatched to drain the coffee pot in Ian's kitchen. An hour later I wandered back, full of trepidation and expecting bad news. Jason greeted me with a broad smile. 'Done', he said.

'What?'

'Done. It was just the rudder.'

'So ... ?'

'So we stuck it in a vice and beat the crap out of it,' supplied Tony. 'Sorted!'

The repair was complete, and the boat was fit for purpose again in the time it had taken me to drink a very good cup of coffee. I also had a pot of marmalade. It was a win all round. With a little goodwill and Tony's strong arm, the damage had been repaired. *Tinker* was whole again; and I was beginning to feel a little better myself.

'You can bugger off now', said Tony.

'I'm not sure I want to,' I said, meeting his eye. *Oh dear*. Spring time. The sap is rising.

The Other Way

from Boat in Dry Dock

for Tony
[...]
She floats again. She bobs
and bumps her nose against the gate.
She holds. The welcome shift
of everything, the balance
and the give!

There was pear blossom in the dockside orchard, warblers were warbling and buntings bunting. At last, I was free to explore the K&A by water. I did so with Semington as my base, returning every few days to giggle with the princesses or to spend an evening at the Semington Arms with the dock family. One thing to explore was the unlikely concentration of pillboxes on the GHQ Blue Line. Improbably, the Kennet and Avon was a top-secret military boundary during the Second World War. Machine gun emplacements and secret strongholds were nestled in the hedgerows. Had the Nazis invaded, this corridor of blossom would have been the last line of resistance for the Home Guard. Happily, Field Marshal Montgomery pointed out that the resources being put into this rearguard defence might be better spent on making sure we weren't invaded in the first place. The towpaths of Semington were never muddied by the regimental boots of storm troopers.

As I travelled, I chatted to boaters and discovered just how unusual the K&A is. It was a community apart, like one of those inland lakes where strange species are discovered after millions of years evolving in isolation. Mark, from a boat called *Nutty Noah*, talked to me about his PhD and explained that he would be a Romanian prince 'when my grandfather dies'. His dog appeared from the cabin and joined us. 'That's Maggie', said the prince. Maggie fell gently sideways, resting her weight against my leg. She was recovering from a broken back, explained Mark, and could not stand for long. 'I've trained her,' he said, 'to lean against women.' This seemed oddly specific, but I could see that if I stepped away the dog would fall over. 'It's hard to meet women when you're a shepherd, you see,' said Mark enigmatically.

As we spoke, a young man appeared beside us on the towpath. He was carrying a wok. 'Are you the person who wanted the wok?' he asked. I was not. 'Right. Sorry,' he said. 'Someone down here wanted a wok.' He was downsizing, from a sixty-foot boat to a twenty-eight-foot boat, and getting rid of possessions. 'I hope you're a tidy person,' I said, telling him about the twenty-four-foot Springer on which I had cooked the ill-fated Christmas goose. He laughed. 'In London you'd pay £500 a week for a space like that,' he said.

I tied up at Semington once more that evening, to meet the boat-yard crew. We were going to the pub for a summit meeting. It was time to think about moving on. I was already full of that strange near-nostalgia that boaters are familiar with. It's the opposite of homesickness; you have a sense of missing a place before you have actually left. This place and its people were magical, but I wanted clear, shallow water between me and Calum. I had itchy feet again, and if I were to head north at all, I had better do it while my old friendships and working contacts were still intact. That luscious mooring in Stone beckoned me with its plot of land and nodding elderflowers. I needed to figure out my route to Roger Fuller's boatyard.

'You don't *have* to go at all,' said Tony wistfully. It was true. The West Country had welcomed me: the people peculiarly charming and charmingly peculiar. Yet it was not my country. I had never felt more northern than in this south-western idyll. I needed high chimneys and low drystone walls spotted with lichen. My country had stone edges and moorland heather in it, not white horses and crop circles.

A huddle of friends awaited me when I got to the bar with a sheaf of Nicholson guides under my arm. There were several routes to consider, especially around Birmingham. I could dawdle and explore, or I could press on. All options would be time-consuming. Another boater walked into the bar as I started turning the pages.

'Planning an invasion of Normandy?' he asked, looking over the outspread Nicholson guides. He was a former sailor, I recalled. We explained my forthcoming journey. 'How long is it going to take you?' he asked.

'Well, it took me just over a month to get down here last summer,' I said, 'and it took a lot of organising. I'm not really looking forward to doing it all again, to be honest.'

'You don't have to,' he said. He took a swig of his pint. 'You could go the Other Way.'

I wasn't quite with him. Tony, a former merchant sailor, got the gist immediately. 'In a *narrow boat*?' he cackled. 'No chance!'

It dawned on me what they meant. I laughed too. 'Oh, bloody hell,' I said. 'I'm daft. But I'm not that daft!'

'Suit yourself,' said the stranger with a shrug. 'But it would only take nine days.'

Reader, I *am* that daft. I went the Other Way.

I blame it on Marcus Aurelius. 'You can see what needs to be done. If you can see the road, follow it. Cheerfully, without turning back,' he advised.

The usual way from the luscious orchards to the purple elderflower bush of Limekiln Wharf would be to simply reverse the southward journey of the previous summer. I would go up the twenty-nine locks of Caen Hill, and east: past Honeystreet, past The Barge, past the Alton Barnes White Horse, and on through Newbury to Reading. At the spot where the little gods of the Kennet met the larger gods of the Thames, I would turn left (giving them a piece of my mind as I went, for a fat lot of good they had done me) and head north to Oxford. I would slalom once more through Brindley's curves, around the obstinate windmill at Wormleighton; then past Napton, where I had first seen *Tinker* with Skipper Jon, and on through the urban waters of Birmingham and Stoke to reach Stone. At least I would stop before reaching the grim portal of the Harecastle Tunnel.

In each and every place, I would remember how hopeful the earlier journey had been, as *Tinker* ploughed towards Calum the previous year. It would be an exercise in poking at an open wound repeatedly; and each day I would be joined by friends who knew very well that I was returning in a spirit of shame and disappointment. I would travel 200 miles with my tail between my legs. It sounded unappealing.

The Other Way bypassed nearly the whole of this long route. It would take, as the man in the pub had said, nine days. I would be going quickly, in a spirit of adventure, with my head held high. This did not sound like defeat. It was a whole new adventure. *I am woman, hear me roar,* etc.

The only hitch was that short cut, which took twenty days off the journey: a stretch of water that a sensible narrow boat skipper would not contemplate. *Tinker*, who was at home bumbling around the untroubled canals, would have to dip her toes into the second-highest tidal range in the world – the Bristol Channel, and the estuary of the Severn.

Underneath the south coast of Wales, Severn is in her full pomp. Any river is a living thing but this one is more alive than most, and her potency is partly a question of volume. The tidal rise and drop of the Severn is the second highest in the world: only the Bay of Fundy in Canada has a greater range. Between high tide and low, there is up to fourteen metres of difference. At high tide the whole landscape is full of water, glimmering and deep. A few hours later the whole estuary is a broad, shallow bed of rich mud, picked over by oystercatchers and waders until the water rushes back in, millions of tons of liquid repossessing the inlet.

It isn't just water that comes back, but the rich deposits that make the banks shift shape each day. Every day the river lifts, shifts and deposits up to ten million tonnes of silt, bundling it along in cloudy currents at up to seven metres per second. It drops it in newly formed sand banks or bars of mud. Some of these barriers are fixed. Others change from one week to the next. If *Tinker* and I should tip into these velvet currents or hit one of the shifting hazards, we would be swallowed up without a moment's notice. I had always thought of Severn as a drowning river, thick with eels and mysteries. I looked it up on the Canal and River Trust website. 'The section below Sharpness,' it advised, 'is not recommended for inland craft, unless they are equipped for a short sea voyage.'

'What could possibly go wrong?' I said to Tony.

'No idea, but I'm coming for the ride,' he said.

Westward Ho!

Rolt said of the pottery workers around Stoke that among them 'there is no social distinction but that of capability', and the same is true of boaters. It doesn't matter if you are a rocket scientist or a road sweeper; on the canal, you will be judged by how you handle a boat and how much you know about fixing a leak. Among the most capable boaters on the K&A were Dru and Suzanne, skippers of *Eve* and *Electra* respectively. Suzanne was a musician, Dru an artist and travelling bicycle fixer; both were experimental, curious, and indifferent to convention. Each of them had rolled up to help me through the Caen Hill locks, and then locked me into their own network.

As I told Dru and Suzanne of my plan, their ears pricked up. They liked an adventure. By the time we had finished our conversation, both were resolved to join me on the trip in Suzanne's boat *Electra*. There was no stopping them, and we all liked the idea of a shared adventure. Within days, Suzanne had signed up for a VHF radio course. Dru was an old hand at sailing on the briny deep, and needed nothing but an excuse to join us. It wasn't quite circumnavigating the globe but for a few exciting hours, we would certainly sail off the edge of the world described on Nicholson's linear maps. 'Here be dragons!' said Suzanne in her most Gothic voice.

Tinker and *Electra* leapfrogged each other westward along the canal, sometimes travelling together and sometimes apart. Boating in company was a joy, as we shared the broad locks and the work of getting through them. We hopped off to share a towpath walk from time to time. In Bradford-on-Avon we strolled through the small town with author Richard Beard, an old friend of Dru's, and stood in the medieval tithe barn as the sun threw triangular wedges of light into the dark space. Bradford has a Quaker meeting house which, by chance, I found on a Sunday morning just as the meeting was about to begin. Many of the people I most admire are Quakers: in my experience they always wear a fleece and sensible shoes, and a woman in that uniform was just going in to the meeting house. She gave me an encouraging smile. 'Would you like to come and join us for the meeting?' she said.

'Thank you but, er, I'm not ... '

'It doesn't matter. Come in.'

So I did. There were no Bibles, no large Christian posters exhorting me to look at footsteps in the sand; just a circle of people sitting together on comfortable chairs, in comfortable silence. 'Together' was the key word. It was the simplest and most perfect form of community.

To my surprise, emotion welled up inside me as we sat peacefully sharing the minutes. The recent weeks of break-up and boat repair, of settling and almost immediately deciding to leave, overflowed and the tears came spilling out – silently, of course. A couple of people nodded understandingly. Overwhelm was welcome here, and perhaps not new. One or two people stood to speak when moved to do so – about family, about gratitude – and sat again. After half an hour, the lady who had encouraged me in to the building stood up.

Quietly, she said: 'Since our friend Helen's death, I have been thinking about grace. The loss of love is very sad. I was thinking that when we are sad, then we experience grace in love, the love of other people round us.'

She sat down. It was a moment of great intimacy. Her words were spoken without ego or a desire to impress. They were exactly the words I needed to hear at that moment. I walked back to the dappled water, to meet another friendly crew for lunch at the Lock Inn Café; vastly encouraged, and lucky to have so much grace about me.

Tony was with me, full of smiles and smelling of sun cream as *Tinker* arrived at Bath Deep Lock, the second deepest in the country. The deepest on the whole system is Tuel Lane Lock near Rochdale, and I have been through that one too. There are three inches difference between them. It's not the three inches that you notice: it's the nineteen-foot fall. As the boat descended into this minor canyon, Tony was far above me, working the lock gear. There was an unnerving feeling of being lowered into a grave as the boat dropped, and dropped, and kept dropping, descending twice as far as in most locks.

It did that because this *is* really two locks. Not even the most ambitious engineer of the canal age would have dared to create a single chamber of this depth; it was built in 1976 by combining two locks. That explained the curiosity of a lock with two numbers. Bath Deep Lock is number 8/9. When Tony leant over the edge to check on me, I saw only his silhouette against the bright blue sky, a man-shaped outline at the top of a man-made cliff. Steering *Tinker* out, I felt the gentle tug of current as we joined the mild river Avon.

The Romans famously called this city Aquae Sulis, prudently naming it after the local river goddess who made hot water run out of the ground. If the little gods of the Kennet and Avon were disgruntled enough with me to hang up my boat on a lock cill, who knows how a grumpy Sulis might have punished the colonising Romans when they built a new town on top of her shrines and filled it with frolicking sex tourists. So, they did their usual trick of keeping the site sacred, and rebranding it. Among my favourite archaeological relics are the lead curse tablets that were thrown into the water by Roman bathers. If someone stole your best cloak or hat while you were bathing, you could buy a small sheet of lead alloy and write a curse on it with a sharp point, then offer it to Sulis by throwing it into the green water. Here's a typical one:

> Docimedis has lost two gloves. He asks that the person who stole them should lose his mind and his eyes in the temple where she appoints.

It seems excessive. Perhaps they were very nice gloves.

If you laid all the layers of the time map on top of one another in Bath, you would see a Roman constellation of black dots around the hot springs: temples, buildings, a small garrison. In later layers, there would be great blanks as Angles, Saxons, and Normans ranged over a largely abandoned site. An Anglo-Saxon poet of the eighth or ninth century stood in the mysterious, half-broken buildings and wrote a poem called 'The Ruin': 'What walls and gables, wonders still of workmanship!' The eighteenth-century layer would add a new flurry of dots to the map: some on the line of the new canal, with its warehouses and stable yards, and others in grand curves where the famous Adam crescents housed the well-to-do. They came to take the waters and give Jane Austen her raw material, but some of those who passed through were canal builders, engineers and navvies. Stone masons left their angular, chiselled marks in the lock walls and bridges to show which blocks they had cut, and to make sure they were paid for them. Most of them are as anonymous as the Anglo-Saxon poet. I thought of them all as I read Jacob Polley's translation of 'The Ruin':

> And what of the wrights
> and hammer-men, the mortar-mixers and heavers
> of slab? A long time laid off, fast in the earth.

Tony walked down from the lock to join me.

We enjoyed the peace of the boat, now quiet after hours of chugging, and sat on the roof to eat lunch. It was a perfect city mooring, just below the railway station and within easy reach of the town. The citizens and tourists of Bath were hardly aware of this spot, while for us the busy streets were no more than a quiet backdrop to the river. My back yard was full of Georgian buildings, modern supermarkets, and the rich cultural life of a fine European city. Next morning, the river was flat as a mirror, reflecting the waterside warehouses – and lifting over them, the same suspended fig shape that Gilbert White had seen over Selborne in 1784: a hot-air balloon. As the balloon drifted out of sight, something more urgent, more sleek, made a bump in the river. It headed towards some invisible landmark, and began to play in an outfall of water at the foot of the nearby lock. Never before had I seen an otter in a navigation like this. They are bio-indicators, who need clean water and a rich source of food to thrive. They are back on our canals after years of decline caused by industry, pesticides, and hostile landowners; and here was one, cheekily playing in the middle of Bath in broad daylight.

Boaters don't have a monopoly on these special moments. The house-dwellers of Bath may well have seen the balloon, and a few people walking the dog might have seen the otter: but we had a unique perspective as both local residents and newcomers, with the open eyes of travellers greedy to notice everything. For one morning the local buildings, regional foods, the landmarks, or dialect that belong to this place belonged briefly to me too. The balloon, the otter, and the bright blue morning were added to my ownership of the Avon.

Bristol, Brunel and Telford

In my whole journey since leaving Macclesfield, I had only touched on one major city. That was Birmingham, the true capital of our alternative England. Now, as *Electra* and *Tinker* joined up to travel onwards, we arrived in Bristol – one of the great river cities which, like Newcastle or Liverpool, loves its river and has a confident sense of its own identity. Our two boats cruised into the floating harbour through a wide corridor of warehouses and grand barges, with plastic cruisers and seagoing ships tied alongside. We could smell the sea, or the idea of the sea.

We drew up to the floating pontoon in front of the Arnolfini gallery, and as I bent to loop the ropes through the mooring rings a huge cheer went up from the quayside bar opposite. *How very gratifying.* I knew my skills had improved since my early days of boating, but this seemed like an extreme reaction to the tying of a half hitch. It turned out that the cheers were from a bar full of tennis fans. *Tinker* and *Electra* had come to rest at the exact moment when Andy Murray hit the winning stroke to take his first Wimbledon title. The floating harbour is the liveliest part of Bristol, surrounded by drinking holes and crossed by a striking bridge. A few narrow boats make their homes here, nestling against the high harbour walls, but they look weedy in the company of the swelling barges and tug boats.

To our left were the huge travelling cranes of the M Shed, a former transhipment warehouse. It is now a museum, and inside it is an unusual exhibit: the paint-daubed statue of eighteenth-century slaver and city worthy, Edward Colston. The tipping of this effigy into the harbour in 2020 was a deliberate nod to the fate of thousands of Africans who were drowned on the Middle Passage. Each generation addresses itself to the past with different accusations, old omissions and new inclusions. This monument has its part to play in that conversation. The past is what happened: history is what we tell ourselves about what happened. As Colston's statue lies on its back, bespattered with paint in a museum case, its meaning has changed: and a damn good thing too.

It was early evening. The sky over the harbour was turning violet: it was one of those summer evenings when you are particularly aware of warm air on your skin, and when sound travels across water most clearly. We were relaxing in preparation for our first taste of the Bristol Channel. Around us were a lot of people who were more relaxed still. The neighbouring boat was hosting a party: dozens of women were spilling around it, standing on the pontoon in groups or perching their bottoms on the gunnels. Dru, Suzanne and I looked sideways at them. Unlike us, they had make-up on. Unlike us, their hair was beautifully arranged and clean. Entirely unlike us, they were wearing floaty summer dresses and strappy shoes. Tony was delighted by our new neighbours, but they did not look like typical boaters.

A woman of about sixty walked down the pontoon to greet us, slightly uncertain in her step. 'Sorry about all this noise!' she said. 'It's my daughter's fortieth birthday. I've come to ask if you would like to join us.' We declined to gatecrash, but raised a cheery glass in the direction of the party.

'Can I join *you* for a moment?' said the woman. We hadn't expected that.

She seemed glad of a moment's peace. 'It's the first time I've been out in a while,' she said quietly. When she explained why, we marvelled that she was able to come out at all. A few weeks before, she and her partner had been walking back from one of the nearby bars to their boat. 'That one over there,' she nodded across the harbour.

They were too close to the edge. The man stumbled; the woman made a grab to catch him as he overbalanced; they fell in together. It was midsummer and the water was not cold, but her partner was unfit, or a weak swimmer. Perhaps he was stunned by the shock of falling. Whatever the reason, as the woman struggled towards the harbour wall and the steps that would give her a safe route out, she realised that he was no longer swimming with her.

Six weeks later this lady put on her dress, her waterproof mascara, and her bravest face for her daughter's birthday party in the same spot. 'The show must go on,' she said. We stood in silence for a moment as the women at the other end of the pontoon shared a landmark birthday. I remembered the Quaker meeting at Bradford-on-Avon, and the woman who had stood to speak there. The loss of love, she said in that kindly circle, is very sad; but 'we experience grace in the love of other people round us'. Here in Bristol, this boater – half-cut, wholly grief-stricken, but surrounded by laughter — seemed to have plenty of opportunities for grace.

'Wait there,' I said.

She did so without question, swaying gently with a glass of fizz in her hand. I walked into the boat and lifted from the wall the bright turquoise plaque that had hung there since my first week aboard. It was inscribed with the Raymond Carver poem I read at my father's funeral, 'Late Fragment'. The poem was a reminder of my dad's great achievement:

And did you get what
you wanted from this life, even so?
I did.
And what did you want?
To call myself beloved, to feel myself
beloved on the earth

Back on the pontoon, I handed it to the woman. 'Are you sure?' she said.

'Absolutely.' Poetry doesn't fix anything, I knew; but sometimes it helps.

The next morning we swung out of the floating harbour and headed for the lock that would take us onto the tidal Avon. In the early sunlight, we slid past two historic ships; two monuments to bloody-minded determination. The first was the replica of the *Matthew*, the astonishingly tiny ship that John Cabot took across the Atlantic in 1497 to make landfall at Newfoundland. The *Matthew* was only eleven feet longer than *Tinker*, and carried a payload of around fifty tonnes – slightly more than two working canal boats. I would have been nervous taking it across the Solent, let alone the Atlantic. The second was the steamer *SS Great Britain*, built by Isambard Kingdom Brunel at the height of his fame and launched here in 1843. *Great Britan* was a giant, 100 feet longer than anything else on the seas, and a floating showcase for British ironmasters: she had an iron hull, iron masts, iron railings, even iron hawsers in the rigging instead of hemp ropes. She rolled like a barrel in high seas and went hard aground twice in her first two years of service; but as we passed her on our way to the river lock, she looked lean and proud.

Dru and Suzanne reached the lock before me, in *Electra*. We locked out together, onto the river Avon. It was fast flowing, channelled between the steep and wooded sides of the Avon Gorge; and soon we reached its best known landmark, another brainchild of Brunel, the rock star engineer. The *Great Britain* belonged to his years of fame, but the Clifton Suspension Bridge marked his emergence into the limelight.

In 1829, Bristol had growing pains. It needed a bridge over the Avon Gorge; and it wanted a fine one. The Society of Merchant Venturers launched a competition to design it, and wanting a high-status judge they turned to the man nicknamed 'Pontifex Maximus', or the great bridge builder. By now Thomas Telford was the most famous engineer of his time. He had changed the landscape of Britain and Europe; he had put in place dozens of bridges, harbours and aqueducts, seventeen canals and thousands of miles of road, opening up the inhospitable terrain of Snowdonia and the Scottish Highlands. Telford had recently completed the largest suspension bridge in the world over the Menai Straits, 'a wonder then and now' as his biographer Julian Glover says.

Just as the *Great Britain* was not Brunel's finest hour, the competition for the Clifton crossing was not Telford's. The competition attracted a handful of entries, including an audacious one from Brunel, twenty-three years old and just at the beginning of his career. Telford, seventy-two years old, and at the end of his, did not like Brunel's design. He didn't like any of the others either; and in an unfortunate display of hubris, Thomas Telford awarded the prize to – himself. The Society of Merchant Venturers were taken aback. At first they consented: but on closer examination of Telford's design, they realised that it was, not to put too fine a point on it, ugly as hell. They ran the competition again, and this time excluded him from the running.

It is no surprise that Telford was more cautious than Brunel. Everyone was more cautious than Brunel. Telford's design had foundations deep in the riverbed: Brunel's perched high above, in the sides of the gorge. Telford's bridge would be wide at the bottom, but narrow at road level because he was reluctant to take a suspension bridge across more than 600 feet. Brunel's track bed was 702 feet long. Telford's architectural flourish was a pair of Gothic-looking structures in the bottom of the gorge; Brunel's was a daring pair of Egyptian-style towers standing high above the road.

Even then, Brunel did not win the competition. The committee chose a design by Smith and Hawkes of the Eagle Foundry in

Birmingham. At this point Brunel drew himself up to his full five feet and came in, all guns blazing, to persuade them to change their mind again. Committee members do not seem to have been very strong-minded men. Once again, they blinked; they changed their decision; Brunel got the gig. Telford, presumably, went back to building the Macclesfield Canal, which was close to completion.

Brunel's bridge was not opened in his lifetime. Expensive and difficult, it only opened to traffic in 1864; but it is an absolute corker. *Electra* led the way underneath it, and we revelled in its monumental towers, the elegant curve of the suspension chains. The Bristol Avon was tidal but gentle, a magical river whose most impressive trick is to disappear entirely. When we left the city at breakfast time, the river carried us easily under the hanging bridge. The water was broad, gentle, and for all we knew, thirty feet deep; but if you look down from the bridge at low tide, you will see that even a paper boat would struggle to pass in the muddy ditch that is left behind as the tide pulls back through Clifton Gorge.

At high tide, we had no difficulty. The gnarly cliffs were walls of red sandstone banded with limestone, making *Electra* look like a toy boat as she motored forward between them. The landscape grew altogether larger and the river began to gather force. *We're not in Kansas anymore, Toto.* In the high trees on the city side, a heronry was full of squawking pterodactyls. It felt like a prehistoric place, but the sturdy shape of *Electra* was one proof that it was not.

We were approaching Avonmouth where river debouches into the wide Bristol Channel. This would be our first taste of the great channel and its famously turbulent waters. The river would draw us briefly west – 'As if to America!' Suzanne had said cheerily that morning. We would be dipping into the channel for only twenty minutes or so, en route to the harbour at Portishead: this was just a momentary experience of the estuary. Nonetheless as the giant wind turbines and transhipment docks of Avonmouth appeared, misty silhouettes in the early morning light, it all felt unsettlingly maritime.

Suzanne and I throttled up at the same moment, pushing our two boats out into waters greater than they had ever handled before. *Tinker* pushed her nose out into a channel spangled with sunshine, and bucked slightly as the current took hold. She and *Electra* both turned on a sixpence to travel with the tide. It was heading west, pulling unimaginable volumes of water towards the Irish Sea, and we were riding it. The propeller bit willingly into the new depths, and for twenty-five minutes we bowled along in summer breeze. *Electra* had the unaccustomed froth of a bow wave at the front as I looked across at her. Suzanne was grinning as she stood at the tiller, her long hair whipping around her face.

We swung round a harbour wall into the river lock, and rose into the safe haven of Portishead Marina. Our two boats tied up alongside dozens of sleek, white seagoing vessels; we filled our water tanks, ran our washing machines with their electricity and set up collapsible chairs on the pontoon for an impromptu picnic. It had been an exhilarating sample of what was to come. *What the hell am I doing?* I thought. The answer came back loud and clear: *I am having the time of my life.*

Portishead

I've always thought that the map of Wales looks rather like a pig's head. Under its jowls, the wide stretch of water that separates it from Devon and Somerset is the Bristol Channel, where the Atlantic makes its last hurrah on its approach to the British mainland. At its widest, the channel is about forty-two miles across: the Welsh call it Môr Hafren (the Severn Sea). *Tinker* and *Electra* would not be venturing onto that grand expanse, thank God. We would nose out of Portishead and drop into the water almost in the very crease of the pig's chinny chin chin, where the channel narrows.

'The water,' said Dru reassuringly, 'is only five miles wide here.' Dru spent some years in the merchant navy, and has a sanguine approach to wide expanses of water. Suzanne and I were more accustomed to the thirty-foot breadth of the K&A. Five miles seemed quite wide enough to us. Once we were settled in Portishead's pristine marina, I wandered to the quayside to look out over the estuary at sunset. The tide was coming in at just this moment, and the surface of the channel was rumpled with purposeful threads of seawater, pushing on towards the land. I knew the whole length of this river, to varying degrees. I had once visited its source, wanting it to be something mystical: of course it was only a wet field in mid-Wales. I knew the river in its well-trafficked inland sections too. My first time at the helm of a working boat had been that memorable, skin-tingling first trip steering *Cepheus* at Worcester. Now, at last, I was looking at the business end of the Severn. It would soon be right behind us on our journey, pushing us north-east to river lock at Sharpness, where we would be back in still waters.

It isn't unheard of for a narrow boat to make this trip. About fifty boats a year do it nowadays, but it is daunting for any inland skipper with a sense of scale. 'Second-highest tidal range in the world,' said Suzanne brightly. I recalled the familiar mantra: 'One rule on the river: the river rules.' *No shit.* As I looked out into the Bristol Channel, I noticed that I had stopped breathing.

Our river pilot, Carl, stood in an ancient tradition of people who have guided vessels into harbour. Their usual work is to guide huge container ships and cargo vessels in these waters, but sometimes they hop on to a narrow boat to do the same. Our boats must seem like scale models to them, compared with the bread-and-butter work. Carl said that we needed two things: an incoming tide and very kind weather. 'We'll go tomorrow, on the evening tide,' he said. 'Be ready to go at 6.30 p.m.' *No problem.* My crew were Oxfordian therapist Alan and Semington diehard Tony, now my boon companion. We could eat lunch, write our wills and drop out of the Portishead river lock into the channel. By bedtime, we would be rising in the equivalent lock at Sharpness, to plug ourselves back into the inland waters where we belonged.

Perhaps now is a good time to explain why it is such a bad idea to take a narrow boat onto tidal waters like these. Firstly, there *are no* tidal waters like these. Severn has more oomph than most rivers in the world, and you don't want to be on the receiving end of it. You want to stay oomph-adjacent, but in control. That means that you need to travel faster than the river. Fall behind, and you are no longer the captain of your ship but a passenger on a raft, which will go where the river takes it. Most narrow boats have an engine fitted for the low speeds of the inland waterways. That was fine for us: *Tinker* should have no problem with her sturdy, unglamorous Barras Shire.

A seagoing boat, be it ever so modest, has a keel. Its hull below the water is curved, and thins to a narrow point like the seam of a pea pod. There are many versions of this shape: what all of them have in common is that they stabilise the craft in a choppy sea. A narrow boat has no *intention* of going to sea, thank you very much. It intends to pootle slowly up and down the tranquil waters of a man-made ditch with not so much as a slight current, let alone a tidal force travelling at seven metres per second. If such a force hits it sideways, a narrow boat is far, far more likely to capsize than a keeled boat.

I had it on good authority from a drunk boatbuilder in the Semington Arms that a seagoing yacht can heel over by as much as 60 degrees and right itself. A narrow boat, he maintained, is likely to go over if it tips by only 16 degrees – as it might well do if pushed by a very strong wind or a sudden sideways current, or millions of tons of water flowing between England and Wales. If his figures were wrong, I did not want to test them. Given a substantial sideways current, *Tinker* might capsize. My steel shell would go to the bottom of the estuary, taking with it the bright wood burner, the pink sofa bed and its wine-stained covers; the bookshelf where Marcus Aurelius and Tom Rolt rubbed shoulders; the cosy cabin with its high bed and its bull's-eye glass; the little bathtub, the trough of lettuces; the blue lace plate that Richard had grudgingly given me in a moment of generosity.

I did not, however, expect that to happen. The estuary would be an adventure, but not a totally foolhardy one.

The phone rang. 'Change of plan', said Carl cheerfully. 'The forecast isn't good for tomorrow afternoon. We're going in the morning. See you at 5.00 a.m.' The crew were about to start a serious programme of whisky tasting when I broke it to them. 'Bedtime, chaps,' I said.

At 5.00 a.m., I stood half-awake in the dawn light in Portishead harbour and gazed into the water. There was something flimsy and pale in the water at the back of the boat; I leaned over to investigate. I have seen many things floating in the canal. Coal sacks, beer bottles and fag packets in the outskirts of Manchester or Loughborough; a swan-shaped pedalo, listing under the weight of obese fundraisers; the odd dead rat. I have seen coconut shells tied with red ribbons in Walsall, where Hindu offerings begin their long journey to the Ganges by way of the Birmingham Canal Navigations. One thing you never, ever see on the canal is a jellyfish. I was looking at one now. It pulsed softly in the water by *Tinker's* dark hull like an animated mob cap.

The narrow boat belongs to the shallow and prosaic canals, the jellyfish to the constantly motive world of salt water and whale song. One of them was in the wrong place, and I knew which one it was. I remembered the bit in *Jurassic Park* where a jovial Richard Attenborough explains that his crazy admixture of dinosaurs from different periods will work out just *fine*, honestly. The jellyfish trembled, a little wet ghost waiting to return through the river lock into the estuary. Around us in the marina were the pleasure boats, all sheen and guard rail, whose clean lines made *Tinker* and I shiver ourselves. Next to us on the pontoon sat our friend *Electra*. We looked like chimney sweeps at a debutantes' ball.

Tinker bobbed innocently back and forth against the floating pontoons. She was built in a tradition of waterborne wheelbarrows. She was no pleasure boat herself, but she was mine. I felt deeply protective and curiously proud. We had come a long way together. This morning's journey would be an adventure, and we were up to it. On the pink chalkboard in the kitchen, I had jokingly written a quote from *Swallows and Amazons* to cheer us on: 'BETTER DROWNED THAN DUFFERS. IF NOT DUFFERS, WON'T DROWN'.

We didn't expect to drown in the Bristol Channel. Still, it does not do to be disrespectful. I had already contrived a near-sinking on flat water four feet deep, and it was certainly within my skill set to do it in the turbulent channel ahead of us. If I had a sense of apprehension about this short trip, it was at least proportionate. Apparently not everyone shared that approach. 'Do people make this journey without a river pilot?' I asked Carl.

'Oh yes,' he said brightly. 'There was a bloke called Ken. He did it with an AA road map.'

The AA road map is admirable, but has very little information about sand banks in the Bristol Channel. I had a feeling that Ken might represent the triumph of hope over experience.

'What happened to Ken?' I asked.

'Went aground ten minutes out of the harbour,' Carl said. 'Boat sank. Had to be floated at the next tide.'

Mermaids

The seventh-season-floating brings *this* river – Severn,
goddess, eel-queen. The tall masts, bone-damp in the banks
are text enough to tell us who is judge, and who the judged.

A wide and drowning-water, spitting silt at every turn.
One rule on the river; the river rules.
I ask safe passage, Severn. I accept your terms.
– *from* 'Untitled'

It is very early, neither dark nor day. In the water I see my own reflection alongside that of the paling moon. I said that we wouldn't go into the estuary unless I could see my face in the water: and here it is, looking tired and with a somewhat wiggy mop of spiky hair, but with a willing smile. There is not a breath of wind. The water is still as a millpond.

Suzanne and Dru, early risers both, are merrily eating toast and discussing marmalade recipes as they balance on the gunnels of *Electra*. They tidy ropes and stow away the fenders. My crew – one hairy poet, one hairy-arsed sailor with whom I have been having a joyous, post-traumatic fling – are putting lifejackets on. The day is turning pink, and *Tinker* and *Electra* are slowly pirouetting like trained elephants, making their way towards the huge river lock that separates us from the epic currents of the Bristol Channel.

The oligarchs' yachts sleep like swans as we ugly ducklings creep forward at tick-over speed, past the shining glass tower of the harbour master and into the river lock that separates this calm haven from the torrent outside. The lock is the size of a canal winding hole, and our two boats look ridiculous as we sit inside a space made for huge yachts and fishing boats. At each side of the chamber is a floating pontoon. *Electra* ties to one, *Tinker* to another and the platforms slide down with us, holding us close against the lock walls as we drop from harbour level down to the estuary. We slip the engines into gear and inch forward as the gates open, feeling a little like Christians about to meet the lion. I exaggerate, but not by much. The two boats nudge out into the yolk-bright sunrise.

Normally a lock releases you into another twenty-foot ribbon of canal. This time, as our eyes adjust to the clarity of a bright July day we are looking at the south coast of Wales. It is five miles away. On the distant shore opposite us is Newport where the river Usk floods into the channel, just in case there didn't seem to be enough water in it already. 'Come on in', says Severn. 'The water's lovely.' This is probably what the sirens sounded like as they sang to Odysseus. The river surface shifts in the sun, and spreads in front of us a dancing carpet of light; five miles of diamonds.

At this moment we are protected from the great push of the tide by the harbour wall, but when we reach the end of that wall we'll be out and in it, punched sideways by an elemental force. Suddenly, we're in it all right. Severn takes hold of us – *Tinker* first, *Electra* hot on her heels. The muscle of the river slams into us from the left as Severn impresses upon us that *she* will be determining the direction of travel. She is pushing us up towards Sharpness, like a croupier's rake pushing gaming chips across a table.

We slink into the estuary proper, low shapes against the silhouettes of Avonmouth's gigantic wind turbines. Both boats are rocking sideways a little, as they never do on the canals. Now we are properly part of the dancing channel of sunlit water. Those five miles of diamonds shift and glimmer and sparkle around us. Our two skippers throttle up. For the next three hours both boats will be running at full tilt, racing to stay just a little faster than the tide and earn the right to steer. If we slip into a slower pace, the river will be steering us – towards whatever sand bank or obstacle she has concealed in her thick folds.

The boats can tell that they are in a grown-up environment, and able to stretch themselves to full capacity. Like a pit pony released onto a race course, *Tinker* grabs the moment. She meets the river's force respectfully and sits as steady as I could wish, cutting a path through it with her little snub nose. The potted geraniums on my cabin top jiggle excitedly.

We are all grinning now. My two crew members are leaning into the fresh air, laughing at the novel sight of white water breaking around *Tinker*'s bows. The water isn't clear or flinty like the sea, but thick and brown like chocolate sauce. We can see particles of silt swirling in the currents around the hull. As we reach the part of the channel called the Slime Road, Carl takes us through in a series of inexplicable zig-zags and turns. At one stage he definitely says the word 'whirlpool'.

Looking back to *Electra*, I see Dru and Suzanne as silhouettes on the counter, tiny figures on a tiny boat against the backdrop of the Welsh coast. Suzanne's long wavy hair streams behind her like a mermaid's. Dru's distinctive red hat is wedged in place over her cherry-cheeked face as she keeps her eye fixed ahead. She is watching Carl as he reads the water. Occasionally their voices crackle on the VHF as Carl gives instruction. Sometimes he wants *Electra* at a distance – 'Stay back, back, and follow my path' to swerve us around an invisible bar. At other times it's 'come in right up behind us, so close we can almost touch you'. At these moments, close as a motor and butty on a short rope, we are passing through a deeper strait between two shallows.

'Get the kettle on,' says Carl. I expected sea monsters and krakens; instead it's mostly tea and biscuits, and seems entirely run of the mill to him. Only once does a great silver shape leap out of the water and curve back in, giving itself to the tumbling tonnes of silt. 'Salmon!' says the pilot cheerfully. *Bollocks*, I think. I know a mermaid when I see one.

We pass under the two immense bridges of the Bristol channel, first the egg-slicer wires of the Prince of Wales bridge carrying the M4 over a part of the estuary called 'The Shoots', then Bill Brown's Severn Bridge. Its titanic suspension chains hang in the sunlight like slack ropes, bearing up bored commuters as they head in and out of Bristol. If any of the drivers look down to the river below, they will see two tiny dots making their almost-invisible mark on the time map, the actual map, on the wide map of this wide water. *Tinker* and *Electra* are on a rollicking, glorious sunlit ride, driven by the river faster than a narrow boat ever dreams of. The silt-thickened water crests gently at their bows. Severn throws her shapes, the great bridges cut into the bright sky, and the two sister boats press on in their journey, scooting along the ancient waterway that boats have braved for millennia as the road traffic passes blithely overhead.

Three hours later, we are approaching the river lock at Sharpness as the water begins to slacken. If we were much slower, the tide would be going out again and it would pull us right back with it, heading for Portishead again. Instead, we arrive just when our engines have most agency. 'Don't panic as we come in to the lock,' says Carl as the buoy marking our progress looms ahead. *Panic?* The very thought. 'We will be coming in so close around that buoy that you will be able to reach out and touch it with a paintbrush.'

I'm not sure why he has a paintbrush in mind, but he's not wrong. We scoot neatly around the sea wall at Sharpness and into another lock the size of a canal basin. A swing bridge opens for us, sticking slightly in the heat. It is nine o'clock in the morning, and we slide onto the glassy waters of the Gloucester and Sharpness Canal, feeling like Odysseus. Nobody falls in. Nobody even gets wet. My geraniums remain undisturbed on the roof.

We slide past what I take to be a high blue wall, until Tony points out that it is actually the side of a massive container ship waiting to go out to sea, and tie up in bright sunshine on the canal near Purton. *Tinker* and *Electra* nuzzle at each other like horses after a gallop. The canal lies close to the river here, separated by a spit of land and a curious, moving collection of boat carcases called the Purton Hulks which were driven into the eroding embankment to shore it up. *Tinker* and *Electra*'s crews step off, alive in this graveyard of past river craft. All around us are great rib cages of oak and elm, sticking out of the sand and marram grass. Below us in the great estuary, the Severn is suddenly huge in its own absence; the sullen waters are visibly withdrawing from a plain of silt.

Oystercatchers and curlews stalk the mud. Flurries of sand martins start up from the banks as they prepare for a far longer migration than ours.

Once again no hordes are lining the canal banks. There is still not a brass band to be seen. No crowds of small children with flags and bunting. We celebrate with a cup of tea and a photograph; Dru and Suzanne, me and my crew sitting on a wall pulling faces and congratulating ourselves for making what, in narrow boat terms, qualifies as an epic journey.

We are once more on the canal network. I have defeated monsters, crossed great oceans and it isn't even breakfast time. Behind me lies a long winter, a wounded boat and a broken heart. Ahead of me is a warm sunny morning, a bacon butty and sixteen miles of unknown canal. We make our own adventures. For this one, and the company I was lucky to have during it, I am properly grateful. I head inside and chalk a new slogan on the noticeboard. NOT DUFFERS, DIDN'T DROWN it says.

Mid-way on our journey towards Sharpness, either Dru or Suzanne took a picture of *Tinker* heading for the great bridge unimaginatively named 'the second Severn crossing' when it was put up in 1996. In the photo, its struts and sharp lines spans the estuary like the entry to a spaceport. Underneath it, beetling towards its great columns like a determined Lego brick, is the little, lonely silhouette of *Tinker*. She is a slender case of steel and wood, unimaginably small in the face of great forces; but she is pushing forward anyway. Her ordinary little nose is up in the unfamiliar foam. If she were a dog she would be paddling bravely and pretending that she didn't have water in her eyes. My home; my stubborn little boat doing whatever she is asked to do. She presses on unnoticed by the hundreds of drivers on motorway bridge above, unnoticed by the planes flying still above them, unnoticed by the krakens and mythical monsters that probably sleep at the bottom of the Bristol Channel. I am the captain of my ship. It is only a little ship, and I am only a little captain – but still. *I can see the road, and I am following it: cheerfully, without turning back.*

Gloucester

Grebes were rearing their silly humbug-striped chicks on the Gloucester and Sharpness Canal, a sure sign that the water supports a lively mix of creatures. As friend Phil walked down the towpath with his teenager to join the boat, we heard the *plop* of a water vole dropping into the channel; a happy sound, because the dastardly mink have made them an endangered animal.

Suzanne's boat *Electra* was still close by. We were travelling together in boaterly fellowship, sharing dinner or texting each other from moorings a few feet apart. 'Are you awake? Come for a coffee!' or 'I see you're back from London, can I cook dinner?' She and Phil, musicians both, sat playing the guitar in my lounge as beside a tangled heap of teenage limbs. Such relaxed, happenstance meetings are a part of boat-dwelling life; there are quick-and-easy friendships that form in a few weeks but last for years.

The Gloucester and Sharpness is a ship canal, sometimes called 'The Sixteen' because it's sixteen miles long and sixteen feet deep, with sixteen swing bridges. It was commissioned in 1793 to bypass a wicked oxbow in the Severn, and to give ships a short cut from the Bristol Channel to the dock at Gloucester. It lies on the very fringes of the inland network, and it took more than thirty years to complete.

Unsurprisingly, it was the ubiquitous Thomas Telford who saw it to completion in 1827, as a masterpiece of Georgian civil engineering.

The canal was clearly man-made, with neat edges and automated swing bridges that opened without any effort from us, but it was river-like in its scale; broad, calm and tree-lined, with swans and coots patrolling the dappled surfaces. Suzanne and I travelled together, leap-frogging occasionally and greeting passing boats. 'Morning!' called our river pilot Carl as he cruised past us the next day, on a boat called *Indefatigable*. 'I'm headed the other way today!' The skipper, about to travel from Sharpness to Portishead, looked nervous. I did not reassure him. The anticipation was part of the pleasure, I told myself with a smirk. At Saul Junction, our two boats moored by a great canopied warehouse within sight of the Cotswold ridge, under an ivory half-moon and bright stars, as we prepared to go on our separate journeys. Suzanne and I parted company with a hug, and I drank my coffee alone the next morning on the sunny cabin top, giving thanks for the whole experiment. The friendships, the collapsed love affair, the new waters I was travelling on; they were not a gift I had asked for but, as I often tell myself, *it's not pain; it's raw material.*

The waterway became more suburban: tennis courts, waterside houses, and a few slender sculls rowed by grim, healthy people in base-ball caps. Not all of the local wildlife was as endearing as the grebe chicks. At Quedgeley, the dry soil crumbled when I hammered a mooring spike into the bank. I was a little grumpy, because I had just been stung on the arm by a wasp. I moved the pin a few inches to the left and tried again, bashing it angrily with a hammer. Only now did I understand that the first wasp was a lookout. I had driven a long metal spike firmly into the middle of a wasps' nest.

The wasps expressed themselves with great clarity. 'Exit, pursued by wasps,' as Shakespeare so nearly said. The people of Quedgeley watched me calmly from their waterside flats as I ran down the towpath with a sledgehammer, arms and legs flailing in a cloud of stings. 'Are you all right?' asked a passer-by, in the hostile tone of a person who asks 'Can I help you?' when he actually means 'Are you trying to steal my car?' I was moving too fast to reply, but enjoyed watching him retreat at full speed a few moments later, his limbs a cartoonish blur.

Our boats usually carry not only their name but also their place of origin. On the Kennet and Avon, relatively far from the Midlands network, I had seen 'Bradford-on-Avon' or 'Semington Dock' on the cabin sides. In Gloucestershire, the place names began to have a Midlands accent. 'Dadford's Wharf', 'Fazeley', 'Coven Heath'; these are landmarks on the water map, unknown to most people who live on the ordinary one.

Gloucester, however, is known to both. It was ten years since I had visited Richard and his shipwright friends in the spice-scented holds of the tall ships at Tommi Nielsen's yard, and raced across the dock for a glass of beer. The inland waterways had been a novelty to me then. Now I watched the familiar lift bridge open its arms for me, and steered into Gloucester Dock on my own boat. The wharfside buildings had been refurbished and refreshed, with a new comb of visitor pontoons by Philpott's Warehouse. There was of course a man standing on the bank with his arms folded, who watched me attentively as I moored. I was ready for him, but as I slid in neatly to join the ranked narrow boats he said, approvingly, 'You can see you've done that before. Immense confidence!' Perhaps the dock wasn't the only thing to have changed in the past ten years. I remembered my wobbling progress in Richard's coracle: 'Thanks,' I said. 'Last time I was here, I fell in.'

The Middle Lands

It was the height of an English summer; I was cruising with friends on the Severn, and within reach of the Boat Inn at Ashleworth. 'Earth has not anything to show more fair', as that nice Mr Wordsworth said, and he didn't even have a pint in his hand.

The ship canal had taken us across a tight bend of the river in a straight line typical of Telford's uncompromising eye; now we had reached the end of that bypass, and were delivered back onto the Severn. Twenty miles inland it was no longer the lively serpent we had met in the Bristol Channel, but one of the loveliest stretches of water in the British Isles. The river was a wide green corridor furnished with trees so full and perfect that they looked like pictures of trees, and with butterflies. We were heading upstream, but still we travelled faster than any canal would allow – a dizzying rate of six or seven miles an hour. 'People suffocate at this speed, you know,' I said to my friend Ruth, who had joined me for this section of the journey. We stuck to the centre of the channel, with plenty of water underneath us. In the silted bends we often saw a heron, standing disgruntled on the bank and reminding me of Paul Farley's poem about it:

> One of the most begrudging avian take-offs
> is the heron's 'fucking hell, all right, all right,
> I'll go to the garage for your flaming fags.'
> – *from* 'The Heron'

The silk-shuttle dart of a kingfisher shot along the surface sometimes, and every now and then we saw the scimitar curve of a fish flipping out of the water. Severn, in short, looked as if butter wouldn't melt in her mouth. Of course, she was lulling us into a false sense of security. Around the next bend was the medieval town of Tewkesbury, where we drew up to the river lock and found a narrow boat perilously balanced on the edge of a high harbour wall twenty feet above us. It looked like a car in a movie scene, hanging over a precipice. I wondered if it would fall on us. The lock keeper was a friendly hobbit, who glanced up at the hanging boat. 'Oh no,' he said. 'You're all right. It's stuck there well and good.' In the latest floods, Severn had lifted this boat off its mooring and taken it for a joyride. When the floods receded, the boat dropped with the water levels – and was impaled on a lamp post. It was pinned above us, high and dry, a reminder from the river gods. *One rule on the river.*

Worcester's houses and public buildings began to speckle the river bank, and I decided not to turn straight into the canal, as I had done years ago on *Cepheus.* I was reluctant to leave the Severn and its rich thread of summer life just yet. I tied up on the river moorings below the cathedral, as it eased its Gothic bones in the August sun. Inside the stone ribs of this church lay King John. I remembered him from my mooring by the castle in Newark, where he died of dysentery. His heart and intestines were buried (in haste, one imagines) at Croxton Abbey in Leicestershire, but the rest of him came here to Worcester and the shrine of St Wulfstan.

Tinker and I were travelling not only in the middle lands of England, but in the Middle Ages. The places *Tinker* cruised by were not just old towns on the river: they were old towns *because* of the river. They stood for centuries of marketplace trading, local politics, worship, and every kind of old-fashioned human behaviour from lechery to money-lending. Gloucester, Tewkesbury, Upton-upon-Severn, Worcester, and

Shrewsbury were trading hubs, with guildhalls and merchants' wharves. They were religious centres with friaries and abbeys. They were garrison towns of castle and city wall. The street names of Worcester stood for any riverside town of the Middle Ages. Church Street, Friary Street, City Walls Road, Quay Street spoke for themselves: Fish Street and The Shambles (or slaughterhouses) were for food shopping, The Butts for archery practice.

Britain then had a culture where everyone lived in the country, except a few weirdos who made a living by trade, brewing, building or money-lending. These unusual people had to *buy* their butter and their woollen clothes, instead of making them like normal people. The towns of pre-industrial Britain were outliers in a nation where almost everyone lived on the land. Within the space of seventy years, we became a culture where everyone lived in the towns, except a few weirdos who made a living as arable farmers or cattle breeders. No prizes for guessing which seventy years they were; the canal years, the Age of Wonder.

In the interests of historical research I went to the pub. The Cardinal's Hat on Friar Street was a sort of medieval Travelodge, and in it I had a minor epiphany. It may have been the cider that brought it on. I was about to drop out of the river channel and rejoin the canal system, back at Worcester where I had first made that transition years before. A lot of water, as it were, had passed under the bridge since then; and suddenly I had the strongest, clearest sense ever of what the canals had achieved. It came home to me not just as textbook knowledge, but as a fact confirmed in every boat trip *Tinker* had ever made. When Worcester or Bristol first thrived, the water map was only a fringe of rivers at the edges of Britain, with occasional notches cut deep inland. The Severn and Avon, Trent and Thames were the ageless waterways that first allowed settlement and heavy traffic. True inland areas were, well, backwaters. Only when technology called for more iron, more copper, more lead, and above all more coal, were the Midlands and North at last in a seller's market.

Within a few decades the owners and makers had found people like Brindley or Telford who understood water and building: and they simply, quickly stitched together the great arteries with threads of water. Manchester, Stoke-on-Trent, Sheffield; once they had access to water transport, they were unstoppable. The canals are a gigantic set of jump leads which connected the terminals of pre-industrial Britain – the navigable rivers – and completed the circuits necessary to make goods, ideas and money flow freely. That shock changed Britain and sent its people rushing into the towns, into an environment full of opportunity and hazard.

At my next stop *Tinker* squeezed out of a lock wide enough for only one narrow boat, for the first time in a year, and glided into a busy canal centre. When the engineers first cut a canal terminus into meadows near Low Milton, a village with a population of twelve, they didn't know what to call their new development. They tried Stourmouth, then Newport. Around 1771, they settled on Stourport. By the end of the century there were around 1,500 people living in it, and it was a thriving inland harbour. The staircase locks and the busy basins of the town brought us back onto the system, and the Staffordshire and Worcestershire Canal.

As Worcestershire became Staffordshire, the accents of local people changed to something resembling a Stokie accent. The bedrock around us changed too. The canal banks closed in through a channel of deep red sandstone. At Kinver we rose through locks to see the curious Flintstone-style residences of the last cave-dwellers in England, the

Martindale Caves, lived in until the 1960s by people from the nearby ironworks. It was a sinuous canal, with lots of curves and the occasional 90 degree turn. *Ah, Mr Brindley, we meet again.* There were other old friends too. I began to see working boats; the familiar motor *Roach*, and an unnamed motor manoeuvring the town class butty *Gosport* around a tight corner. At last, we rounded a familiar bend in the canal to see the water broadening ahead of us. The last stop but one before Stone was a familiar one, and one that I had been particularly looking forward to.

It was a busy August weekend at Tixall Wide. Tinker slotted in to the very last space available, overlooking the mad folly where the cupolas of Thomas Clifford's gate house overlook the artificial lake made by Brindley and Brown to improve his view. I stepped off to tie up, glancing at the back of the neighbouring boat. There was a small horse standing in the doorway. I stood up and looked again. It was not a horse but an enormous black Great Dane, as shiny as Chinese lacquer. As I approached, it walked backwards into the cabin.

The boat was, of course, *Ventus* – Skipper Jon's flying fart. Jon emerged, grinning and joyous as ever. 'Ah, Jo Bell!' He greeted me as boaters often do, with the sense that it is not at all unusual to bump into one another 100 miles from where you last met. After all, ours is a small town with residents who are bound to meet every now and then; it's just a very long high street.

Jon had a meaningful and triumphant glint in his eye. He was bobbing up and down with outright glee, delighted to see me for a reason I couldn't quite grasp. Judy stuck her head out of the side hatch, 'Oh.

Hello Jo! I'll put the kettle on.' By now Jon had the eager look of a young Border Collie waiting for its owner to throw a stick.

'Go on then,' I said, 'tell me.'

'I've done it,' he said in a stage whisper, his face almost cracking in two with the breadth of his grin.

'Done what?'

He was positively gleeful.

'I finally persuaded her to live on the boat!'

After forty years of marriage, Judy had surrendered. We were all delighted with the synchronicity of the moment. As I headed towards Stone to take up a new mooring, they were heading away from it to begin life afloat. 'One in, one out!' laughed Jon. It was the very first night of their new life as liveaboard boaters. I took the proffered cup of tea and read Judy's eloquent eyebrows. *It was always going to happen,* they said. *I just wanted to make him wait.*

Still waters

The Irish say that you shouldn't arrive at someone's home 'with both arms the same length'. When my last guests of the journey reported to my mooring on a rural towpath, they had arms full of food and drink. Alan and Angi appeared through an opening in the hedgerow as I set up a table on the towpath; smiling as they always are, wise and gentle as they always are. The young man tagging gamely along in their wake was their son Chris. I had found a perfect mooring in which to wait for them: *Tinker* was moored on a raised embankment, overlooking a

blanket of summer fields. We were the only boat in sight. All of Staffordshire was ours. It sounded like sheep and blackbirds, and it smelt
of sausages and chicken drumsticks. We dined in a haze of barbecue
smoke, welcoming the local ducks as they politely enquired after bread.
In Staffordshire everyone is a 'duck' but the ducks, of course, are more
so. After dinner, Angi and I sat watching the two men as they strolled
down the towpath in a summer sunset, an image of father-and-son
closeness. *Peace comes dropping slow.*

It was the last part of the nine-day journey from Honeystreet,
and there was warm air on our skin as we travelled. We took it slow and
paid attention, with the deep pleasure of boaters in no hurry. Angi
and Chris walked ahead to work the locks at Weston and Aston, paus-
ing to take pictures of birds and beetles. Alan and I took turns to steer.
I was, he tells me, rather philosophical that day. We talked about the
risks of new relationships, and the challenges people face at pivotal
moments. Both must have been on my mind. Angi and Chris worked
the paddles slowly, *dinkdinkdink-ing* us through the narrow chambers
and enjoying the trickle-and-bump soundtrack. As *Tinker* rose in the
lock at Aston I read the black-and-white milepost that located us
within the water map. On one side it said SHARDLOW – 46 MILES,
and on the other PRESTON BROOK – 46 MILES. We were precisely
halfway along the Trent and Mersey, between two landmark points
that few people on the real map have ever heard of.

Stone has a handful of locks. My new mooring was at Roger Fuller's
yard, right next to the top one. With a mile or so to go, we approached
the bottom one in the flight, and Alan hopped off the boat. His manly
reputation was at stake if he allowed Angi and Chris to work the lock
without him, because it is practically inside the beer garden of the Star
Inn, and on this sunny afternoon there were scores of gongoozlers for

whom we were the in-house entertainment. They watched, keenly interested and with no intention of helping. The crew made their gentle, ergonomic dance steps; they closed gates, wound the paddles up and the boat rose like a slow magic trick. *Now you see me, now you don't.*

Mother, father and son walked slowly up the path through the town of Stone, with *Tinker* following close behind as they saw me through the locks. We passed the memorial to Christina Collins, a woman who was murdered by a canal boat crew in 1839. We entered the lock where Skipper Jon had once been steering a trip boat full of merrymakers, when all the water suddenly disappeared into a void under the lock, and the boat fell six feet through the air. We passed the oldest dry dock on the system, where in 1951 Tom Rolt arrived with *Cressy*, tied the boat up for the very last time and walked away to a new life with Sonia South. Behind it on the High Street stood the Crown Hotel, where in 1766 Josiah Wedgwood set about persuading investors to finance a new canal, joining the Trent to the Mersey.

Tinker slipped into Stone Top Lock, and the familiar gentle surge of water rushed into the chamber, jostling her slightly. As she rose, I peeked through the gap beneath the black-and-white balance beam, and saw a bright stretch of water ahead of us. Here was the little yard where famous working boats, the grubby queens of the waterway, were healed and relaunched. Here Roger Fuller collected signal boxes and old railway cars and unusual, ragged machinery, and brought it all back to wholeness with a mixture of love and welding. Next to it was the most perfect mooring I had ever seen; a small patch of lawn at the end of a basin filled with working boats. There was a riot of brambles along one edge, and a rich purple elderflower bush in full foliage.

The lock gates opened, and my three beaming crew members saw me in to the new mooring. I tied up to a small but sincere round of applause. Yet again, I was disappointed by the absence of brass bands and small children; but there were, at least, biscuits. We were soon joined by another friend, Jayne, with her young son William – raised on a working boat. The welcome committee spread out across my new estate, picking blackberries and revelling in the luxury of a private garden with its own little gate. Roger was nowhere to be seen but an hour or so later, I saw two of him – the Trilby Crew – moving slowly in the evening sunshine as the Fuller twins brought a working pair into the basin.

'I've just seen the chalkboard in the kitchen,' said Jayne as she handed me a glass of fizz. 'Very good.' I was delighted to be complimented on my chalk work by a teacher. 'I should hope so too,' I said. 'It took me ages.' I had brought my best signwriting skills to the task, and a number of coloured chalks, sitting on the floor with my tongue sticking out as I wrote it. It was an audit; a final reckoning of the journey from Macclesfield to Honeystreet, and now here to Stone. It read:

Months – 13
Miles – 439
Crew – 50
Locks – 274 (at least)
Heartbreak – 1(old)
Friends – 100s (old and new)
SURRENDER – O

Underneath it I wrote, in defiant capitals: TO BE CONTINUED.

Still waters do not run deep. They run to about four feet, as a rule. They are deep enough for me, and for thousands of boaters who call them home. The narrow and broad canals, the navigations and rivers, the many miles of channelled water that we circulate on in a slow game of musical chairs, are the highways of an alternative England. Our waterway system was built for a purpose. It is one of humankind's great achievements. It is a map-within-a-map; a parallel country, with its own landmarks and place names. We live on the other side of your map, in a narrow country; and we navigate by different stars.

Afterword: Return to the Macc

Tinker and I had spent a dozen years together. Our travels together changed my life, and my entire outlook on life. But all good things come to an end, and it is rare for boaters to live their whole waterborne life on a single vessel. As *Tinker* grew older and my needs changed slightly, I decided to let her go, and to build a new boat. *Tinker* was released to a new, loving owner. It made me sad, in a way that selling a house could never do; but she has since been sighted in the wild, apparently happy and living in the Midlands.

My new boat had to be craned into the water somewhere, in the unnerving manoeuvre called a boat lift. It occurred to me that it would be a nice gesture to do that at the Macclesfield Home for the Unusual. I rang Kevin. He had not heard from me in four years. The conversation went like this:

'Hello Kevin.'

'Oh, it's you. Do you want your old mooring back, then?'

'Erm. Well ...'

Why not? In the 1730s, a young millwright called James Brindley served his apprenticeship a couple of miles from this mooring. Eighty years later, an ageing Thomas Telford paced out the route of the Macclesfield Canal and drew his very last line on the finished water map. The little Cheshire town where I had pulled up many years before and found myself surrounded by Elvises had a curious importance to both of these men, and to me too. For years, I had resisted the idea of calling any particular place 'home'. Home was where the boat was; home was the seventy feet of towpath or boatyard where I tied up. To *settle* anywhere had felt like a failure.

Now, in Kevin's gruff tones, there was familiarity, welcome, and the promise of closure for a particularly pleasing circle.

On the day of the boat lift, I arrived at the yard ahead of the huge lorry that carried my new boat, and watched it nudging slowly into place alongside the crane. I went in to the boatyard toilet. There was a laminated sign on the wall. IF I CATCH YOU SMOKING IN HERE, YOU HAD BETTER BE ON FIRE, it said.

The sides of the new boat were blank, awaiting a signwriter. The renowned Phil Speight had offered to do it, and who was I to refuse such a doyen of traditional canal painting scene? He rolled up in an old Alfa Romeo, his jeans covered in bright smears of paint and a roll-up hanging from his mouth. His hair was long and silver, with a mind of its own; he looked like an escapee from a 1970s folk rock band, which indeed he was. As Phil stepped out of the car, he immediately clocked my face. It was not the proud face of a new boat owner, but the slightly conflicted face of someone who has just parted with an old friend, and isn't yet sure about the new one. He understood immediately.

'It will be all right, you know,' he said. *It will be all right.* He understood this particular mix of loss and gain.

The name he was about to paint on the cabin sides was a careful choice. I had run it past Roger Fuller, boat builder and working boat devotee. 'I like that,' he said thoughtfully. 'It's a good name: a strong name.' She was to be called *Stoic*, in a nod to Marcus Aurelius. As Phil chalked the freehand swirls of her name around the portholes, this boat took on her own personality. She carried the same potential as any other for a homely, mobile life on the unique water map that boaters occupy; a network that exists on so many layers of the time map, speckled with so many unnamed lives and so many living characters. I hung up the Eric Gaskell linocuts of canal scenes, and put my copy of

Narrow Boat on the bookshelf. I unpacked the red kettle, and set it on the woodburning stove.

'It will be all right, you know,' said Phil. He had a twinkle in his eye which I would come to know much better. And he was perfectly correct: it was going to be all right. I knew by now that it wasn't the man I was falling in love with – though admittedly, there was that too. It was the boat.

Glossary

Balance beam – the big black-and-white beam on the lock gate.

Barge – the wide-beam cargo boat traditionally seen on rivers and wide canals.

Beam – the width of a boat.

Breasted up – when two boats are lashed together side by side, either on a mooring or as they travel. This effectively makes a single, slightly unwieldy craft that can be steered by one person.

Butty – the unpowered boat that travels with a motor boat, either towed behind it or tied alongside.

Cill (not sill) – the deep stone shelf at the bottom of the top lock gate, which can be a hazard for boats going downhill if they get caught on it.

Contour canal – a canal (usually early) which follows a single level for as long as possible, rather than taking the shortest line between two points. This sometimes made for a long and winding route, but avoided the expense and difficulty of building locks, embankments or aqueducts to get boats across uneven ground.

Draft – the depth of a boat under the water. A boat is said to 'draw three feet' if the depth is three feet. Most modern narrow boats draw about 2ft 6.

Ellum – the substantial rudder on a butty boat.

Fender – the rope or plastic 'bumper' attached to the front, back or sides of a boat to protect it from damage in locks and on moorings: traditionally made of knotted rope.

Flight – a series of locks.

Gongoozler – someone who watches boats go by, usually with their arms folded. The number of gongoozlers watching is inversely proportional to the difficulty of the manoeuvre you are undertaking.

Gunnel – the widest part of the boat. On the outside it makes a walkway a few inches wide, or a space to perch your bottom when chatting on the towpath.

Lock gear – the standing element of a lock, where you attach a windlass to wind up the paddles and release water.

Motor – the boat in a working pair which has an engine, and tows the butty boat behind it.

Paddles – the sliding doors in the middle of a lock gate, which open or close a hole and thereby release water into the lock, or drain water out of it. On some locks there are two kinds – the usual gate paddles are accompanied by ground paddles, which release water into the bottom of the lock first.

Pawl – the safety catch on lock gear which stops the windlass spinning round and hitting you in the face. You should always have the pawl DOWN when winding UP (so that it makes the distinctive clicking noise), and lift it UP when winding DOWN.

Pound – the stretch between two locks on a canal. Sometimes very short, sometimes twenty miles long.

Reach – a stretch of river; the equivalent of a pound on the canal.

Side pond – ponds at the side of a lock which act as mini-reservoirs and help in conserving water. Nowadays, although they would be very useful, they are not generally in use because modern boaters don't know how to use them.

Stemmed up – gone aground.

Stop lock – a very shallow lock, which drops only a few inches and acts as a sort of tourniquet to stop the water of one canal flowing into another. A relic of days when canals were built by private companies, who wanted to safeguard the water it had cost them a fortune to supply. The stop lock is also a means of draining a section of canal, without emptying the whole waterway.

Stop planks – the set of timbers you will often see beside a canal bridge, which drop into slots in the bridge to form a temporary gate so that water can be drained from a section of canal for repairs or inspection.

The system – the available canal network. There are supposedly 2,000 miles of canal and navigable river at present. It used to be 4,000 and it will soon diminish further if we don't invest in our canals.

Top gates, Bottom gates – the gates at the upper and lower end of a lock, respectively.

Top lock, Bottom lock – the top and bottom locks in a flight.

Tumblehome – the sloping sides of the cabin, which lean inwards so that the boat can slide through arched bridges with inches to spare.

Windlass (not lock key) – the angled metal handle with one or two holes in it, which allows you to wind up the lock gear.

Working boat – any boat that worked on the canals. Usually it refers to the cargo boats that carried around twenty tons of coal, stone or anything else. It also covers tug boats, which drew trains of boats through long tunnels; maintenance boats like dredgers or piling rigs; icebreakers; and the hoppers or 'joey boats' which were essentially large trailers.

Working pair – the familiar formation for working narrow boats, with a motor boat and a butty boat working together. Sometimes the butty was on 'long lines' like a long tow rope, sometimes on short lines making a sort of articulated vehicle with the motor, and sometimes they breasted up side by side.

Bibliography

If you are looking for a good grounding in canal history, have a particular look at the titles marked with an asterisk (*) below.

*Aickman, Robert (JM Pearson & Son, 1986) *The River Runs Uphill*

Aubertin, CJ (Shepperton Swan, 1982) *A Caravan Afloat*

Babbs, Helen (Icon Books Ltd, 2016) *Adrift: A Secret life of London's Waterways*

Bachelard, Gaston (Beacon Press, 1994) *The Poetics of Space*

Baines, Sir Edward (H Fisher, R Fisher and P Jackson, 1835) *A History of the Cotton Manufacture*

Barrett, Jeff et al (Cassell Illustrated, 2009) *Caught by the River: A Collection of Words on Water*

Bogart, Dan (University of California, 2004) *Turnpike Trusts and the Transportation Revolution in 18th Century England*

Broadbridge, Stanley Robertson (David & Charles, 1974) *The Birmingham Canal Navigations*

*Burton, Anthony (Pen & Sword Transport, 2024) *The Canal Builders: The Men Who Constructed Britain's Canals*

*Burton, Anthony (Pen & Sword Books, 2017) *The Canal Pioneers: Canal Construction from 2,500 BC to the Early 20th Century*

Cobbett, William (ed. John Derry) (Parkgate Books, 1997) *Cobbett's England: A Selection from the Writings of William Cobbett*

Corble, Nick (Tempus, 2005) *James Brindley: The First Canal Builder*

Dutton, Julian (The History Press, 2021) *Water Gypsies: A History of Life on Britain's Rivers and Canals*

Gibbings, Robert (Cox & Wyman Ltd, 1967) *Sweet Thames Run Softly*

*Glover, Julian (Bloomsbury, 2017) *Man of Iron: Thomas Telford and the Building of Britain*

Griffin, Emma (Yale University Press, 2014) *Liberty's Dawn: A People's History of the Industrial Revolution*

*Hadfield, Charles (Latimer Trend & Company, 1968) *The Canal Age*

Hartley, Dorothy (Macdonald, 1964) *Water in England*

Holmes, Richard (HarperPress, 2009) *The Age of Wonder: How the Romantic Generation Discovered the Beauty and Terror of Science*

Hopkins, Tony and Brassley, Pat (Moorland Publishing, 1982) *Wildlife of Rivers and Canals*

*Hunt, Tristram (Allen Lane, 2021) *The Radical Potter: Josiah Wedgwood and the Transformation of Britain*

Kitching, Tom (Tom Kitching, 2024) *Where There's Brass: A Love Letter to the Waterways of England*

Matthews, Jodie (Intersections in Literature and Science, 2023) *The British Industrial Canal: Reading the Waterways from the Eighteenth Century to the Anthropocene*

Midgley, Clare (Routledge, 1992) *Women Against Slavery: The British Campaigns 1780-1870*

Nichols, Wallace J (Abacus Books, 2014) *Blue Mind*

O'Connor, John (Unicorn Press, 2014) *Canals, Barges and People*

Owens, Victoria (Amberley, 2015) *James Brindley and the Duke of Bridgewater: Canal Visionaries*

*Richardson, Christine (Waterways World, 2005) *James Brindley: Canal Pioneer*

Rolt, LTC (Alan Sutton Publishing Limited, 1986) *Landscape with Canals*

*Rolt, LTC (Eyre & Spottiswoode, 1957) *Narrow Boat*

Rolt, LTC (Allen & Unwin, 1970) *The Inland Waterways of England*

Rolt, Sonia (The History Press, 2009) *A Canal People: The Photographs of Robert Longden*

Sadler, Nigel (Amberley Publishing, 2018) *The Legacy of Slavery in Britain*

Samuel, Raphael (ed. John Merrick) (Verso, 2024) *Workshop of the World: Essays in People's History*

Schama, Simon (Vintage Books, 2009) *Rough Crossings: Britain, the Slaves and the American Revolution*

*Smiles, Samuel (John Murray, 1874) *Lives of the Engineers with an Account of their Principal Works: Comprising also A History of Inland Communication in Britain*

Shaw, Martin (Chelsea Green Publishing, 2021) *Smoke Hole: Looking to the Wild in the Time of the Spyglass*

Sullivan, Dick (Coracle Books, 1983) *Navvyman*

Thurston, ET (David & Charles, 1972) *The 'Flower of Gloster'*

Turchi, Peter (Trinity University Press, 2007) *Maps of the Imagination: The Writer as Cartographer*

Ware, Michael E (Moorland Publishing, 1989) *Britain's Lost Waterways*

Weaver, CP and CR (David & Charles, 1983) *Steam on Canals*

White, Gilbert (ed. Walter Johnson), (Routledge & Kegan Paul, 1970) *Gilbert White's Journals*

Yorke, Stan (Countryside Books, 2004) *English Canals Explained*

Acknowledgements

This is all Thomas Telford's fault. There are others to thank too, and they are as follows:

The Society of Authors for a vital grant which saw me through the early stages of writing this book; the Ann Atkinson writers who have supported, critiqued and shaped it from beginning to end; Rach Crawford at Wolf Literary Services for remote agenting; and all in the HarperNorth family for giving *Boater* a home and a warm welcome. Thanks to Jodie Matthews and Julian Glover for giving me time, advice, and new perspectives on canal writing and Thomas Telford.

I thank my essential kith, especially my boat-and-bank life support system, Heather and Jen who both lent me their homes to write in and to Sarah Jasmon, the mooring yin to my boating yang. Thanks to Jane, the Wharf Woollies and Phil Speight (MBE) for their deep and supportive friendships; to the people of The Poetic Licence, who are at my side whatever I do; and the many, many writers and literary friends who have encouraged me.

Annette Simpson and Eliza Botham gave me a job when I was patently not the right woman to do it, though I may have become that woman now; Judith Palmer gave me another as Canal Laureate; Tim Eastop, Ed Fox, Tony Hales and Richard Parry at CRT supported me in that role. I thank the Wiltshire friends and crew including Tony, Dru, Suzanne, Ian and Liz, and every crew on every journey from the beginning, including those who think I have forgotten them. Thanks, too, to Joe Hollinshead; Ray Wain; Roger Fuller; Brian McGuigan; to all at the Macclesfield Home for the Unusual; to Marcus Aurelius; and, of course, to Nigel and Elizabeth.

Above all, this book would not exist without my editor, Ben McConnell, who suggested that I write it, never let go of it even when I was tempted to, and has championed it without fail since first discussing it.